RETREAT, HELL!

RETREAT, HELL!

WE'RE JUST ATTACKING IN ANOTHER DIRECTION

JIM WILSON

WILLIAM MORROW AND COMAPANY, INC.

NEW YORK

Library of Congress Cataloging-in-Publication Data

Wilson, Jim, 1929–
    Retreat, hell : we're just attacking in another direction / Jim
Wilson.
        p.   cm.
    ISBN 0-688-07576-2
    1. Korean War, 1950–1953—Campaigns.   2. United States.   Marine
Corps—History—Korean War, 1950–1953.   I. Title.
DS918.W54   1989
951.9′042—dc19   88–23143
                                                                                    CIP

Printed in the United States of America

First Edition

1 2 3 4 5 6 7 8 9 10

BOOK DESIGN BY MARK STEIN

CONTENTS

INTRODUCTION

Korea is a country forged in war. Fighting has been a way of life there for centuries: Tribes, clans, provincial armies, one feudal lord against another, all battled to see who would rule. And when they were not fighting each other, they were defending their country against outside aggression.

The tiny peninsulalike nation—the north is the size of Mississippi, the South that of Indiana—has been kicked around, threatened, influenced, invaded, looted, brutalized, occupied, and divided. Its geographic location and ability to produce great quantities of agricultural products have always whetted the appetite of its larger, more powerful neighbors: China, Japan, and Russia.

For many, many years Koreans have felt strongly that their destiny was controlled not by events within their country but by events that occurred outside Korea. Largely, this has been true. There's an old saying on the peninsula that Korea is merely a "shrimp among whales."

Rugged, mountainous, with temperatures that range from bone-chilling cold to great heat, Korea juts southward from the northeastern rim of the Asian mainland, separates the Sea of Japan and the Yellow Sea, and points like the deadly tip of a spear at Japan. It is a perfect buffer between two old enemies: China and Japan.

For centuries, China, Japan, and the Mongols have preyed on Korea. Because of this, the Yi rulers in the fourteenth century closed their borders to the north, shut tight their seaports, and withdrew from the rest of the world, thus earning Korea the sobriquet of the "Hermit Kingdom." But this didn't put an end to harassment from its aggressive neighbors, and when the outside world discovered that, in addition to rice, wheat, and millet, Korea possessed great quantities of mineral resources, it wasn't long before the big fellows were back.

Finally, under great pressure from the outside, Korea allowed foreigners to reenter, granting trade concessions to all. As the years passed, China, Japan, and Russia developed a thirst for Korea that only war could quench. First, China and Japan clashed in 1894–95, with Japan winning handily. The first thing Japan did was make a move toward Korea by sending troops there to "protect" Japan's legation from just exactly what no one ever seemed to know.

Once Japan had a foot in the door, it wasn't long before Korea fell completely under Japanese influence.

Meanwhile, the other great power in the region, Czarist Russia, watched with concern as Japan extended its sphere of influence. Ultimately this led to war and, in 1904–5, Japan crushed Russia, destroying its fleet, and overnight became a great power.

Then, to solidify its hold on Korea, Japan occupied the peninsula in 1910 and closed it to the rest of the world. It became the most brutal, repressive period in Korea's long history that dates back to 2333 B.C.

No level of Korean life went untouched during the thirty-five-year occupation. It reached into every home, each family. Banking, industry, agriculture, the courts, and newspapers suffered the most. Japan tried to force Koreans to discard their language and learn Japanese. Then, when the Sino-Japanese war broke out in 1937, Japan turned Korea into a staging area, a giant logistical base. Korea's mineral riches in the North were developed to the utmost. Koreans were forced to work in the mines and mills. Those of military age were dragged into the Japanese Army.

Japan built huge hydroelectric power plants in the North. Factories were constructed to turn out products needed in Japan's growing war effort. In the South, vast amounts of farm products were grown with the help of fertilizers the Japanese developed.

The Korean peninsula was now an integral part of Japan; it remained so throughout World War II.

As the fighting in the Pacific neared an end and it became apparent that Japan would lose, it seemed that Korea might once again become a free nation.

For the United States, however, a great problem was in its infancy.

At this point in history, Korea was like a tiny thorn in one's foot. You knew it was there, but it really didn't hurt. But if you didn't deal with the problem, infection could set in.

The problem surfaced in December 1943 at Cairo, when the United States, Britain, and China decided that the Allies would strip Japan of all the territory it had taken after the Sino-Japanese war of 1894–95 and that "in due course Korea shall become free and independent."

Korea reappeared at the Potsdam Conference in July 1945, when the same three powers reaffirmed the Cairo declaration. They added: "Japanese sovereignty shall be limited to the islands of Honshu, Hokkaido, Kyushu, and Shikoku and such minor islands as we shall determine."

But in the final days of the war, another problem arose. The Soviet Union declared war on Japan on August 8, 1945, and sent troops rushing toward Korea.

Quickly, the United States pushed for agreement to an earlier proposal that Russia accept the surrender of all Japanese troops on the peninsula above the thirty-eighth parallel, and the U.S. accept the surrender of those below the thirty-eighth. Surprisingly, the Russians agreed. At the time it appeared to be a good plan, for it gave the United States two good seaports, Inchon in the North and Pusan, far to the south, from which to repatriate Japanese prisoners of war.

The United States viewed the thirty-eighth parallel as a line of convenience to facilitate the surrender of many thousands of Japanese troops. It was not looked upon as a permanent dividing line between the North and the South.

But the Russians felt otherwise from the outset.

As soon as Soviet troops reached the thirty-eighth, they tore up all the railroad tracks, cut all lines of communication, destroyed the roads, and closed traffic in both directions. Then they constructed huge barricades so there was no movement whatsoever.

Gen. John R. Hodge, commander of American forces in Korea, reported to Washington that almost immediately there was "dissatisfaction with the division of the country. . . ."

Dean Acheson, undersecretary of state, remarked: "We soon found that the Soviet Union considered the thirty-eighth parallel not as a line of military administrative convenience but as a wall around their preserve. . . ."

Once again, Korea had fallen victim to the whales. And once again, outside forces were controlling the destiny of Koreans.

Nevertheless, in an effort to overcome the differences between North and South, the United States and Russia worked out an agreement whereby a Joint Commission for the Unity and Independence of Korea would be established. But little came of it, and by early 1947, President Harry S. Truman had all but given up hope that the two Koreas would get together and become one again.

Meanwhile, small patrols from both sides stepped up forays across the thirty-eighth parallel, and life went on as best it could in a situation that each day became a bit more tense in a country that was now divided.

The United States now had troops bogged down in Korea, an area where it had no desire to be. The GI's were needed elsewhere—in Europe, in Germany, in Berlin. But if they left, Communist forces almost surely would try to take over the South. Yet if they didn't leave, they might never get out.

The Joint Chiefs of Staff had already determined that "from the standpoint of military security, the United States has little strategic interest in maintaining the present troops and bases in Korea."

Gen. George C. Marshall, the secretary of state from 1947 to 1949, and various State Department advisers agreed, saying: "Ultimately, the U.S. position in Korea is untenable even with the expenditure of considerable U.S. money and effort."

So U.S. policy from September 1947 was to get out as quickly as possible.

But how could we do this gracefully?

The answer, Washington decided, was the United Nations. So the question of Korea's future was submitted to the world body, and in November 1947, over Soviet objections, the General Assembly adopted a resolution specifying that elected representatives of the Korean people, North and South, should establish conditions of unification and determine their own form of government through a nationwide election. The United Nations would oversee the voting.

However, it was clear from the outset that this would not work. The Communists had no intention of letting the question of unification be resolved at the ballot box. To emphasize this, the rulers of the North further strengthened the border so that it was impossible to move in either direction. A worm couldn't squeeze through.

As a result of the North's refusal to permit voting, the UN-supervised elections were held throughout the South on May 10, 1948, and the Republic of Korea was officially born. Its first president was Syngman Rhee, a crusty old patriot who, through his country's darkest hours, never let the world forget Korea.

Rhee was born April 26, 1875, and educated in the United States at George Washington University and at Harvard, where he received a master's degree in history and political science. Almost from the start, he had been a radical, a revolutionary. He spent time in prison, was tortured, and was in continual trouble with the Japanese occupiers, but he remained determined to work for one thing: independence for Korea, no strings attached.

Not to be outdone, the Russians established the Democratic People's Republic of Korea in September 1948. Its first leader was Kim Il Sung. Kim's real name was Kim Song Ju. When he was fourteen he became active in the Korean Communist movement. Later, in the 1930s, he assumed the name of a deceased guerrilla leader and became Kim Il Sung. After that, his career becomes hazy. His past is murky. All we know for certain is that he was born in 1912 and that in 1945 he appeared as a Communist leader in the northern half of Korea.

In August 1948 the American occupation of South Korea ended, and the Americans began to go home. John J. Muccio arrived in Seoul as the first U.S. ambassador to South Korea. At the same time, American advisers were training a constabulary force, one the United States hoped would be capable of maintaining order in the South and strong enough to handle any attack from above the thirty-eighth parallel. This force, however, could not be so strong that it posed a threat to the North. Washington didn't want the North to invade the South under the guise that ROK troops were so strong that they posed a major threat to North Korea. It was a delicate situation.

By early 1949, American military advisers were still in South Korea, still training the constabulary, which was slowly growing in size, if not in ability. In fact, in the first few months of 1949, the Korean Military Advisory Group training staff cabled their superiors in Washington about the sorry state of the ROK troops. Not only that, they had no tanks, no planes, only a few light artillery pieces, and only enough small arms and ammunition for a few days of combat. Most of the vehicles had long since broken down.

Nevertheless, Rhee felt pleased with the situation. He had a country now. And he had an army, of sorts.

And the United States was feeling pleased with itself, too. It had gotten out of Korea gracefully, and had turned the problem over to the people to whom it belonged.

But this feeling of euphoria didn't last too long.

On August 29, 1949, Russia exploded an atomic bomb, ending the *withdrew military aid (Vietnam 1974!!)*

United States' four-year monopoly in the nuclear world. No longer could we expect the "bomb" to keep aggressors in line. *only after we*

Then, in December 1949, following one crushing defeat after another, the Nationalist forces of Chiang Kai-shek were driven from the mainland of China to the offshore island of Formosa by the Communist forces of Mao Tse-tung.

Because of these two earth-shattering events, the United States quickly had to rethink its plans—or lack thereof—for Asia. For instance, the Joint Chiefs of Staff revised their thinking. They now believed that if Russia were to launch an all-out war, the major aim of the United States in Asia would be to defend Japan and Okinawa so they could be used as bases for air warfare against the Soviet Union.

In Washington, the word had been out for some time: Reduce the federal budget. Slash, cut, pare, trim. Nothing in it was sacred. Everything was fair game. Particularly vulnerable was the defense budget, totaling fifteen billion dollars. World War II was still too vivid in the eyes of many Americans, so no one wanted a large military establishment. Where better to save than in the production of arms and manpower?

And no service was hit harder than the Marine Corps, *w/so the Army as they soon proved* whose manpower dropped dramatically, from a postwar level of 155,592 in 1946 to a low of 74,270 in 1950. And only 40,364 were in fighting trim.

Times were so hard for the corps that if the 1st and 2nd divisions were combined, the total strength would still be 20 percent less than the twenty-one thousand men called for in a standard battle-ready division.

Marine pilots, whose skills are so vital in close air support of men on the ground, used film at gunnery practice because there was little or no ammunition. But neither were there funds to develop the film, so pilots did a lot of their own maintenance on their planes. A marine air group in June 1950 carried 136 pilots at full strength. But few were close to that figure; several had only twenty-six or twenty-seven pilots. For every plane in the sky, there were three on the ground for lack of parts. Fuel was so scarce that many pilots removed armor on planes so they could remain in the air longer.

At Camp Pendleton, the giant marine base in California, facilities were woefully inadequate. Many buildings hadn't been used since the end of World War II. Barracks were dilapidated. Supplies and equipment were hard to come by.

But once the Russians let the world know they had the "bomb," all this began to change.

Suddenly there was a ringing call to arms in Washington. The president's fifteen-billion-dollar defense budget was now called "skimpy" and would have to be increased severalfold.

Meanwhile, in North Korea, the Communists were flexing muscles. Raids across the border were becoming larger and more frequent.

Below the thirty-eighth parallel, our advisers were working around the clock with Korean troops, but the result was anything but gratifying. There was a lack of leadership among the Koreans; and while the size of the army was growing, the amount of weapons and supplies was not.

To put it bluntly, the South Koreans were not good soldiers.

In fact, on June 15, the Korea Military Advisory Group training staff cabled its superiors in Washington that the Korean Army was in such sad shape and that equipment and supplies were so scarce that "Korea is threatened with the same disaster that befell China."

There were persistent reports from foreign diplomats and various intelligence sources that North Korea was on the verge of launching a major attack against South Korea. Reports, or rumors, such as these were commonplace. They had been popping up for some time, from both North and South. Nevertheless, they were cause for concern.

And no one was more interested in the situation than Gen. Omar Bradley, chairman of the Joint Chiefs of Staff. Bradley was in Tokyo conferring with Gen. Douglas MacArthur, the American commander in the Far East, about a myriad of problems. While there, Bradley ran into an old friend and former West Point classmate, Brig. Gen. William L. Roberts, who was heading home for retirement after spending the final two years of his career as chief of KMAG. Bradley thought it time to check out the rumors and get a solid briefing on the situation in Korea. They met on June 20, 1950, in MacArthur's headquarters in the Dai Ichi Building in downtown Tokyo. Bradley questioned Roberts closely about the reports concerning North Korea and about the ability of the ROK Army to repel an attack.

"Roberts was completely reassuring," Bradley said. "The ROK army could meet any test the North Koreans imposed on it," Roberts told Bradley.

"Since I knew Roberts to be a professional soldier of good judgment," Bradley said, "I took his word on it, feeling greatly relieved that we had no cause for concern in Korea."

Bradley, however, was not privy to the feelings of the on-the-ground KMAG advisers. Nor was there a sound explanation for the great disparity in evaluation of the ROK troops by the KMAG rank and file and their commanding officer.

Then Bradley, who caught some sort of bug during his stay in the Far East, left for home, arriving at Fort Myer, Virginia, on June 24, and immediately went to bed for much-needed rest. why?

Thus was the stage set for North Korea's invasion of South Korea on June 25, 1950.

RETREAT, HELL!

CHAPTER 1
CABLE 925

Saturday, June 24, 1950, Washington, D.C.:

At 9:26 P.M. in the code room of the State Department, a clattering teletype machine began to spew forth Cable 925 from the American ambassador in Korea, John J. Muccio, to the secretary of state:

"Confidential

"NIACT

"925. According to Korean Army reports, which partly confirmed by KMAG field adviser reports, North Korean forces invaded ROK territory at several points this morning. Action was initiated about 4:00 A.M. Ongjin blasted by North Korean artillery fire. About 6:00 A.M. North Korean infantry commenced crossing parallel. . . . It would appear from nature of attack and manner in which it was launched that it constitutes all-out offensive against ROK."

Although the security classification was only "confidential," Cable 925 did carry the all-important designation "NIACT," which told those in the code room to decipher it immediately and make certain someone at the very top is made aware of its contents as quickly as possible.

Frank E. Duval, the chief watch officer at the department that night, began to have those contacted who were on standby should a crisis occur. Each was asked to report to the department as quickly as possible, but for security reasons they were not told the contents of 925.

Dean Rusk, assistant secretary of state for Far Eastern affairs, and Frank Pace, secretary of the Army, were the first to arrive. They came straight from a party. Within the hour they were joined by H. Freeman Matthews, deputy undersecretary of state, and John D. Hickerson, assistant secretary of state for United Nations affairs.

Dean Acheson, the secretary of state from 1949 to 1953, was at his home, Harewood, in nearby Maryland, resting after a hectic week—the governors' conference on Tuesday, a graduation address at Harvard on Thursday, a long session with the Washington press corps and, finally, a lengthy briefing for an upcoming appearance before a congressional committee. Just getting away from the ringing telephone was a welcome change. The more they rang, it seemed, the louder they got.

He had puttered around in his garden most of the day, planting, pruning, pulling a few weeds, paying little attention to the security people hovering in the background. He had an early dinner and retired

19

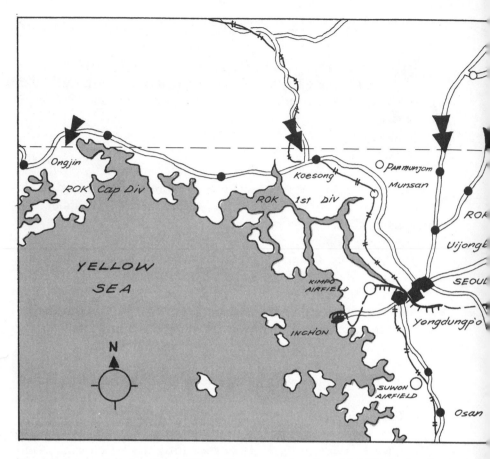

Map 1—Arrows show locations of North Korean attack on June 25, 1950. Broken line that begins west of Seoul and runs to the east shows South Korean defensive line on the southern side of the Han River on June 28, 1950.

for the night. Close by was the "white phone," which was connected to the switchboard at the White House. He hoped it wouldn't ring. It was used sparingly by his staff, but when it rang, it meant big trouble.

That night it rang at 10:00 P.M. It was Hickerson. He quickly read the contents of 925 to a stunned Acheson. After several moments of silence, they discussed what course of action to take. Hickerson suggested that the situation be placed before the United Nations at the earliest possible moment, which would be in the morning, Sunday, June 25, just a few hours away. Hopefully by daybreak a little more information would be forthcoming from Seoul. At this moment the only other

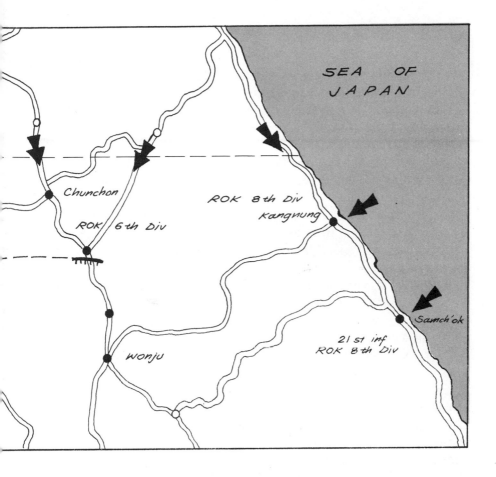

indication of trouble in Korea was a story out of Seoul carried by United Press news agency that reported the invasion. In fact, it was this very brief news bulletin that first alerted the State Department that there was a crisis brewing in Korea. At the same time that 925 was arriving, the department had drafted and sent the following message to the embassy in Seoul:

"Plain. 612. UP bulletins report tonight North Korean forces launched general offensive across border. Heavy tanks in use; First Army defeated. Story by Jack James. Advise urgently."

Gen. Omar Bradley was very ill and fast asleep in Quarters One at

Fort Myer, Virginia. The chairman of the Joint Chiefs of Staff and Louis Johnson, the secretary of defense, had just returned from an arduous trip to the Far East and talks with American commanders, including Gen. Douglas MacArthur. One of the major problems discussed was Korea, and the recurring rumors of an impending invasion from the North.

At 10:00 P.M. UP reporter Dayton Moore telephoned the general's residence, got him out of bed, and asked for comment on the situation in Korea.

"Situation in Korea?" Bradley asked. "What situation?" Moore then read him the bulletin from Seoul.

"I was stunned speechless and, of course, had no comment," the general said.

At 10:00 P.M. a copy of 925 was sent to the Department of the Army. Another went to the Pentagon. Two were dispatched to the White House for transmission to the president, who was vacationing with his family in Missouri.

Harry S. Truman had planned what he hoped would be a quiet weekend, but he was up early. He first wrote a brief note to an old friend, Stanley Woodward, the newly appointed ambassador to Canada, inviting him to visit the Florida White House the following winter. Then he flew to Baltimore, Maryland, to shake a few hands and say a few words at the dedication of Friendship Airport. ". . . why, I don't know," Truman said in his note to Woodward. "I guess because the governor of Maryland, the two senators from that great state, and the congressmen, and the mayor of Baltimore high-pressured me into doing it. . . ."

Nevertheless, he seemed to enjoy it, and was in a great frame of mind when the presidential plane *Independence* took off for Kansas City. He went by car to his home in Independence, waved to well-wishers, talked to a few close friends, then settled down to a nice family dinner and a weekend of small talk.

So far, the president's weekend had been everything he hoped it would. At no time did he have a sense of impending trouble.

This changed at 9:20 P.M. Missouri time when his telephone rang. It was a somber secretary of state who said:

"Mr. President, I have very serious news. The North Koreans have invaded South Korea."

Truman was at a loss for words. When he was able to speak again, he wondered aloud if he should return immediately to Washington. The president and Acheson discussed this for several minutes, then agreed that for the time being he should remain in Independence and do exactly as he had planned. To do otherwise, to return to Washington in the dark, would be both dangerous and might create panic in the nation, perhaps the world.

Acheson then brought up Hickerson's suggestion that the invasion be taken to the United Nations, and the president agreed. They discussed the lack of solid information from Seoul, and Acheson told Truman he would keep him informed throughout the night should any details be forthcoming. Regardless, they planned to talk again Sunday morning.

Official Washington, at best a slumbering giant and on weekends more so, was beginning to stir. Switchboards around town were coming alive. Information officers at the Pentagon, the Army, Navy, and Air Force departments were fending off reporters who were trying to find out exactly what was happening in Korea. At this point there wasn't much to tell them.

Phillip Jessup, ambassador at large, had arrived at State. So had Theodore Achilles, director of the Office of European Affairs. David Wainhouse, deputy director of the Office of United Nations Political and Security Affairs, was there, too. Then Miss Ruth Bacon of the Bureau of Far Eastern Affairs walked in.

The crisis team—those who would deal with the fighting in Korea that first night and into Sunday morning—was now in position.

Hickerson tried to reach members of the U.S. delegation to the United Nations. Warren R. Austin, the permanent representative, was on vacation and could not be reached. Nor could Ernest Gross, the deputy ambassador, be found.

So Hickerson did it himself. At 11:30 P.M. he telephoned UN secretary general Trygve Lie and told him of the North Korean invasion. Lie was stunned. Hickerson then told him that the United States would bring the invasion before the Security Council at the earliest possible moment Sunday morning.

Wainhouse and Bacon then began drafting the document.

It was a crafty move on the part of Acheson and Hickerson. Jacob Malik, the Soviet representative at the UN, was in Moscow. He hadn't attended a session for some time in protest over the seating of Nationalist China and the lack of a representative from Red China. So there was no chance of a Soviet veto of the resolution.

The decision to go to the United Nations was made on the basis of that one cable, 925, a tribute to Muccio and an indication of how seriously the United States viewed the news.

Just before midnight, copies of 925 were transmitted to London, Paris, Moscow, Ottawa, Tokyo, Canberra, Manila, Wellington, New Delhi, Djakarta and Taipei.

Then the first day of the Korean War passed into history on a note of ominous silence between Washington and Seoul. The State Department could not reach Muccio. There was no more information from the ambassador on the fighting.

Washington, D.C., Sunday, June 25, 1950: The next word from Muccio, at 2:05 A.M., was a plea for ammunition for South Korean troops. Cable 929 asked for a ten-day supply for ninety 105mm howitzers, seven hundred 60mm mortars, and forty thousand .30-caliber carbines. The message left no doubt that there was heavy fighting along a wide front.

In Tokyo, Gen. Douglas MacArthur said that South Korean troops would get all the weapons and ammunition in his command.

By 3:00 A.M. Gross had arrived in his New York office and was on the telephone to Trygue Lie, reading him the formal request that the Security Council be convened immediately to consider the fighting in Korea. It read:

"The American ambassador to the Republic of Korea has informed the Department of State that North Korean forces invaded the territory of the Republic of Korea at several points in the early morning hours of June 25 (Korea time).

"Pyongyang Radio under the control of the North Korean regime, it is reported, has broadcast a declaration of war against the Republic of Korea effective 9:00 P.M. EDT June 24.

"An attack of the forces of the North Korean regime under the circumstances referred to above constitutes a breach of the peace and an act of aggression.

"Upon the urgent request of my government, I ask you to call an immediate meeting of the Security Council of the United Nations."

At 4:00 A.M. Rusk spoke by telephone with William J. Sebold, the acting political adviser in Japan, and tried to obtain more details on the fighting. Sebold could give him none.

A few hours later, at 6:46 A.M., Cable 935, from Muccio to Acheson added a grim new dimension to the fighting. Four North Korean MIGs attacked Kimpo Air Base, near Seoul, shot up a U.S. Air Force transport, a fuel truck, and set fire to several buildings and a number of other planes.

"The future of the fighting could well depend on whether the United States will provide air support to the South Koreans," Muccio stressed.

Then, at 8:44 A.M., the Army, trying to get a better picture of what was happening in Korea, set up a top secret teletype conference between Washington and Tokyo, between the intelligence apparatus that included the Army, Navy, and the Central Intelligence Agency, and MacArthur's Far East Command, and came up with the first solid information on the fighting.

Washington: What North Korean units were committed?

Tokyo: Reports indicate the 3rd Border Constabulary Brigade on Ongjin Peninsula; two divisions, possibly 1st and 2nd, attacking south toward Pochon and Uijongbu; forty tanks reported several miles north of Uijongbu; 1st Border Constabulary Brigade, minus two battalions, reportedly landed on the eastern coast; two battalions of 1st Border Constabulary Brigade attacking south along eastern coastal road; 7th Border Constabulary Brigade attacking near Pochon; 6th Division reportedly in Sariwon moving south toward Kaesong; independent mixed brigade, possibly the 4th Division, in general reserve, location unknown.

Washington: Resistance of South Korea?

Tokyo: Reports indicate orderliness of withdrawal of South Korean units.

Washington: Is South Korean government standing firm?

Tokyo: Government standing firm and maintaining internal order. Martial law declared in most towns. Curfew in Seoul.

Washington: What is your estimate of objective of current North Korean effort?

Tokyo: There is no evidence to substantiate a belief that the North Koreans are engaged in a limited-objective offensive or in a raid. On the contrary, the size of the North Korean forces employed, the depth of penetration, the intensity of attack, and the landings made miles south of the parallel on the eastern coast indicate that the North Koreans are engaged in an all-out offensive to subjugate South Korea.

Washington: Do you have any information regarding numbers of North Korean naval forces involved in amphibious landings on Korean eastern coast?

Tokyo: We have no information as to number of ships involved. However, landing of thirty-two hundred to thirty-eight hundred reported at four points.

Washington: We assume Far East Command will assume responsibility to assist the U.S. ambassador to Korea in providing for safety of U.S. nationals in emergency.

Tokyo: In view of proximity of enemy tanks to American embassy we have plans to evacuate American women and children tomorrow through Inchon on available transportation. Will provide American naval and air protection. General situation now points to a tank breakthrough via Uijongbu.

Washington: Are there any indications of Soviet military participation?

Tokyo: There is no evidence of Soviet military participation in invasion.

Washington: What casualties are reported?

Tokyo: KMAG has been queried on casualties.

Washington: Is there anything you request from the United States at this time? Have you anything further?

Tokyo: We have last-minute information from KMAG in Seoul. Seventy tanks concentrated in night bivouac five miles north of Uijongbu. As of midnight tonight morale of South Korean troops reported good. Civilian population disturbed but fairly stable.

The next cable from the Far East was the most ominous to be received so far. It raised for the first time the specter of American troops being drawn into the fighting. It was from Sebold in Japan to Acheson and contained the thoughts of veteran diplomat John Foster Dulles and John Allison, director of the Office of Northeast Asian Affairs, who were in Tokyo at the time of the invasion.

"Top Secret

"619. For Acheson and Rusk from Dulles and Allison. It is possible that South Koreans may themselves contain and repulse attacks and, if so, this is the best way. If, however, it appears they cannot do so then we believe that U.S. forces should be used even though this risks Russian countermoves. To sit by while Korea is overrun by unprovoked armed attack would start disastrous chain of events leading most probably to world war. . . ."

When Acheson talked to Truman on Sunday, the news was all bad: North Korean tanks and infantry were closing on Seoul. Kimpo Air Base was in danger. American dependents were being evacuated, and there were reports that Rhee's government was getting ready to flee south. What had been termed as an orderly withdrawal was now becoming a rout.

At this point Truman told Acheson that he was returning to Washington immediately. He wanted all his advisers at dinner at Blair House that evening at 8:00 P.M., followed by a war conference. Included were Acheson, Rusk, Jessup, Hickerson, Bradley, Johnson, the service secretaries, and the Joint Chiefs of Staff.

The *Independence* touched down at St. Louis at midday to pick up Secretary of the Treasury John Snyder, then continued on to Washington. While still in the air, the president received the first good news in more than twenty hours: The UN Security Council had approved, 9–0, the resolution condemning North Korea's "act of aggression."

The *Independence* landed at 7:15 P.M., and Truman went straight to Blair House (the White House was being remodeled) and dinner with his diplomats and generals. Several subjects were discussed, none of which pertained to Korea. The president had asked that this not be brought up until they had their coffee and the servants had withdrawn. At that point Acheson read the latest cables and added what bits of information he had gathered from other sources. The evacuation was discussed. So was the resupply of South Korean troops. Then the president ordered that MacArthur send a survey party to Korea immediately "to get the facts."

Then they began to discuss what was on everyone's mind: sending American ground troops to Korea. By now everyone realized that if Korea were to remain free, American assistance would be needed.

After much talk, Truman ended the session by directing that orders be issued for the eighty-thousand-man garrison force in Japan to get ready to go to Korea.

On Monday, June 26, the evacuation of women and children was continuing, with Air Force jets flying cover. Then, because of the rapid disintegration of the ROK Army, Muccio ordered the evacuation of all women who for one reason or another had elected to remain behind; they were sent on the way south by convoy. Enemy planes were strafing military and civilian airfields near Seoul. President Rhee, his cabinet, and most other government officials were fleeing south by car and train. The city's residents were told by loudspeakers to remain indoors as the first North Korean tanks entered the outskirts. Muccio cabled Acheson that he intended to remain in Seoul to the bitter end, but he was told to get out while he could.

At 9:00 P.M. the president met again with his advisers. He opened the session by reading a message from MacArthur: "Tanks are in the city and heading for the Han River, where ROK troops have thrown up a defense line on the south bank." Acheson said the situation was so bad that State had lost contact with Seoul. The Army said it still had contact, but only with a ham operator and wasn't getting much information.

The president wondered if he should call up National Guard and fleet reserve units, including the marine reserves, but Bradley suggested he wait forty-eight hours before making that decision.

Next day, Tuesday, June 27, the Security Council adopted without amendment a resolution that "recommended that the members of the United Nations furnish such assistance to the Republic of Korea as may be necessary to repel the armed attack and to restore international peace and security to the area."

By this time, Muccio had arrived in Taejon and located Rhee, who was attempting to set up a temporary government. The survey party that Truman had ordered to Korea returned to Tokyo and reported to MacArthur that only U.S. ground troops could stop the North Koreans. Disturbed, the general flew to Korea the following morning. His plane, the *Bataan,* landed at Suwon, about thirty miles south of Seoul. He met with Muccio and Rhee, who drove up from Taejon, then left for the front. From a position overlooking the Han River he watched a defeated army in full retreat. He returned to Tokyo and sent this cable to the State Department:

"Top Secret

". . . the Korean Army and coastal forces are in confusion, have not seriously fought, and lack leadership. South Korean military strength estimated at twenty-five thousand effectives. The Korean Army is entirely incapable of counteraction and there is grave danger of a further breakthrough. . . . If the enemy advance continues much further it will threaten the fall of the republic. The only assurance for holding of the present line . . . is through the introduction of U.S. ground combat forces into the Korean battle area. . . . If authorized, it is my intention to immediately move a U.S. regimental combat team to the reinforcement of the vital area discussed and to provide buildup of up to a two-division strength from the troops in Japan for an early counteroffensive."

The response was immediate. At 3:40 A.M. on June 29, Washington time, the Army messaged MacArthur: "Okay to send RCT to Pusan, not into combat." *Bradley type decision — the not starts from the Top!*

The general was furious and cabled his superiors: ". . . it does not satisfy the basic requirement in my message. . . ."

Within minutes the Army responded, saying: "Will take it to the president right away, get back within half an hour."

Meanwhile, ROK defenses along the Han had cracked wide open, and tanks and infantry were streaming south virtually unchecked. Roads were clogged with refugees. South Korean troops had suffered an estimated 60 percent casualties and were outnumbered four to one.

Twenty minutes later, MacArthur got the word he wanted so desperately: "Your recommendation to move one RCT into combat is approved. You will be advised later as to further buildup."

At Camp Wood in southern Japan it was Friday night, June 30, and Lt. Col. Charles B. Smith, his junior officers, and his sergeants were hurriedly trying to round up the men of Companies B and C, 1st Battalion, 21st Infantry Regiment, 24th Division, and get them aboard trucks that would take them some eighty miles to Itazuke Air Base. From there they would fly to Korea to become the first American ground combat troops to face the enemy. Cooks, truck drivers, clerks, bakers, anyone who could be found that night—about 450 in all— became members of Task Force Smith, the Army's ill-fated attempt to slow the onrushing North Koreans. The two understrength rifle companies, far below the size of a regimental combat team, poorly trained, *poorly led* poorly armed, possessing nothing that would stop a Russian T-34 tank, were the best the Army could offer. *General Walker was in charge of the 8th Army!*

At 9:30 P.M. the president again gathered his advisers together and told them that in addition to the RCT, more American combat troops were headed for Korea.

The next day, June 30, Washington time, Congress extended the draft act for one year and gave the president power to call up National Guard units.

In Japan, meanwhile, the rest of the 24th Division was preparing to sail for Korea as soon as enough transports could be found. The 1st Cavalry Division (infantry) and the 25th Division would follow. Once there, they would become part of a new command, the U.S. Eighth Army, Korea (EUSAK), and would be under the command of Lt. Gen. Walton H. Walker, a crusty, tough old bird just past fifty with World War II experience under Gen. George S. Patton, who referred to him as "my toughest son-of-a-bitch."

At this time the news from Korea was as bad as it could be. Task Force Smith had met the enemy on the morning of Wednesday, July 5, and almost immediately ceased to be a viable fighting force. North Korean tanks raced through the inexperienced GI's without slowing. Then came the infantry, and for Task Force Smith, this was the end.

In the first few days of July, MacArthur pressured Washington for a battle-ready marine division with the necessary air support. He confidently told the Joint Chiefs that it was his intention, once the North Koreans had been halted, "to exploit our air and sea control and, by amphibious maneuver, strike him [the enemy] behind his mass of ground force."

But the only troops available to him at this time were those in Japan on soft occupation duty—the 1st Cavalry, 7th, 24th, and 25th divisions —all of them understrength, with no more than 12,000 men in any one division. The only division in the United States in fighting trim was the 82nd Airborne Division, and the Joint Chiefs made it clear to the general that he would never get his hands on this elite fighting force. No National Guard divisions would be ready until after March 15 the following year. No new divisions could be built through the draft before March 1. And there could not be a steady stream of replacements until after January 1.

The marines, for instance, couldn't put together a battle-ready division unless their reserves were called up. The 1st Provisional Marine Brigade (reinforced) was activated on July 7 at Camp Pendleton, about eighty miles south of Los Angeles. The sixty-five hundred ground and air marines were regulars—well trained and combat-ready. But after that, the pickings were slim. The brigade weighed anchor seven days later, bound for Kobe, Japan, but the fighting was so intense that it was diverted to Korea while still at sea.

Meanwhile, MacArthur continued to press for a full-size marine division and an air wing. After much nagging, the Joint Chiefs relented; the marine reserves were called up.

Events began to move rapidly. Overnight, a sprawling Camp Pendleton, a sleepy marine base caught in the throes of steep budget cuts, became a hub of activity as thousands of regulars from 105 posts and stations throughout the United States began to report to Pendleton.

Young marine lieutenants Ty Hill, Chuck Kiser, and Don Floyd were at the Keyport, Washington, naval torpedo station at a clambake when the telephone rang at 11:00 P.M. It was for Hill. He listened, smiled. It was from the wife of the executive officer at the marine barracks at nearby Bangor. She told him that he, Kiser, and Floyd were to report immediately to Treasure Island at San Francisco and join the first replacement unit for Korea.

"We thought that she was playing a little joke on us," Hill recalled, "so I said, 'Okay, Margaret, what's the telephone number back there that called you?' "

She gave Hill the number and he dialed and got the sandblasting shop at the Bremerton Navy Yard.

"We knew for sure then that it was a joke," Hill said, and the party continued.

The next morning they discovered it was no joke when a copy of the message arrived from the communications center at Bremerton.

And the wrong number the night before?

"Quite a bit of booze was flowing," Hill remembers, "and that might have had something to do with it."

They arrived at Treasure Island the next day only to discover that, as so often happens in the corps, their orders were changed en route. They were to report instead to Camp Pendleton, where they were to fill out the ranks of the Marine 1st Division.

There was a feeling of apprehension when they arrived. To many, it was reminiscent of another time when they had shipped out to such strange-sounding places as Guadalcanal, Tarawa, and Iwo Jima.

The flow of regulars quickly became a torrent, and the torrent quickly became a flood as more than twenty-five thousand new arrivals taxed the base beyond capacity. Supplies poured in. Quarters were readied. Tent cities popped up everywhere. Marines got off one train and set about preparing for those on the next train. And the trains arrived day and night for many days.

If you asked each incoming marine how well trained he was, he'd tell you he was combat-ready. But the truth was that very few reservists had received much in the way of training. Many had never fired their rifles. In the confusion of full mobilization, most of their personnel records were either lost or misplaced. It was impossible to know who was ready for Korea and who was not. So the marines did the next best thing. Each man was personally interviewed and then placed in one of two categories: combat-ready or noncombat-ready.

On July 25, the Joint Chiefs alerted corps headquarters that they wanted the division combat-ready, minus one regiment, in time to ship out for Korea between August 10 and 15. Then, just before the division sailed from San Diego, the marines were ordered to activate the 7th Regiment and have it on the way to Korea by September 1.

The division was now intact, although scattered in three different locations. The 5th Regiment, the primary component of the brigade, was at sea. The 1st Regiment was formed and about to board troop transports, and the 7th Regiment was just being assembled at Pendleton.

Hill, Kiser, and Floyd were members of the 81 Club at Pendleton: Check in at 8:00 A.M. and again at 1:00 P.M. to see if you had been assigned to a unit. They waited. Two days, three, four. For a while it appeared as if they might miss this one, and no marine ever wants to do that. How would you explain it to your children? The grandchildren. "They gave a war and I didn't go!"

Then it happened: All three were assigned to the 1st Battalion, 7th Regiment. Now that they had a permanent address, they could draw their 782 gear—cartridge belt, canteen, compass, map, poncho, everything that a marine officer in a line company needs—by signing Form 782.

Next, they met their troops. "The company commander was a disappointment," Kiser remembers. "He had come from a marine detachment at the World's Fair and all he had was his multiple suits of dress blues, whites, swords, white gloves, and a parade background."

At first sight, the battalion commander was an even greater disappointment.

"The first time I saw him he had a set of dungarees on that had never been to a laundry," Kiser recalled. "They were all wrinkled. They had just come off the shelf. They had been folded for years."

They didn't fit him well at all. He was short, perhaps five-six or five-eight, pencil-thin. The shoulders hung down two or three inches, and the sleeves were too long. Each was rolled up two or three turns. And the hat. It came down to his ears, bending them down and out. "He looked like [backwoods movie character] Percy Kilbride," Kiser said.

"Oh, Jesus Christ," Kiser thought.

Then word spread through the ranks: This was Raymond G. Davis, battalion commander during much of the island-hopping campaigns in the Pacific, winner of the Navy Cross, a tough, resourceful marine's marine.

"You only had to be around him a few minutes to realize he was an exceptionally intelligent person," Kiser remembers, "and that he was very knowledgeable in everything that pertained to the infantry."

John Yancey was thirty, tough, outspoken, one who would offer an opinion on anything at any time, which isn't the smart thing to do in a small, tightly knit organization such as the Marine Corps, where every stone has its place. He had heard his first shot fired in anger on Guadalcanal. He and several others once charged what they thought was a small band of Japanese only to find instead that they had stumbled onto a company. They killed seventy-six. Out of it came a Navy Cross and a commission for Yancey.

"But I couldn't take the horseshit," he said, so he got out after the war and joined the reserves.

Now he was back, recalled to active duty to see if he had one more war in him. A warrant officer interviewed him and asked if he would volunteer for combat.

"I'm probably the best damn combat leader you got," Yancey shot back, loud and clear.

The interviewer grabbed the phone to Col. Homer Litzenberg, who was fleshing out the 7th Regiment, and shouted:

"Colonel, I've got a live one!"

"I'll send a jeep right over for him."

"When I got to Litzenberg's headquarters, he asked, 'Are you the one that volunteered?'"

"Yes, sir!"

"Go get a haircut." Yancey was in the 7th Regiment.

After a second interview, he was given a platoon, but not a company, as he had hoped. When he saw his men, he was horrified. Eight were straight out of the brig and still had on their prison garb.

"One of them, though, was the best damn soldier I ever had," Yancey said. "Pvt. Stanley Robinson. He took a special delight in killing people. He was only nineteen or twenty. He always had this silly grin, no matter what the situation was. He did so many, so damn many great things, I was always sending citations on him to Litzenberg."

Why was he in the brig?

"He told me he beat up an officer," Yancey said. "Hell, he probably needed it."

Right away Yancey started to shake down his platoon, get to know the NCO's, the men. All his squad leaders had fought in the Pacific.

"He called us all together one day," recalled PFC Marshall McCann, his radio operator and runner, then said, 'Anyone who doesn't want to be in a line company, step forward one pace.'"

Three men stepped forward.

"Tough shit!"

Now that he had his platoon, he had little time to work with it. He never had the opportunity to take the men out at night. They never went to the rifle range. All their time was spent getting shots, their gear, having their records updated, if they could be found.

Two days later they were at sea, bound for Korea. Ahead were twenty-two days of chalk talks on the bulkheads, firing off the fantail at orange crates tossed overboard, and endless hours of cleaning weapons.

Between July 7 and September 1, the corps put together a division almost from scratch, consisting of twenty-four thousand marines and 1,145 Navy personnel and had it on the way to Korea.

Meanwhile, by the end of July there were more than ninety thousand United Nations troops in South Korea, almost as many as there were North Koreans.

The Army's 1st Cavalry, the 24th and the 25th divisions were in the line now, and the 7th Division would soon be leaving Japan for Korea, an army of young kids and old weapons.

The only bright spot in the war so far was the marine brigade that had been thrust into the western sector of the perimeter around Pusan opposite North Korea's veteran 6th Division. Although outnumbered, the marines fought them to a standstill around the cities of Masan and Chinju. Then, early in September, the brigade was pulled back, re-armed, rested briefly, its ranks filled by a few replacements, and it joined with the 1st Marine Regiment for an assault landing at a place called Inchon, far up the coast and just west of Seoul.

It was the worst possible location for an amphibious assault.

The president had serious misgivings about MacArthur's plan when he first heard about it. The Joint Chiefs were more concerned than the president. The admirals and generals who would have to pull it off had grave doubts about it, too.

Adm. James H. Doyle, the commander of American naval forces in the area, thought it was a big gamble that was far too risky. Gen. Oliver P. Smith, commander of the 1st Marine Division that would have to make the assault, liked the idea even less.

About the only brass who really liked the idea besides MacArthur were members of his staff.

There were just too many important questions that had to be an-swered, and the Joint Chiefs felt that they were not getting these an-swers, or that they were not getting straight answers. The Joint Chiefs became so concerned that General Bradley sent two members—Gen. J. Lawton Collins, of the Army, and Adm. Forrest P. Sherman—to Tokyo to discuss it with MacArthur. They met in the general's head-quarters in the Dai Ichi Building in Tokyo on August 23.

The supreme commander in the Pacific listened with great patience for three hours, much as a father would listen to his children, while the visitors ticked off their concerns.

What about seawalls of undetermined height?

Do we know the length of the scaling ladders?

Then there were the mudflats that could ensnare landing craft if the tide were not right.

Would not the element of surprise be lost once the softening-up bombardment began?

And the "beaches," "Red" and "Blue": They were not real beaches but two widely separated landing zones in the heart of the industrial section of the city that featured many structures. Wouldn't this afford good cover for the defenders?

These were but a few of the many questions MacArthur and his chief of staff, Gen. Edward M. Almond, were asked.

Many were answered, but just as many went unanswered, by the time MacArthur took the floor to explain the purpose of Inchon.

Inchon was chosen as the landing site because it was close to Seoul —about thirty-five miles to the west—and he felt that it was psychologically important to recapture the city.

He felt, too, that the North Koreans were stretched paper thin from the thirty-eighth parallel to the southern tip of the peninsula and very soon they would have to slow or even halt their advance so that food and ammunition could catch up to the troops. All he had to do to end the war, he said, was land behind the enemy and cut the lines of communication and supply and the war would be over.

At the same time, the Eighth Army would break out of the Pusan perimeter and shove north, ultimately catching the bulk of the North Korean Army in a giant pincers just below and slightly to the east of Seoul.

As for losing the element of surprise, MacArthur viewed this differently than did his detractors, who listened to him as if in a trance.

All the fears, the potential drawbacks, would actually serve to ensure the element of surprise, because no one would dare dream that a landing would take place at a location as precarious as Inchon.

September 15 was selected as D-Day, his staff explained, because on that date water conditions would be such that landing craft could get very close to the seawalls.

"Now is the time to strike," MacArthur told the hushed gathering.

"I can almost hear the tick of the second hand of destiny. . . . We shall land at Inchon, and I shall crush them."

The general simply overwhelmed his audience.

Collins and Sherman returned to Washington, explained in detail the landing operation, and the Joint Chiefs approved it. So did the president.

The marines stormed ashore at 5:30 P.M., the 1st Regiment at Red Beach, the 5th Regiment at Blue Beach. Rocks, shoals, and mudflats really didn't cause them too much trouble, although several landing vehicles did get stuck in the mud for a few hours. And the Navy missed several landing areas, but the assault, nevertheless, was a huge success.

The heavy bombardment had turned Inchon into a pile of rubble. As the first waves climbed over the seawalls they saw a wall of flame, for everything before them was burning. The engineers blasted holes in the rock walls for the tanks and other tracked vehicles. The first waves then got out of the dock area as quickly as possible and headed for the heart of the city. Korean Marine troops followed and held the city that night as the 1st and 5th regiments headed toward Seoul.

By morning, more than eighteen thousand men had come ashore. The Eighth Army broke out of the perimeter around Pusan and slowly moved north.

The assault landing had cost the marines twenty dead and 174 wounded. The North Koreans lost 1,350 dead, wounded, and captured.

MacArthur's great gamble had paid off. He had placed his reputation, his career, on the line, and he had won.

Congratulations poured in from everywhere; even the Joint Chiefs of Staff had a kind word for him.

A day later, Walker's Eighth Army had the enemy on the run. South Korean troops were moving up the eastern coast, and the marines were well on their way toward Seoul. The 7th Division had come ashore at Inchon and was right behind the marines. Soon it would swing a bit more to the east and try to hook up with the Eighth Army, which was charging north from the Pusan Perimeter. The marines and the Army's 7th Division were now part of what had become X Corps and were under the overall command of General Almond.

The 1st and 5th regiments of the marine division were well on their way to Seoul before the North Korean People's Army fully understood that a major enemy force had landed far to their rear and that they were in grave danger of being trapped. Burning T-34s and North Korean dead littered the highway to Seoul as the marines moved quickly toward the capital. But the closer the marines got, the tougher the fighting became. When they entered the city they were met by ten thousand fresh, heavily armed troops who fought house-to-house.

By September 25 the marines were in the center of the city, which had been reduced to rubble. There were three more days of heavy fighting before the city fell.

On September 27, infantrymen from the 31st Regiment, 7th Division linked up with advance units of the Eighth Army near Suwon, just below Seoul, trapping thousands of enemy troops. But for the rest of the NKPA, the only hope was to escape above the thirty-eighth parallel.

The major question at this point was how far MacArthur's troops should chase the North Koreans. All the way to the thirty-eighth parallel? Across the parallel? If so, how far? To the Yalu River, the boundary with Manchuria? These questions were answered to some extent in a cable from the Joint Chiefs on September 27 to MacArthur:

"Your military objective is the destruction of the North Korean armed forces. In attaining this objective you are authorized to conduct military operations, including amphibious and airborne landings or ground operations north of the thirty-eighth parallel in Korea. . . ."

MacArthur and his staff needed no more than this, the go-ahead to pursue the North Koreans as far as necessary to destroy them. This was the green light to cross the thirty-eighth parallel and wage war in the enemy's territory. The rest of the message contained what Washington at that time felt were sufficient safeguards, restraints, restrictions, paragraph after paragraph of cautions on what he could or could not do in following the directive, but they were either circumvented, misinterpreted, or disregarded.

MacArthur was perhaps at the apex of his career. Inchon had been the crowning achievement, the greatest gamble of his illustrious military life. Accolades were still pouring in from the free world. But in the process he did something military commanders never do: He had divided his forces in the face of the enemy. Yet he had won. So why not again? Why not another amphibious assault in the enemy's backyard?

MacArthur's plans and operations staff in Tokyo already had two proposals on the drawing board. One had the Eighth Army driving north and northwest toward Pyongyang, while an amphibious force would seize the port of Chinnampo on the Yellow Sea. The other had the Eighth Army striking north and northeast along the Seoul-to-Wonsan corridor while an amphibious assault would be made at Wonsan, far up the eastern coast and well above the thirty-eighth parallel.

There was a definite need for a port such as Wonsan if the war were to be carried into the North and to the east because huge amounts of supplies, weapons, vehicles, and replacements would be needed. Under the Japanese, Wonsan had become Korea's petroleum refining center. It was situated on a good harbor. Railways and roads were among the best in Korea. Port facilities were good. There was ample storage areas.

And the port city was the eastern terminus of the Seoul–Wonsan corridor, the best of the few natural routes across the mountainous country.

The question was: How to take the port? Would it be by a 115-mile overland march? Or would it be a seven-hundred-mile voyage down the western coast and back up the eastern coast?

There was still the delicate situation of two separate commands operating in Korea: the Eighth Army under Walker, and X Corps under Almond. Both men had assumed that once the Inchon operation had taken place, X Corps would become part of the Eighth Army. But this did not happen. Thus, at a critical time in the fighting, there would be a divided command in Korea, with poor communications, their flanks exposed and separated by 115 to 150 miles of mountain ranges as high as five thousand feet. None of the division commanders liked this setup.

As for taking Wonsan, Walker and his staff favored an overland march. So did the Navy. Three generals on MacArthur's staff in Tokyo also favored this plan. All voiced strong objections to an amphibious landing. But most of these objections never reached MacArthur, and those that did were too feeble to carry much weight. Later, when the obvious drawbacks were pointed out, no strong objections were made even then.

MacArthur's plan called for the marines to ship out of Inchon and the 7th Division to depart from Pusan, arriving at Wonsan a few days after the marines had stormed ashore.

But this would tie up both ports with outgoing troops and equipment at a time when both were vitally needed for the off-loading of incoming supplies for the Eighth Army. For instance, none of the soldiers had winter clothing, and Korean winters are harsh. All the railways and roads would be clogged with southbound traffic at a time when everything should be moving north.

About the best that could be said for the general's proposed assault on Wonsan is that it was hastily conceived and very poorly planned.

As Gen. Matthew Ridgway, the army's deputy chief of staff, noted: "A more subtle result of the Inchon triumph was the development of an almost superstitious regard for MacArthur's infallibility. Even his superiors, it seemed, began to doubt if they should question any of MacArthur's decisions and as a result he was deprived of forthright and informed criticism, such as every commander should have—particularly when he is trying to run a war from seven hundred miles away."

Ridgway also noted that a good many military leaders have recognized that it takes a special kind of person, a special kind of courage to stand up to your superior and tell him that your think his plan is wrong.

As General Marshall said so often, "That is the time when you put your commission on the line."

MacArthur opted for the amphibious assault. He felt that the rugged Taebek mountain range that separated the two coasts was too formidable an obstacle to cross, despite a relatively good road between Seoul and Wonsan. Almond supported this view, adding that he didn't think the road was passable.

The marines passed through Seoul in late September and were pushing north when the division was pulled from the line and replaced by Eighth Army troops. The marines were trucked back to Inchon and loaded aboard transports for the long, dreary voyage to Wonsan, on the other side of the peninsula. The other part of X Corps, the 7th Division, was already moving south by truck and train toward Pusan to climb aboard troop ships for the trip up the eastern coast.

Walker's Eighth Army was racing north now with virtually no opposition in what MacArthur called his general offensive to wipe out the North Korean Army and end the war.

On October 9 armored forces of the 1st Cavalry Division roared across the thirty-eighth parallel and raced toward Sariwan and the North Korean capital of Pyongyang. The 24th Division was moving up along the coast, to the left of the 1st Cavalry. Sariwan fell a few days later, and the 1st Cavalry entered Pyongyang on October 19. The city fell three days later. Elements of the 1st Cavalry then occupied the port city of Chinnampo, about thirty-five miles southwest of Pyongyang.

The ROK Army, restructured and attached to the Eighth Army, was doing equally well.

In rugged central Korea, where each hill seemed to grow taller and steeper the closer you got to it, the ROK 6th Division had captured Hwachwon, Chorwon, and Kumwha. On October 22, the 6th Division had moved slightly west and was bearing down on Kunu-ri, about forty-five miles by air north of Pyongyang.

ROK troops moving swiftly up the eastern coast had already captured the marines' objective, Wonsan, with hardly a shot fired. The marines, now at sea en route to Wonsan, had received new orders: Make an administrative landing at Wonsan, then deploy rapidly to the west along the Pyongyang–Wonsan axis and hook up with Eighth Army troops, thus trapping the rest of the North Korean Army.

In his Tokyo headquarters, a confident MacArthur predicted that the war would soon be over.

What had taken place in Korea could be classified as incredible.

A few weeks earlier, MacArthur had been defending a toehold on the southeastern tip of the peninsula. At any moment his forces could have been shoved into the sea. Now, with the success at Inchon, all of Korea was MacArthur's for the taking. And he intended to take it—all of it.

If there was any question about this, it was removed in an exchange of cables between Marshall, the new secretary of defense, and MacArthur.

Marshall, in his message, told MacArthur: "We want you to feel unhampered tactically and strategically to proceed north of the thirty-eighth parallel."

MacArthur's immediate response was brief and to the point: "I regard all Korea as open for our military operations."

Yet despite his great success, cracks were beginning to appear in his grand plan to end the fighting. His luck, it appeared, was beginning to change.

- The problem of a divided command had seeped down to the Eighth Army, which was now rushing toward the Yalu in four separate columns as opposed to advancing along a broad west-to-east front.
- There was very little, if any, flank protection for the four columns.
- There was extremely poor lateral connections and very poor communications between the columns.
- The offensive was being run from MacArthur's headquarters in Tokyo based on questionable intelligence from Korea. The most damaging area was in trying to evaluate the intent of the Chinese. Would they intervene, or not? The closer MacArthur's forces got to the Yalu, the more important the answer became.
- There seemed to be a war's-over atmosphere among the troops. Many infantrymen hadn't heard a shot, or fired their weapons, in days. They were tossing away their equipment along the roadside

41

—helmets, gas masks, extra ammunition, anything to make their load lighter. They walked in bunches, not the normal five to seven yards apart along both sides of the road. They were doing all the things you shouldn't do in a situation like this.

- The command structure was deteriorating from the top down.
- There was increasing confusion as far as X Corps was concerned. Its mission had already been changed once and would be changed again and again and again.

In describing the events that took place during the next few weeks after MacArthur crossed the thirty-eighth parallel, Secretary of State Acheson said: "It was the greatest defeat suffered by American arms since the Battle of Manassas and an international disaster of the first water."

CHAPTER 2
OPERATION YO-YO

Those Tough and Fighting Gyrenes,
Wherever They May Be,
Are Always Bringing Up the Rear,
Behind Bob Hope and the USO.

Thus another verse was added to the Marine Corps Hymn, this by the U.S. soldiers who accompanied the ROK Army's I Corps into Wonsan days ahead of the Marines' 1st Division.

When the convoy of seventy-two ships arrived off Wonsan, the marines discovered that the harbor had been sown with two thousand sophisticated mines. Although minesweepers had been working for a week, it would be another seven to ten days before a path could be cleared to the beach.

In the meantime, the ships would have to sail up the coast for twelve hours, turn around and sail back for twelve hours, then repeat this again and again until it was safe to approach the landing areas.

The marines dubbed this "Operation Yo-Yo," and they didn't like it. Food ran short. Aboard one vessel the menu was mustard sandwiches three times a day. Morale dropped. Tempers flared. Dysentery swept through several ships. One, the *Marine Phoenix,* had a sick call of 750. Smallpox was discovered on another transport.

And had the ground marines known that the air marines were already ashore and had set up shop, they would have been irate.

Now, on the evening of October 24, Bob Hope and Marilyn Maxwell were putting on a USO show, and the marines still at sea were the objects of many of the comedian's jokes.

What had started out as an assault landing on an enemy-held beach was now reduced to an administrative landing, a routine over-the-side-and-into-the-landing-craft operation followed by a slow and easy ride to the sand. When the marines waded ashore with their fighting gear it was a little embarrassing because the GI's were there to greet them, singing that new but not popular addition to the "Marine Hymn."

At 9:00 A.M. on October 26, the 1st and 3rd battalions of the 1st Regiment landed on Yellow Beach, the first of thirty-nine waves that brought the division ashore. Troops of the 7th Regiment went ashore at Blue Beach at 1:00 P.M. Advance parties of the 5th Regiment landed at both Yellow and Blue beaches, and by morning all three regiments were on land.

By now it was clear to everyone that the transpeninsula march was

45

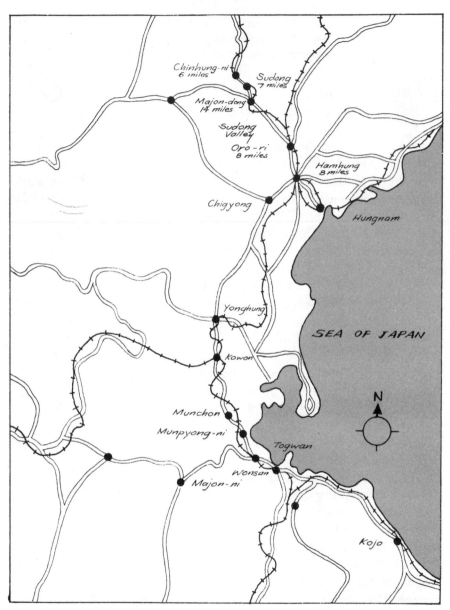

Map 2—Marines landed at Wonsan, deployed briefly to Kojo and Majon-ni, then went by rail and truck to Hamhung to begin the seventy-eight-mile march to the Chosin Reservoir.

46

no longer practicable. The Eighth Army was well beyond Pyongyang, and the marines, because of the delay brought about by the mines, could not move west in time to close the gap along the Pyongyang–Wonsan axis and trap the fleeing North Koreans.

Once ashore after twenty-three days of inactivity, the same "war's over" atmosphere that plagued the Eighth Army now prevailed among the marines.

Signs began to appear everywhere: "Drive Carefully: The Marine You Hit May Be Your Replacement."

General Smith, the marine commander, received a message from naval headquarters in the Far East informing him that upon cessation of hostilities the Navy would recommend that the marine division be sent home, minus one regiment, which would remain in Japan.

A few days later, Smith became aware of a letter circulating in the Far East disclosing that Almond, the corps commander, would soon become commanding officer of the occupation forces.

And then there was MacArthur's remark that "the boys will be home for Christmas."

So it's easy to see why the marines at this point were thinking of home more than of fighting.

MacArthur, meanwhile, had issued new orders for X Corps. He instructed Almond to get his troops up to the border with China as quickly as possible and to disregard any previous restrictions placed upon him. Prior to this there had been a restraining line that ran across North Korea, west to east, from forty to fifty miles below the northern border. Only South Korean troops could operate beyond this line. But now the rules were changed, and both Walker and Almond were told to use whatever forces were necessary to capture all of North Korea and ". . . to drive forward with all speed. . . ."

MacArthur also told Almond that he wanted the marines to seize the Chosin Reservoir and the 7th Division to secure the Fusen Reservoir. Both were fifty to sixty air miles from the port of Hungnam. The Fusen Reservoir was about twenty miles east of the Chosin Reservoir.

The 7th Division was still at sea and was due to land shortly at Wonsan. Now it was directed to land at Iwon, about a hundred miles northeast of Wonsan. As soon as the GI's touched land they headed north, toward the Fusen Reservoir.

The marines, meanwhile, had been given a sector three hundred miles north by south, and fifty miles wide west to east, and five of their specific orders were those of an occupation force. The sixth was not. It read: "Advance rapidly to the border."

Smith's staff then broke down this far-reaching order and assigned the following to each of the three regiments:

- 1st Regiment: Relieve elements of the ROK Army's I Corps in the Wonsan–Kojo–Majon–ni area, patrol the roads, and destroy the enemy.
- 7th Regiment: Relieve elements of the ROK I Corps along the Hamhung–Chosin Reservoir road, advance rapidly to the northern tip of the reservoir. Be prepared for further advance to the northern border of Korea, and destroy the enemy in the zone.
- 5th Regiment: Move to position behind the 7th Regiment, relieve elements of the ROK I Corps in the vicinity of the Fusen Reservoir, establish necessary roadblocks to prevent enemy movement into the area, patrol the roads, and destroy the enemy.

The order did not indicate that the marines would encounter heavy resistance from anyone—guerrillas, fleeing North Korean troops, or the Chinese.

As soon as the marines were ashore, the 1st Battalion of the 1st Regiment was dispatched to Kojo to relieve ROK troops and guard a supply dump that no longer existed. Along the thirty-nine-mile route from Wonsan there was no sign of the enemy, but later in the afternoon, as the trucks were pulling into Kojo, a few shots were fired at a jeep, a truck, and several wiremen. This brought the ground-pounders out of their lethargy and let them know that a person could get killed here.

Then, at 10:00 P.M., North Korean troops surprised the marines, and the fighting was so heavy that come morning the 2nd Battalion was sent from Wonsan to help. By this time the fighting was over and the North Koreans had fled. The marines suffered twenty-three dead, forty-seven wounded, and four missing, and word spread quickly through the division that the war was not over.

Later, the two battalions at Kojo and the third at Majon-ni were replaced by newly arrived U.S. Army troops. The three battalions returned to Wonsan, and the 1st Regiment was intact again. Then it moved by rail to Hamhung and fell in behind the 7th and 5th regiments to begin the advance up the treacherous seventy-eight-mile road to the Chosin Reservoir.

The road began at Hungnam, which was just to the right of where the Songchan River flows into the Sea of Japan. From Hungnam to Hamhung is eight miles; from Hamhung to Sudong is twenty-nine miles; from Sudong to Chinhung-ni, six miles; from Chinhung-ni to Koto-ri, ten miles; from Koto-ri to Hagaru-ri, eleven miles, and from Hagaru-ri to Yudam-ni, fourteen miles.

Not a mile was easy.

It was narrow and winding. Oxcarts had a hard time passing, let alone tanks, trucks, and artillery. Most of the road was dirt and gravel. At times it seemed to go straight up; at other times, straight down. It went from low country to towering peaks.

On one side were cliffs hundreds of feet high; on the other, sheer drops.

The most difficult stretch was Funchilin Pass, a slow, steady climb of eight miles to the high country, twenty-five hundred feet up, to Koto-ri. North of Koto-ri the road runs into a high plateau, then continues on to Hagaru-ri, most of which had been flattened by bombing.

Above Hagaru-ri, at the southern tip of the Chosin Reservoir, the road climbs and winds up to Toktong Pass, four thousand feet high, then drops into Yudam-ni Valley. There it splits, one route continuing north, another west.

This, then, is the road—or Main Supply Route (MSR)—that will become so terribly important to the marines in the days ahead and on which the eyes of the world will soon focus.

In the last days of October, the 7th Regiment moved from Wonsan to Hamhung by rail, received a little cold weather clothing, then started up the road toward the reservoir, with Davis's 1st Battalion leading the way. Three jeeps raced ahead to the command post of the 26th Regiment of the ROK 3rd Division, the regiment that the 7th Marines was to replace in the hills near Sudong, and for the first time marines saw their new enemy—a Chinese soldier, a prisoner. He wore a tattered quilted uniform, old tennis shoes, and carried a single-shot rifle so dirty that it probably wouldn't have fired. At the time the new enemy didn't seem formidable.

But when the 7th Marines arrived to replace the ROK troops they found the Koreans upset and anxious to leave. They were already on the way out, and a few were running.

"Many, many Chinese up there," the marines were told.

49

Next day, November 1, the marines received word that the Army's 1st Calvary Division in the northwest had run into a lot of Chinese and had gotten beaten up pretty badly. Then the Chinese withdrew as mysteriously as they had appeared.

Despite this, it was difficult to get MacArthur's intelligence people to accept the fact that China had entered the war. Almond, for instance, was continually pushing Smith to get the marines up the road toward the reservoir as quickly as possible.

Perhaps the general's staff didn't want to believe that large numbers of Chinese had crossed the Yalu.

At Wake Island on October 16, when President Truman and MacArthur met to discuss the status of the fighting, the president asked MacArthur what the chances were of Chinese or Soviet intervention in Korea, and the general replied:

"Very little. Had they intervened in the first or second months it would have been decisive. We are no longer fearful of their intervention. We no longer stand hat in hand. The Chinese have three hundred thousand men in Manchuria. Of these, probably not more than a hundred thousand to 125,000 are spread along the Yalu River. They have no Air Force. Now that we have bases for our Air Force in Korea, if the Chinese tried to get down to Pyongyang, there would be the greatest slaughter. . . ."

But the Chinese knew otherwise.

They were already across the Yalu in great numbers and, by late November, there would be more than three hundred thousand soldiers poised to attack the Eighth Army along the Chongchon River in the northwest and the marines at the Chosin Reservoir.

And the first major battle for the marines was but a few hours away, near Sudong, where the 7th Regiment was digging in for a cold and what the marines thought would be a relatively peaceful night.

CHAPTER 3
A NEW ENEMY

November 2, 1950; headquarters, 7th Regiment, 6:00 P.M.:

The atmosphere was tense as key officers hurried toward Litzenberg's tent in the Sudong Valley, a mile south of the village. His men were in the hills, cold, weary, waiting for first light when they would begin the division's attack north to the Chosin Reservoir power complex and then on to the border with China.

Litzenberg wanted to make certain that every man in the regiment was aware that a new enemy was in front of them, more menacing, better equipped, much better led than the North Koreans. He felt certain that his men would encounter this new enemy head-on—very soon—so he told his officers:

"We can expect to meet Chinese Communist troops, and it is important that we win the first battle. The result of that action will reverberate around the world, and we want to make certain the outcome has an adverse effect in Moscow as well as Peking."

He was so concerned that he told them their regiment "might be taking part in the opening engagement of World War III."

Ray Davis's 1st Battalion was at the northern end of the valley, just south of Sudong. Capt. David W. Banks's A Company was on the right of the road, on Hill 532. Capt. William E. Shea's C Company was on the front of Hill 698, on the left of the road and up a few hundred yards. Close behind and on both sides of the road and into the hills were the men of Capt. Myron E. Wilcox's B Company. Not far behind and close to the road was Davis's battalion command post. The 2nd Battalion command post of Maj. Webb D. Sawyer was a few hundred yards behind Davis's. Sawyer's three rifle companies were high in the hills on both sides of the road behind the 1st Battalion positions. Capt. Elmer J. Zorn's F Company was high on Hill 727 on the right. Capt. Walter D. Phillips's E Company was on the left side of the road on Hill 698, just a few hundred yards from the top. Capt. Milt Hull's D Company was on the lower backside of the same hill and not too far from the road. The 7th Regiment's headquarters was alongside the road, close to Hull's company and several hundred yards behind the 2nd Battalion's command post.

Just behind regimental headquarters was the command post of Maj. Maurice Roach's 3rd Battalion, which brought up the rear of the 7th

53

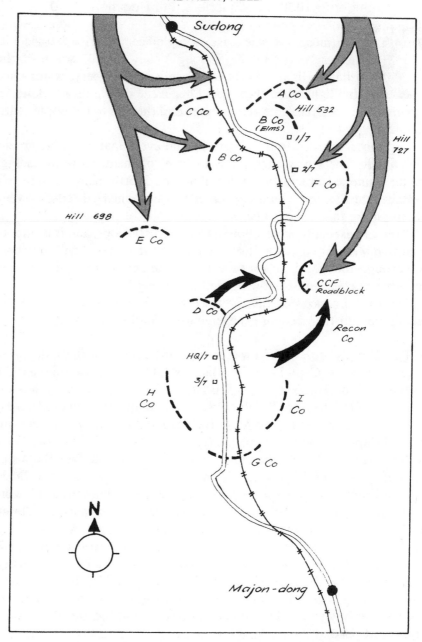

Map 3—Arrows coming from the north indicate route of Chinese attack during the Battle of Sudong. Dark arrows show marine attack on Chinese roadblock.

Regiment in a horseshoe formation: H Company was in the hills on the left; I Company was in the hills on the right; and back a short distance was G Company, astride the road.

Although a late-afternoon helicopter flight revealed no Chinese in the hills, they were out there, well concealed and in great strength, waiting for nightfall. The 371st Regiment of the Chinese 124th Division was hidden to the north and west of the valley. The 370th Regiment was concealed on the high ground east of the road. A few miles farther back and just north of Sudong was the 372nd Regiment in reserve but within easy striking distance of the valley.

The 124th, 125th, and 126th divisions were part of the Chinese Communist Forces (CCF) Forty-second Army, which crossed the Yalu River between October 14 and 20. The 124th marched southeast to position itself for the defense of the Chosin Reservoir; the 126th moved a little farther east, to guard the Fusen Reservoir; and the 125th guarded the Forty-second Army's right flank.

When the Chinese discovered the marines on the road north, the 124th was quickly shifted to the hills around Sudong to confront them.

Now, in the early evening hours of November 2, you could hear the faint sound of gunfire in the distance. The marines were exhausted. They had marched most of the day, then climbed into the hills at dusk, and dug their foxholes after dark. Even so, no one dared sleep, or even relax. Every marine had heard the rumors that swept the hilltops: Chinese are everywhere. "We were afraid to close our eyes, we were looking for Chinese behind every rock and tree," Lt. Harrol (Chuck) Kiser remembers.

The outposts were now reporting enemy probes, searching for weak spots, trying to find a seam where one unit tied in with another. Slowly the intensity of fire increased. The probes became bolder, more frequent. Soon Hills 698 and 727 were sheathed in fire and flame. Cries of wounded could be heard. By midnight a full-scale battle was under way.

3rd Platoon, B Company, 1st Battalion, Hill 698, 11:30 P.M.: Kiser's men were stretched thin along a narrow ridge for about a hundred yards on the front of the hill. A .30-caliber machine gun anchored his position on the left. He had an outpost about eighty to a hundred yards above the machine gun at a point from which he figured the Chinese attack would come, "Although you could see that from any one of the ridges around us, the Chinese could come right down to our positions," Kiser said.

Sgt. Joe Hedrick was huddled in his foxhole, cold and wondering about the gunfire he could hear. He thought, too, about the South Korean officer who ran by him earlier in the day, slowed, pointed to the hills, and said, "Many Chinese up there!"

"We all smiled," Hedrick remembered, "and accepted it for what it was—the overexaggeration of an unsophisticated soldier."

Archie Van Winkle, Kiser's platoon sergeant, was on his knees crawling from hole to hole talking to the men, calming some, reassuring others, sharing a joke with the few who had been shot at before. Then he inched his way up the thirty-five-degree slope to spend a little time with the four men there.

"I was just trying to get everyone looking at the world with the same set of eyeballs," he explained.

Lt. Chew En Lee, the company machine gun officer who was with Kiser, slipped into the night to try to locate the Chinese. He was back in minutes and excitedly whispered to Kiser, "They're preparing to attack . . . they're just out of sight. . . ." Before he could finish, the Chinese were there.

Cpl. Richard Germond, nineteen, heard the whistles and bugles, saw the Chinese, then they were past him. They hit the top of the hill so fast that five marines were bayoneted in their holes.

3rd Platoon outpost, Hill 698, 11:45 P.M.: "They were just kids so I sat around and talked about what could happen, what to do if it did happen," Van Winkle said. "They were a little clutched up about the whole thing, so I stayed a little longer than I had planned." The outpost had good communications with the platoon, so Van Winkle cranked up the phone and listened:

"This is Charlie. We hear sounds."

"This is Able. Chinese moving to our left. We can hear them talking."

Van Winkle watched the men and thought, "Obviously they're more scared than I am, and I'm scared as hell. And I've been shot at before."

A corporal on Guadalcanal in World War II, a sergeant at Cape Gloucester. A platoon sergeant on Peleliu. Twice wounded, he left the hospital and switched to marine air as a gunner. The Distinguished Flying Cross, two Air Medals, two Purple Hearts. Then the reserves. Now he was back. Soon his list of decorations would grow by one: the Medal of Honor.

Van Winkle heard the bugles just before midnight. Then the phone went dead and he realized they were cut off, on their own. Five men against an untold number of Chinese. Down below he could see the fighting. Chinese were swarming over the ridge.

"The whole area seemed to explode," Van Winkle said. "There were flares, tracers, grenades. It sounded like a symphony with me in the middle of the orchestra."

Then more Chinese came down the hill from every direction toward the platoon.

"Christ, we were out there to warn the platoon that the Chinese were coming," he said. "Well, the platoon didn't need any goddamn warning to tell them that the war was on."

Then the Chinese spotted the outpost. "Before you knew it, they were close enough to use grenades," Van Winkle said. "That's when it gets very personal." There were more Chinese around the outpost now than they could handle if each had a machine gun, so Van Winkle told them to get ready to go back down the hill to the platoon.

"We're going down the hill with our faces looking up the hill and we'll keep shooting at them," he explained. One man was hit in the arm before they left. There was no time to wrap it. They backed out of their hole facing upward and firing. Then flares burst overhead, lighting the entire area.

"Freeze! Freeze!" Van Winkle shouted. "Get down low, keep your eyes open. You'll see Chinks running by, but if you get up, you're dead . . . !"

"I turned around and they were gone. I don't know if they got hit. I never saw them again," he said.

November 3, 1950; 3rd Platoon, Hill 698, midnight: Kiser was up to his eyeballs in Chinese. You just couldn't shoot fast enough. Once they struck, there wasn't any doubt they were going through.

"You can only shoot what you can see," Kiser said. "It was dark.

They were just forms gliding by in the darkness. You can't aim-fire. They had the advantage in night fighting. They carried Thompsons and could just spray the area. We had rifles and had to aim them."

"We fired one shot at a time, they sprayed, then they were through us, that was it," he said.

The Chinese hit in groups of about thirty all along the platoon line. "In that same distance where there were thirty, there were maybe eight or nine of us," Kiser explained. "If each one of us got off one shot and hit our target, that still left twenty or twenty-one that got through."

Once that happened, and the Chinese headed down the backside toward the valley, half the men had to turn around and face down just in case the Chinese changed their minds and came back up. Then, when the Chinese struck again, when the next wave hit, fewer men faced the front and more of the enemy was able to get through.

Kiser was on the phone talking to Wilcox, whose command post was down in the valley near the road.

"What the hell's going on up there?" he hollered at Kiser.

"The Chinese broke through and they're coming down!" he shouted.

"What are your coordinates and how far are they from you?"

Kiser gave him the coordinates, then the distance.

"They're all over the place, they're in our position, they'll be in your lap in a minute."

"I'll try to get some artillery up there!" Wilcox shouted.

"Hell, they were too busy down there," Kiser said. "They were fighting for their lives."

Van Winkle had reached the left side of the platoon and leaped into a hole close to the machine gun. When he looked around, all he could see were Chinese. The machine gun was still in marine hands, but it looked like the Chinese would have it in a minute or two. "I started shouting orders, but there were more Chinese than marines," he said. "Every time I turned around to try and find someone I knew, I saw another Chinaman."

He tried to fight his way toward the center of the platoon, but he couldn't. He'd lost his carbine but had an old Springfield rifle that he was using as a club. But it broke in two when he smashed it over the head of a Chinese soldier. Grenades were exploding everywhere. Muzzle flashes were so close he suffered powder burns on his face.

Kiser had lost touch with the company CP. The wire had been cut, so he sent a runner down the hill to find Wilcox and tell him exactly what the situation was. Usually, in a situation like this, the runner picks up the wire, runs it through his fingers, and starts walking. Unfortunately, whoever cut the wire is usually waiting for him. Then it comes down to a matter of who shoots first. Or you can say, "To hell with that," and send the runner down in another direction. This is what Kiser did.

Van Winkle was still fighting at the machine-gun position but could see that they couldn't hold it much longer.

"It got very exciting about this time, and somewhere along the line I lost my cool," he remembers. By this time they were fighting hand to hand, and the marines were losing. Then he got hit by shrapnel. And a bullet struck him in the back. The last thing he remembered is the grenade that came "boiling at me."

"It was a potato masher, coming end over end, and I could see the fuse burning in the handle." He took a swipe at it with one hand, missed, and it exploded in front of his face, the full force hitting him in the chest.

"We were all keyed up," Germond remembered. "Ed Koppold threw a grenade out and it came right back. He threw it out and again it came back. It came back three times before he realized that he didn't take the tape off." The grenades came in a canister of three. Each had a strip of tape around it. You first took off the tape, pulled the pin, then threw it.

"We found out later that another guy had thrown a whole case without taking off the tape," Germond said.

A Company, 1st Battalion, Hill 532, 12:25 A.M.: The 1st and 2nd platoons were under attack on three sides. "Everywhere you turned, there were Chinese," Sgt. Robert Olson remembered. "We were spread thin on top. We simply had more ground to cover than we had men, so once the Chinese got to the top, we had to pull back to where our 3rd Platoon was dug in on a spur of Hill 727." As soon as the Chinese got to the top of 532, they forgot about the marines and raced down toward the valley. Hill 727 dwarfed 532. There were Chinese on top firing into the valley. Then the infantry began to descend. When they got to the foxholes, they just ran by. "We kept firing, and we got a lot,

59

but they didn't seem to care. They just wanted to get down to the valley," Olson said.

The marines were hit hard. They had a lot of wounded. The able-bodied helped them down to the aid station. As they did, the Chinese ran by, looked at them, didn't seem to care, and continued running toward the road.

2nd Platoon, B Company, 1st Battalion, Hill 727, 12:45 A.M.: "It was pretty late when we heard the bugles," Lt. William Graeber said. "Then all hell broke loose. Gunfire . . . screaming . . . everywhere. . . ." They were on top in no time. The fighting continued for what seemed like hours. Then Graeber was told to get his men off their hill and back across the road to rejoin B Company. He led them off a knoll and down a draw toward the valley, but they ran into a deadly crossfire. No sooner had they left their holes than the Chinese were up there, firing down at them, over their heads into the valley.

"Chinese were all over the place, we couldn't get through the cross-fire, and we sure couldn't go back up where we were," Graeber said, "so we just stayed where we were and began shooting Chinese." There was no shortage of targets for the next two hours. Then, when the firing eased, he led his men across the main supply route and they rejoined B Company.

By this time the Chinese were swarming down Hill 727. It looked as if someone had kicked over an anthill. The Chinese were so intent on reaching the valley that they ran past the foxholes of F Company and down toward the lightly defended headquarters and support units of the 7th Regiment.

Headquarters, 2nd Battalion, 6:30 A.M.: "When daylight came, we found that we were in a dickens of a mess," Sawyer said. "The rifle companies were up in the hills and the Chinese were occupying the terrain between the CP and the companies." Confusion reigned in the valley. Chinese were everywhere. They captured a 4.2 mortar tube after overrunning a mortar company. Both the 1st and 2nd battalions' command posts were threatened. A huge section of the road was blown away. Most important, the Chinese held the key bend in the road that separated the 1st and 2nd battalions from the 3rd Battalion.

The marine drive north had been stalled by a surprisingly aggressive enemy.

To regain the initiative the marines began very slowly to wipe out the roaming Chinese. Then the heights were cleared of pockets of resistance, particularly the top of Hill 698, from where the Chinese were raking the valley with machine-gun and mortar fire.

This took several hours of savage, close fighting from daybreak until late afternoon. At some points it was hand to hand. Artillery and marine air blasted the ridges with napalm and high explosives, killing and wounding hundreds of enemy soldiers. The marines fired 1,431 artillery rounds that day, as much falling inside the perimeter as outside.

3rd Platoon, B Company, 1st Battalion, Hill 698, 6:30 A.M.: The Chinese who had swarmed over Kiser's men were now running amok in the valley. The machine-gun position was lost at about 4:00 A.M. but later regained. The platoon still held the ridge at daybreak. Bodies were everywhere. From their number the marines estimated that at least two companies had tried to drive them off the hill.

"I won't ever forget that night," said Cpl. Vernon Dyrdahl.

"When we weren't shooting, we were trying to scrape our holes a little deeper," Germond said. "That night you couldn't dig deep enough."

C Company, 1st Battalion, Hill 698, 6:45 A.M.: The enemy had either missed Shea's men or bypassed them intentionally to get to the valley because they were not attacked during the night, and in the morning all the fighting in the northern end of the valley was down on the road. Lt. Ty Hill could see the Chinese behind a railroad embankment about eight hundred yards away firing at the 1st Battalion command post. "I was standing with binoculars, looking at the Chinese, positioning a machine gun to take them under plunging fire when I saw a guy down on the railroad turn around and put a rifle to his shoulder," Hill said. "He looked right at me, at our position. Then he fired. Right about that time I felt a bullet hit me. It felt like I had been kicked in the shin," he said. The bullet tore into his left knee and he went down. A corpsman patched him up and he stayed on top the rest of the day, until the Chinese were driven from the valley.

"The best thing I can figure is that I saw the guy shoot me," Hill explained.

2nd Platoon, E Company, 2nd Battalion, Hill 698, 7:15 A.M.: The fog was so thick at daybreak that Yancey couldn't see five feet in any direction. But he knew the Chinese were close, on the hill above him. They had exchanged gunfire throughout the night. Now he expected them to attack, to try to drive his men from their hilltop, which was situated about 150 to two hundred yards from the top. Even before the fog lifted he could hear movement and passed the word not to shoot until they saw something to shoot at.

Then he heard his first bugle, then a cymbal, and shouting and screaming.

"The first thing I saw were feet as the fog lifted, and they weren't wearing boots," Yancey said.

The first soldier he saw was the bugler, who was about twenty-five yards away.

"I snapped a shot and the bullet went in through the bugle," he said. "Then it was as if someone had lifted a curtain and the Chinese were there. They fought through the morning until the marines counterattacked and the Chinese scrambled away.

That afternoon Yancey was told to take the top of the hill. The Chinese were firing down into the valley and raising too much hell. Hull's D Company had tried to take the top but failed. So had Lt. Robert T. Bey's 3rd Platoon, E Company. Now it was Yancey's turn.

McCann, his runner and radio operator, called the company CP in the valley and asked for napalm and rockets on top. The Corsairs were there in minutes but had no napalm, and their rocket fire was ineffective.

"There's only one way to go," Yancey told his men. "We'll use the basic marine assault formation, 'hi-diddle-diddle, straight up the fucking middle until you're so close they can't use mortars and grenades.' "

He had two rifle squads, about twelve men in each; a machine-gun squad; and a second runner, PFC Rick Marion.

"I also had Robinson and a crazy machine gunner, [Pvt. James Patrick] Gallagher. He was remarkable. With people like this, we couldn't get beat," Yancey said.

They crossed a saddle, then went about fifty yards upward across an open area that was crisscrossed with machine-gun fire. A marine dropped. Then a second. A bullet zipped through the lapel on Yancey's field jacket. Not a scratch. McCann was close by. A Chinese soldier ran toward him, a huge bayonet on the end of his single-shot rifle. McCann dropped him with five rounds in his chest. Robinson had his squad on the right, shot six Chinese, and by the time he reached the top he was the only person alive in his squad. Yancey picked up a Browning Automatic Rifle someone had dropped close to the top and used it to beat back the first of three swift Chinese counterattacks. "I fired it so damn much it caught fire and burned my hands," he said.

"Just when I was about to give up on it, when I thought we'd get kicked off that hill, I looked around and here came that damn Gallagher, firing over our heads into the Chinese, who were counterattacking again."

Gallagher's squad was so shot up he had no one to help so he was carrying that machine gun in his arms, along with two cans of ammunition, and firing.

"I just took off," Gallagher said. "I grabbed that gun and followed him up the hill because he needed more firepower."

"I once asked Gallagher why he did so damn many great things," Yancey said, "and he told me, 'Skipper, my momma didn't raise no cowards.' "

"Yeah, I was a bit crazy then. I've done a few crazy things in my life," Gallagher said. "For instance, my brother-in-law was in a reserve outfit and was called up a few days after the Korean War started. He was ordered to report to Camp Le Jeune, so I said, 'Hey, wait a minute, I'll go with you.' "

So Gallagher, who first snuck into the Corps at the age of sixteen and was later discharged, signed up for Korea at Le Jeune, was shipped to Camp Pendleton a few days later, and joined Yancey's platoon two days before it shipped out.

Gallagher remembers Hill 698, and Yancey.

"He let us know early on that he would give the orders and we would follow them," Gallagher said.

"Yancey never said, 'We'll take that hill,' " Gallagher added. "He said, 'Follow me up the hill.' "

The top of the hill was secure now. "I got there with six men and the remnants of another squad," Yancey recalls, "maybe twelve men in all."

They had beaten back two furious counterattacks and were trying to get ready for another. Yancey and McCann shared a foxhole. "We piled up gooks for sandbags," McCann said.

"I'll live a thousand years and I'll never forget the sound of a bullet hitting a frozen body," Yancey said.

"Radio back that we've secured the hill," Yancey told McCann, then continued digging.

He did and told Phillips they had a lot of wounded on top.

"He said it was a question of whether or not he should go up, or call us back down," McCann told Yancey. The radio operator then shouted into the phone, "You better get the hell up here, you son of a bitch!"

Yancey grabbed the phone and hollered at Phillips, "Get some damn people up here in a hurry!"

"We can't! The machine-gun fire is too heavy!" Phillips answered.

"Hell, we just came through it!" Yancey shouted.

Lt. Leonard Clements overheard the conversation and knew immediately that Yancey, a good friend, was in trouble. Clements's 1st Platoon had the rear guard behind the company CP in the valley, but quickly, on his own, he split his men and led seventeen to the top and not one of them had a scratch. They reached the top in the middle of the third counterattack. Clements shot the officer who was leading the counterattack. Robinson killed seven Chinese.

"It wasn't hand to hand yet, but it sure as hell was belly to belly," McCann said. "It really got messy in a hurry. We sure killed a lot of Chinese in five to ten minutes.

"That's when I wished I was a termite so I could crawl under my helmet and hide," McCann said.

The Chinese had bloodied Yancey's men. There were more dead and wounded on the hill than men who could fight. They couldn't get them down because fighting was raging in the valley, from one end of the perimeter to the other, that stretched two thousand yards north to south and eight hundred yards east to west.

The wounded were bandaged, fed, and made as comfortable as possible. Late in the afternoon his platoon returned to the company CP. Yancey began a search for replacements. His men were out of everything—flares, grenades, ammunition. So McCann asked for an air drop, and in a few minutes two Air Force C-119 Flying Boxcars were over-head, then the parachutes blossomed and the supplies floated to earth: seven hundred rolls of barbed wire.

"You goddamned Air Force assholes!" McCann shouted into the radio. The Air Force quickly realized its mistake, and another flight appeared in the sky and the much-needed supplies arrived.

Headquarters, 1st Battalion, 11:30 A.M.: "Hey, will you look at that!" a marine shouted. Sgt. Roy Pearl, Davis's radio operator, turned and saw more than a company of Chinese walking down the railroad tracks that ran through the valley about a hundred yards away. "They didn't know we were there, waiting," Pearl said. "When they were abreast of us, we fired with machine guns. Very few escaped."

This was the turning point in the fight for the valley.

"I even opened up with my rifle," Pearl remembers. "I was just doing my part." Then he felt a hand on his shoulder and a calm voice said, "Better get back to your radio, Pearl."

"It was Colonel Davis. My job was communications. I learned that then."

By late afternoon the marines had the situation in hand, both in the valley and on the hilltops. They had smashed through the roadblock that had separated the 1st and 2nd battalions from the 3rd Battalion. Trucks were rolling north with replacements and supplies, south with dead and wounded.

Hill was at the 1st Battalion aid station. The young Navy doctor he had met at Camp Pendleton in August and had shown how to pack his gear was taking the bullet out of his knee. Van Winkle was close by, his head propped up, in great pain, waiting to be flown to a hospital in Japan.

His friends who survived the night on Hill 698 dropped by to wish him well, to say good-bye.

"Nice work, Archie. You saved our ass."

"Hey, you did great, really great."

"What do you need, Archie?"

"Can I get you anything?"

"What I wanted was a drink of goddamned water, but they wouldn't give it to me because I had a chest wound," Van Winkle said.

"Archie was whiter than the whitest sheet," Hill said. "I didn't think he was going to make it."

Kiser came over to talk to him, to thank him for what he had done, and thought he was looking at a dead man. "I couldn't believe anyone could be that white," he said.

November 4, 1950; Sudong Valley, 7:00 A.M.: Where had the Chinese gone? And why? No one seemed to know. They had disappeared overnight as stealthily as they had appeared, so as the regiment moved north again, the whereabouts of the enemy was on the minds of everyone along the road.

Out of the fighting at Sudong the marines gained a valuable insight into the Chinese military.

They discovered that Chinese leadership was surprisingly good but that their communications was extremely poor, that you cannot effectively conduct a war using bugles and whistles to direct troops.

Most important, the marines learned that no matter how large the Chinese attacking force, no matter how deep their penetration, if you could hold out until daybreak, artillery and air power would drive the Chinese to cover.

Were the Chinese intent on defeating the marines at Sudong?

Or were they sending a message: "Don't go any farther!"?

No one seemed to know.

What the marines did know was that the two Chinese assault regiments had paid a steep price for failure. The 371st lost the equivalent of five rifle companies in its 1st and 3rd battalions. Their total dead was 793. The 3rd Battalion of the 370th was badly hurt by the destruction of two rifle companies.

In contrast, the marines lost sixty-one dead and 283 wounded.

Yancey was impressed with the Chinese.

"After we took 698, they mounted three damn good counterattacks," he said. "They were a helluva lot better than the North Koreans, better trained, better equipped, and better led.

"One way you judge leadership is the time it takes to launch a counterattack," he said. "They came in minutes, which means you're damn well led. We had a lot of respect for their officers."

"They were excellent soldiers," said Maj. Henry J. Woessner, Litzenberg's operations officer.

And what lay ahead?

McCann recalled the time when E Company's executive officer, Lt. Raymond Ball, called the men together just before they started up the road toward the reservoir. "He read us the orders that we were to secure the Chosin Reservoir for the winter. We all knew we had very little chance of surviving that type of situation."

CHAPTER 4
THE RESERVOIR

Headquarters, 7th Regiment, Sudong Valley, 8:00 A.M.:

"**B**e careful, be cautious, take nothing for granted," Litzenberg told his officers. Then he gave the "go" signal and the jeeps of his Reconnaissance Company with machine guns mounted sped north toward the marines' next objective, the village of Koto-ri, sixteen miles away.

Behind the jeeps and leading the 1st Battalion was Germond's four-man fire team. Then came the 3rd Battalion, with the 2nd Battalion bringing up the rear.

Litzenberg knew the Chinese had inflicted heavy casualties on the 1st Cavalry Division of the Eighth Army to the northwest, sixty miles away. He was aware he would have no flank protection on his left, always a dangerous situation.

He knew, also, that marine pilots had counted three hundred Chinese trucks loaded with troops a few days earlier just after they had crossed the Yalu River, and he knew that they were now just south of the Chosin Reservoir, less than thirty miles in front of his regiment.

There were other problems, too. The marines would have to wind their way up three-thousand-foot-high Funchilin Pass, a treacherous section of the road whose heights afforded the Chinese excellent protection. And the cold—numbing, brutal arctic blasts that swept down from Manchuria, freezing limbs, weapons, plasma, morphine.

Litzenberg's orders had not changed: He was still to advance to the border with China as quickly as possible.

"Under the circumstances, there was no alternative except to continue forward . . ." the division commander, General Smith, said.

This was no time to be careless, so Litzenberg took a few precautions.

He moved his regiment forward as if it were a giant fort, with a perimeter on the left, a perimeter on the right, and the front and rear. "He kept his artillery closed up, he kept his supply lines closed up . . . I think he had a good idea," said Gen. Edward Craig, the assistant division commander.

He used company-size patrols rather than those of platoon and squad strength, and they ranged far and wide to probe the valleys, the canyons, behind the hills, searching for any sign of the enemy.

2nd Platoon, Reconnaissance Company, 7th Regiment, 11:00 A.M.:
Lt. Donald W. Sharon's men raced up and down the road searching for

71

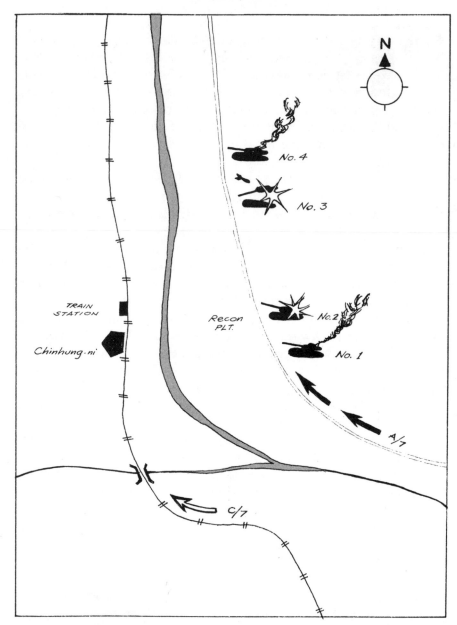

Map 4—Four North Korean tanks surprised the marines at Chinhung-ni but were quickly destroyed.

Chinese, trying to make certain that the marines behind were not caught off guard by an enemy so skilled at catching you by surprise. So well concealed were the four North Korean tanks that no one spotted them at first around a bend and on the right side of the road and across from the railroad station in Chinhung-ni. Sharon's men were interested in a small band of Chinese who had abandoned the tanks and were trying to flee across a dry riverbed and railroad tracks that ran parallel to the road. A few bursts from the .30s sent them scurrying for cover.

"Holy Christ!! They're tanks!" shouted Olson, the first to spot them as he rounded a bend in the road. He sent a runner back to warn Banks, then waited for the inevitable: the turret to start moving. Just as it began to turn, the column rounded the turn and someone shouted for the .75s and the rockets, and the first tank was finished in minutes.

Sharon's men spotted the second tank under a pile of brush about fifty yards beyond the first. He saw the periscope start moving, so he and two others jumped on top, destroyed the periscope, and dropped two grenades inside. Smoke and fire belched from the gunports and the periscope.

The third tank was hidden in a thatched hut about seventy-five yards farther down the road. It smashed through its camouflage and swung toward the advancing marines, its 85mm cannon starting to traverse. But the Corsairs were on station and one zipped earthward and blew the tank to bits with two five-inch rockets.

The fourth tank was just beyond the hut and tight against the hillside. Recoilless rifles put it out of action, and the crew surrendered.

The 344th Tank Regiment of the North Korean People's Army ceased to exist.

Reconnaissance jeeps were on the road again, pushing north but more cautious than before, with the foot marines close behind.

Headquarters, 7th Regiment, Chinhung-ni, 4:00 P.M.: Litzenberg's men had moved up the road about six thousand very careful yards. It was cold but not yet freezing. The sky was clear as his troops began to dig in for the night. Fires were allowed, but only until dark. No one had heard a shot fired in hours. As the heat from the fires seeped through their clothing and penetrated their skin, the men cheered as the night fighters from the marines' 1st Air Wing flew north to attack the Chinese around the reservoir.

In the morning the regiment would begin the tortuous climb to the high plateau and Koto-ri, so Litzenberg ordered a recon jeep patrol to scout about a thousand yards up Funchilin Pass. But this didn't set too well with some of the men in the Reconnaissance Company.

"Hell, we'd already been up there," said Sgt. Ernie DeFazio. "We knew the Chinese were up there, we'd already reported that, so we didn't need another patrol up there.

"But there was nothing we could do about it, so we went," he said.

Six jeeps with four men in each roared through the front perimeter and headed toward the pass and a defensive line set up by the shaken, badly battered Chinese 124th Division, which had fought the marines at Sudong.

2nd Platoon, A Company, 1st Battalion, 7th Regiment, 4:30 P.M.: Olson saw the jeeps race past his men and wondered where they were going and why. He knew there were Chinese ahead. His men had just set up an ambush should they decide to sneak back down after dark and harass the 1st Battalion.

The jeeps got about a mile up the pass and had just rounded a scary hairpin curve when the Chinese opened fire from two towering hills, 987 on the left and 891 on the right. Then a Chinese patrol on the road opened fire on the jeeps and drove them to cover. They were pinned down until dark, when three Corsairs raked the two hills with rockets and machine-gun fire. The jeeps were able to turn around and race back down the road, but it had been a costly foray into enemy territory. Two men were killed and several wounded, and two jeeps were destroyed and the others badly shot up.

Then Olson's platoon got into the fight and for about three hours exchanged long-range machine-gun fire. There didn't seem to be too many Chinese ahead.

November 5, 1950; headquarters, 7th Regiment, Chinhung-ni, 6:15 A.M.: It wasn't the Chinese who worried Litzenberg and Woessner as they prepared to attack the pass again. It was the road. And the cold. Litzenberg knew it would be a very difficult climb and that once they reached the top it would be terribly cold, something the marines had not yet experienced.

So did Woessner, who had flown almost the entire length of the road searching for Chinese. Although he saw no enemy troops or trucks, he did take note of the mountains covered with deep snow and knew the problems that lay ahead.

"The road was ridiculously treacherous," he said, "and it went up a mountain with no alternate route. It was a dangerous road for movement, for resupply. There was no question that if we were opposed, movement was going to be difficult."

Reconnaissance Company, 7th Regiment, Funchilin Pass, 6:45 A.M.: The jeeps were back on the road and heading toward the pass before it was light. Lt. Ernest C. Hargett's 1st Platoon was making its way toward the pass on the right side of the road. Each man had but a single thought: cover. Their world consisted of the twenty yards around them and a place to duck when the shooting began. No sooner had they reached the hairpin turn than they were caught in a crossfire and pinned down again. But the Corsairs were already overhead to bail them out. The jeeps turned around and got out of the line of fire, and Hargett's men backed down the road with their wounded.

Graeber's platoon was on patrol atop Hill 891 to keep an eye out for any Chinese who might try to attack the men on the road. So far all his men had taken was a little rifle fire.

Suddenly they were engulfed in a mortar barrage and Graeber was lifted off the ground and hurled about fifteen feet and wrapped around the base of a large tree. "I got creamed. A couple of my guys got creamed," he said. "I didn't remember anything after that. When I came to, I was on a stretcher down on the road and heading back to Hamhung."

After a few minutes the shelling stopped and the patrol continued.

Roach's 3rd Battalion passed through Davis's 1st Battalion and began to move up into the hills just before the turn in the road. Lt. William E. Johnson's I Company headed toward Hill 987, and Capt. Thomas E. Cooney's G Company started up 891, but neither got far. As soon as the Chinese spotted them, the firing began. So for the rest of the day it was just a matter of keeping your head down, taking a shot or two at not much of anything, then taking cover while Chinese mortars and marine artillery exchanged fire. The pounding continued until nightfall.

Marine artillery lobbed 943 shells onto the two hilltops, but all that came of it was an equally heavy barrage from the 122mm mortars of the Chinese. The result of the day-long exchange of fire: The Chinese still held the mountains and the marines were still stuck at the bottom, unable to get up the pass toward their objective, Koto-ri.

November 6, 1950; headquarters, 3rd Battalion, 7th Regiment, Chin-hung-ni, 8:00 A.M.: Roach ordered H Company up the southwestern slope of Hill 891 and I Company to renew its attack on Hill 987. Corsairs pounded the two peaks time and again. Then the howitzers took over. Finally, the regiment's heavy 4.2 mortars finished the barrage. Then the marines began to inch their way up. It was tough from the start. The soil was powdery, traction was poor. It was a very exhausting climb. By late afternoon they were still a few hundred yards from the top. Ammunition was running low, darkness was approaching, and they were exhausted. When told of this, Litzenberg brought them down, and by 8:00 P.M. they were back inside the regimental perimeter.

November 7, 1950; headquarters, 7th Regiment, Chinhung-ni, 7:00 A.M.: The only sounds during the night came from two hundred Korean laborers who moved ammunition up the road to the forward positions in preparation for the next phase of the assault on Hills 987 and 891. When the marines moved out, caution was the watchword. The 1st Battalion had already suffered enough casualties, so they approached the hairpin turn with extreme caution. Surprisingly, though, the patrols saw no Chinese in the hills or on top. When the marines reached the hairpin turn and rounded the last bend, they drew no fire. The hilltops, the road, and the pass all belonged to the marines.

For some mysterious reason, the Chinese had pulled back toward the reservoir, or beyond. Strangely, they did the same thing in the northwest, breaking off contact with the Eighth Army and disappearing into the hills.

Were the Chinese sending MacArthur a message? Stop. Enough is enough. This is as far as you go. A lot of marines felt this was the case.

The Chinese on Hills 987 and 891 had taken a terrible pounding from artillery and air strikes. It was later estimated that the 124th Division was rendered useless for a year.

The marines spent the rest of the day and the next, November 8,

76

bringing up supplies and replacements, strengthening fortifications along the road in case the Chinese reappeared, sending out patrols. One went all the way to the top of the pass and into the village of Koto-ri, then radioed back to Litzenberg that there were no Chinese to be seen.

The corps commander, General Almond, visited the regiment, passed out medals, and exhorted Litzenberg to get up to the border as soon as possible.

The next morning, November 9, the 3rd Battalion led the regiment up the pass.

November 9, 1950; 2nd Platoon, E Company, 2nd Battalion, 7th Regiment, 9:30 A.M.: Yancey's platoon was trudging toward the hairpin turn when he saw the sleeping bags alongside the road. He slowed so each man could see what can happen if you aren't careful. Seven bags. Seven marines bayoneted. "That's what happens when you get careless, when you fall asleep when you should be watching," he told each man who passed.

November 10, 1950; 1st Battalion, 7th Regiment, Koto-ri, 8:30 A.M.: Davis's men passed through the 3rd Battalion and reached the top of the pass on the Marine Corps' birthday, occupying the village without opposition, and immediately encountered an enemy far more deadly than the Chinese: wintry blasts so fierce that some of the men were blown to the ground.

"Our men were not ready for the cold," Litzenberg said.

"It definitely had an adverse effect on them," Woessner said.

A lot of the men went into shock. Others cried. Some became upset, agitated, very nervous. But all recovered after thawing out in large tents with camp stoves that burned fuel oil. From then on these "warming tents" became a way of life until the division returned to a warmer climate.

There wasn't much to see in Koto-ri. Marine and Navy pilots had worked it over pretty well.

Litzenberg pulled the rest of his regiment up as quickly as he could, then hastily threw up a perimeter around the village.

3rd Platoon, B Company, 1st Battalion, 7th Regiment, Koto-ri, 9:30 A.M.: Kiser reached the village with thirty-eight men, down slightly from the forty-six he had when he left Sudong. No replacements were in sight, but he could make do with the men he had. It didn't seem like there would be too much fighting. Only a shot was heard now and then. His greatest problem was the unexpected cold.

Weapons were beginning to freeze. They were finding out that one of their favorites, the carbine, didn't function well in subzero temperatures.

"Overnight it dropped to twenty-five below, and we weren't ready for it," Dyrdahl said. "I didn't have any winter clothing, a lot of us didn't."

"We really didn't do too much while we were in Koto-ri," Kiser said. "Once in a while we'd get an order to proceed to an area that was receiving fire, but when we got there, the Chinese had gone. But we knew they were watching us from the high peaks."

Most of his time was spent on patrols.

"One of them was a long bastard," Kiser said. "We must have gone fifteen miles, just one peak after another. We interrogated two people in a pretty little village we ran across. We received two rounds of fire all day and didn't see a damn thing. An airplane could have done the same thing in two damn minutes."

"I never understood the reason for this one," he said.

All the homes in this particular village seemed to be new. They were made of wood and stucco and all had new thatched roofs in preparation for winter. There was a big reforestation project under way in the region, too, and all the trees had identification tags. But there was practically no one in the area, so it was difficult to interrogate anyone.

"Here was a pretty little village, practically deserted, and we didn't order the people out, so it must have been the Chinese," Kiser said. "The fact that we couldn't find them didn't reassure us at all," he added. "It really made me feel uneasy."

"I thought the Chinese had probably withdrawn to the border," Kiser added. "So did many other officers and men. Now we were all becoming concerned."

When they returned to Koto-ri, the village had taken on an entirely new appearance. Heavy trucks were rolling in with great amounts of supplies. Tanks were reaching the top. Elements of the 5th Regiment were on the way. Koto-ri was being turned into a big fort. The road up the pass was widened. An airport was being built. Soon the 1st Regiment would arrive to garrison Koto-ri.

"It was reassuring to see the big stuff coming up," Kiser said.

*   *   *

November 14, 1950; headquarters, 7th Regiment, Koto-ri, 8:00 A.M.: It was bitter cold when the marines headed north toward Hagaru-ri and a giant step closer to a night the Marine Corps would always remember. The 5th Regiment was close behind and the 1st Regiment was moving toward this sleepy village and soon would begin turning it into an impregnable fortress and giant supply base because at this point it appeared that the marines would be here through the winter.

Lt. Don Floyd of the antitank platoon remembers well the day, the weather, his feelings as he headed north. In a letter home he wrote, in part:

> Today is the first time for about six days that it's been above freezing. The morning of the 14th we moved north from Koto-ri and it was damned cold. There was about a half inch of snow on the ground and a very cold north wind. It was the worst I've ever seen for a long time. Night before last and yesterday it was terribly cold, also. . . . There's about five inches of ice on the stream and the only way I could keep my canteen from freezing was to keep it empty.
>
> We've had quite a few frozen hands, feet and ears, but that's mostly from kids that have never been in cold weather before and don't know how to take care of themselves.
>
> I've managed pretty good. Of course, I'm plenty cold, but with the clothing we're issued and the sleeping bag, I'm making out.
>
> We got issued heavier shoes yesterday, so now I can keep my feet warm. This is what I'm wearing, and have been for quite some time now: Three pair of sox, heavy shoes, longhandles, dungaree trousers and jacket, parka (fur-lined), cap with ear flaps and two pair of gloves."
>
> Even with all that on I got a little cold yesterday and the day before. At night I take off my parka, gloves and climb in my sleeping bag. Part of the time I even leave my shoes on so I'll be ready to go if the gooks hit us during the night.

November 16, 1950; 2nd Platoon, E Company, 2nd Battalion, 7th Regiment, Hagaru-ri, 10:30 A.M.: It was twenty-one below zero when Yancey walked into the village at the southern tip of the reservoir. The wind that swept down from the north was so cold it felt like a million needles were cutting into his face. "It was so bad that each guy watched someone else's face to check for white spots on the skin," Yancey said. "Then they'd breathe on them until they went away."

They rested and were resupplied. A few replacements arrived. By this time Yancey had the machine guns, too, and the eighteen men he had in his platoon when he left Sudong had grown to sixty-three.

Gallagher was still with him. So was Robinson, who was still a private despite the many citations for bravery that Yancey had written. He was a brig rat and couldn't get a promotion no matter what he did. But his luck wasn't all bad.

At midday Litzenberg's jeep pulled up to where Yancey's men were resting. Yancey jumped to his feet and snapped to attention on limbs that were too cold and stiff to do such foolishness.

"This guy Robinson, the one you keep sending in all those citations on, is he really that good?"

"Better!"

"Go get him. I lost my shotgun."

"So I lost him," Yancey remembers, "but I got him back at Yudam-ni when I needed him most."

It would be Robinson's job to make certain that no harm came to Litzenberg. He would be close by day and night, well armed, ready to go with the regimental commander on a moment's notice.

It was getting colder by the minute, and darker. Once the sun disappeared, the temperature dropped rapidly. Fires were burning for warmth and cooking. Yancey and several of his men were sitting near an old school building, talking. Unexpectedly, a single mortar round came in. "I hit the entranceway to a downstairs potato bin," Yancey recalls. "I slid down and hit the floor and looked around. A few feet away was a fellow I'd known in the Raiders in World War II. He said 'Hello' and reached in his shirt and pulled out a pint of Old Overholt. I had a shot and passed it around to some of my guys."

They scattered the fire, crawled into their sleeping bags, and zipped them partway up.

"That was a nice way to end the day," Yancey said.

It was unbelievably cold now. No one could sleep. Add to that the fact that all hands felt they were getting very close to the Chinese, and you have the ingredients for a miserable night.

But at first light they were up and on patrol, munching on their Hersheys, chewing on Tootsie Rolls and jelly beans.

Headquarters, 7th Regiment, Hagaru-ri, 11:00 A.M.: "We were in a house and relatively comfortable," Woessner remembered. "It had a wooden floor, there were three or four rooms. Outside we set up an operations tent—small, with a couple of bunks at one end. We had our people manning the radios and keeping our map up to date."

They were never more than a few yards from Litzenberg, who needed quick access to communications.

"The trip from Koto was uneventful," he said. "There really wasn't much going on. This caused us to wonder and attempt to get intelligence as to where they were, what their intentions were."

"The Army kept telling us the Chinese were not in the war," Woessner said. "But we didn't believe anything we heard from MacArthur's headquarters. The information from there was a bunch of baloney."

Anti-tank Platoon, 7th Regiment, Hagaru-ri, noon: "We got there with little or no trouble," Floyd recalled. "I still had all my clothes on —I was clumsy but warm—and carried my sleeping bag, the difference between life and death."

Most of his men were eating hamburger patties. They were easy to get out of the can and all you had to do was warm them just a little and they could be eaten half cooked. Your stomach ached a little, but it went away in a short time.

Candy was what everyone craved now, and jelly beans and Tootsie Rolls were the big favorites because they didn't freeze.

"I saw two lieutenants just about fight over the Tootsie Roll ration," Floyd said.

Everyone was eating four times a day because they burned up so much energy. Keeping his canteen from freezing was no longer a problem. "I learned that if you filled it half full with medical alcohol, the water wouldn't freeze. But to this day I can't stand the smell of medical alcohol."

November 23, 1950: The X Corps menu for Thanksgiving Day was roast young tom turkey, sweet potatoes, fruit salad, fruitcake, mince pie, shrimp cocktail, stuffed olives, and hot coffee.

Not much of this found its way to the front.

The men of the 1st Battalion, 7th Regiment, did have a little turkey, sweet potatoes, and hot coffee, but by the time anyone could find a warm place to sit and enjoy the meal, it was frozen. And they ran out of turkey in a hurry, so they switched to canned beans, spaghetti, and sherbet. "They were all frozen," Kiser said, "so we used a little C-4 [plastic explosive] to warm them up. But what this did was to make the outside warm and leave the inside frozen, so we'd stick a knife in the middle and eat it like a Popsicle. We ate a lot of bean Popsicles in those days."

A truckload of fresh bread reached the men as they neared Yudam-ni, at the southern end of the Chosin Reservoir, and each man had one slice. Then a truck with Hersheys arrived.

On this day the marines learned that the 17th Infantry Regiment of the Army's 7th Division had gone up the eastern side of the Chosin Reservoir all the way to the Yalu and had not seen a Chinese soldier.

Meanwhile, the marines' 5th Regiment of Lt. Col. Raymond S. Murray had bypassed the 7th Regiment and, following new X Corps orders, his 2nd Battalion was advancing very slowly, in trucks, up the eastern side of the Chosin Reservoir. The 7th Regiment would continue north, up the western side of the reservoir. Both regiments would meet at the Yalu.

This the marines did not like, and General Smith was upset no end.

"The thing . . . that made me a little jittery was when I found the 2nd Battalion [5th Regiment] going around the east side of the reservoir," Craig said.

"I went up there one afternoon and I saw the positions they were in. . . . I went back and talked to O. P. Smith about it, and he said, 'That's what the Army wants.'

"He said the operation is going to go up there, and it's going to keep going around that side of the reservoir," Craig added.

Craig told Smith that it was a bad situation, that trucks were sliding off the road, ". . . and I'd come across some tanks that had slipped off the road, too.

"The whole thing looked bad to me," Craig said.

"It would have been difficult if not impossible to reinforce the marines up there," he said. "I was very concerned, very jittery, about the situation up there. I didn't like to see the division being split . . . having it on two sides of the reservoir just didn't make sense," Craig explained. "If you have a fighting force and you can keep it together, you ought to do it."

Col. Edward W. Snedeker, General Smith's deputy chief of staff, said that "things became very precarious for them with their long, extended lines . . . without any flank protection.

"This vast extension of lines trying to get up to the border of North Korea . . . General Smith took a very dim view of that," Snedeker said. "He realized that if you get extended that way, your flanks are very vulnerable. The supply situation is vulnerable . . . quite bad . . . in that it would involve great reliance on marine air to give support.

"General Smith was not at all enthusiastic about this and he did not move as fast as the Army commander, General Almond, would have liked," Snedeker added. In fact, Snedeker explained, "He moved in such a fashion that supplies were built up along the way as much as could be done to cover the units advancing there.

"As he moved along," Snedeker said, "precautions were taken to see that the flanks were relatively clear . . . and the slowness with which he moved attributed to the division being able to withdraw when it got ordered to."

"At the same time he was also carrying out the orders to keep advancing. And I know that the pressure was on to go faster," Craig said.

"The main worry for us was this very narrow road we were going up," Craig recalled. "We were going into an area where it was one hairpin turn after another. It was straight up one side, straight down the other, maybe four hundred to five hundred feet."

The road had been built by the Japanese well before World War II. It was made of layers of gravel, rock, dirt, and shored up in many places with timber.

November 24, 1950; headquarters, Eighth Army, 10:00 A.M.: The entire front, west to east, had been quiet for days. It was that way when MacArthur sent his troops north in a massive end-the-war offensive with this stirring communiqué, which was read to all units:

> The United Nations massive compression envelopment in North Korea against the new Red Armies operating there is now approaching its decisive effort. The isolating component of the pincer, our air forces of all types, have for the past three weeks, in a sustained attack of model coordination and effectiveness, successfully interdicted enemy lines of support from the north so that further reinforcement therefrom has been sharply curtailed and essential supplies markedly limited. The eastern sector of the pincer, with noteworthy and effective naval support, has now reached commanding enveloping position, cutting in two the northern reaches of the enemy's geographical potential. This morn-

ing the western sector of the pincer moves forward in general assault in an effort to complete the compression and close the vise. If successful, this should for all practical purposes end the war, restore peace and unity to Korea, enable the prompt withdrawal of United Nations military forces, and permit the complete assumption by the Korean people and nation of full sovereignty and international equality. It is that for which we fight.

The "offensive" began more like a walk in the park than an act of war. There was no opposition. No gunfire. After twenty-four hours the United Nations forces were advancing at the rate of sixteen thousand yards a day, never less than four thousand yards a day. They were fast outrunning their supply lines, much the way the North Koreans had in July and August. Many of the GI's were tossing away equipment because they felt there would be no further use for it.

November 25, 1950; headquarters, marines' 1st Division, Hamhung, 10:00 A.M.: Operations Order 7 from X Corps redirected the marines' attack north so that the division would now provide greater support to the Eighth Army's offensive on the western coast. General Almond, the corps commander, explained to General Smith that his division was to be the northern arm of MacArthur's pincers movement in the "massive compression envelopment." This meant that the Army's 7th Infantry Division that was to the east of the marines and close to the Fusen Reservoir would now assume the marines' mission of advancing to the Yalu.

General Smith's 7th Regiment would, as previously planned, capture Yudam-ni. But the regiment would not continue north to the Yalu. Instead it would establish a perimeter around Yudam-ni, take the high ground, the hilltops, and protect the valley and the road.

Then the much fresher 5th Regiment would pass through the 7th Regiment at Yudam-ni and, on the morning of November 27, launch the division's attack to the west.

The change in orders was a welcome one for the marines. It gave General Smith the chance to tighten his division, to bring the fighting units much closer together. Most important, he could bring his 2nd Battalion, 5th Regiment, back from the eastern side of the reservoir.

Before General Almond left General Smith's command post, he

again stressed the need for speed, saying, "We've got to go barreling down that road [to Yudam-ni]!"

To that General Smith simply said, "No!"

After General Almond left, the marine commander told Craig, "I'm not going to go barreling down that road. I'm not going anywhere until we get the division together and the airfield built at Hagaru."

What General Smith did was to build up the defenses at Koto-ri and Hagaru-ri. The road was widened to Hagaru-ri and beyond. Great stockpiles of supplies were being trucked up the road to both villages. A medical clearing station was set up at Hagaru-ri. He ordered the engineers to work night and day to complete the landing field at Hagaru-ri, and he wanted the runway long enough to accommodate C-47 transports. A smaller landing field was being built at Koto-ri.

Headquarters, 7th Regiment, on the road to Yudam-ni, 1:30 P.M.: Craig flew by helicopter to see Litzenberg, whose troops were approaching the village of Yudam-ni. They talked about the changes in orders, the treacherous road, the formidable hills in front of his men, and the terrible weather.

"He didn't seem worried about the situation," Craig remembers. "If he was worried about something, he'd usually start puffing furiously on his pipe and think, 'What can I do about this?' This day his pipe wasn't even burning."

Litzenberg joined his men on the road north, and a short time later the 7th Regiment captured the village against surprisingly light opposition. But many of those who walked into the village would not be walking out.

November 26, 1950; headquarters, 1st Battalion, 7th Regiment, Yudam-ni, 8:00 A.M.: It was bitterly cold. Bleak, barren. The ground was so hard you couldn't dent it with a pick. What had once been mud and stone huts were stretched along the road. The valley was deserted. Five great ridges surrounded the area, snowcapped, foreboding. It was like being on the rim of the world.

Just behind the hills on the right you could see a finger of the reservoir, frozen and covered with snow. You could tell at a glance that if the Chinese controlled the hills around the valley, then life at the bottom would be miserable.

The men were still exhausted from the climb up four-thousand-foot Toktong Pass that left everyone gasping for air. They were all on double rations because of the great amount of energy each man expended.

Davis knew that the far sides of the ridges were crawling with Chinese. Marine intelligence had reported the capture of three enemy soldiers who said they were from the 60th Division. They said that Yudam-ni would soon be surrounded, that several Chinese divisions were in the area, were closing on Hagaru and Koto-ri. Very soon the road would be cut, isolating the three villages, the prisoners told their interrogators, and then the Chinese would attack the division that was now stretched dangerously thin along the seventy-eight mile road.

But what would peasant soldiers know about grand strategy? So the marines did not place a great amount of credence on what they heard.

Nevertheless, Davis was concerned about the security of the road behind him, so one of the first things he did was send B Company back down that road about three miles, then into the hills on the right, to try to locate the Chinese, but not one was spotted.

Meanwhile, the situation in the northwest had deteriorated rapidly. The ROK II Corps had disintegrated in the face of a powerful Chinese counterattack, exposing the right flank of the Eighth Army to Chinese assault. MacArthur's offensive to end the war had come to an abrupt end before it really got under way, before the marines' attack to the west could begin.

The division's mission had not changed: The 7th Regiment was assigned the task of holding the village, the valley, the surrounding hilltops, and maintaining security along the road all the way back to Hagaru-ri. The 5th Regiment would pass through the 7th Regiment in the morning and launch the division's attack to the west. But now there was a sense of urgency that was not there before the collapse of the ROK II Corps. Originally the marines were intended to be an arm of the giant pincers that hopefully would have trapped a great number of Chinese and North Korean troops. Now it was imperative that the marines move west as rapidly as possible to take the pressure off the exposed right flank, to draw the Chinese away.

No one liked the situation.

"We all had the feeling we were going awfully far from the sea," Woessner said.

"Hagaru was reasonable," he said. "If the division consolidated there, we felt we could take care of any situation that arose. But Yudam-ni was farther, and higher, than anything we had anticipated. It seemed that we were going to be extended beyond our capacity to handle the situation."

Headquarters, 7th Regiment, Yudam-ni, 10:00 P.M.: Litzenberg's officers listened as he explained their mission: He wanted more patrols on the ridges. He wanted to know exactly where the Chinese were. He was particularly interested in the road they had just come up. Had the Chinese slipped behind them and cut it? This would mean a company-size patrol early in the morning. He wanted his 3rd Battalion to extend its position on Northwest Ridge. Specifically, he wanted H Company to occupy Hill 1403, which overlooked the road west. And he wanted D and E companies to patrol more extensively the western side of the reservoir and North Ridge, particularly Hills 1282 and 1240, which overlooked the valley on the eastern side of the road.

It was below zero when the officers left the windblown tent and returned to their units and tried to get some sleep, but no one could close his eyes. It was too cold.

Headquarters, 5th Regiment, Yudam-ni, 10:00 P.M.: Murray briefed his officers for the last time on the plan of attack to the west: The 2nd Battalion early in the morning would pass through the 7th Regiment. A platoon of engineers would be close to the lead element. Two Corsairs and a single-engine spotter plane would be overhead. Capt. Uel D. Peters's F Company would be the point unit and set the pace. Caution was the watchword. Don't take any chances. The target: The road junction at Yongnim, twenty-seven miles to the west. At that time it did not seem to be an unattainable goal for Lt. Col. Harold S. Roisie's 2nd Battalion, 5th Regiment.

General Smith that night had two infantry regiments—about ten thousand men—in Yudam-ni. He had ten rifle companies scattered atop the five ridges—North, South, Southeast, Southwest, and Northwest—so named because of their location from the village. Each had many draws, spurs, saddles, and peaks. As the crisis developed and the fighting shifted, many would increase or diminish in importance.

Supporting the marines was an imposing array of firepower. The 11th Artillery Regiment had forty-eight howitzers—thirty 105's and eighteen 155's—positioned on a long, level area just south of Yudam-ni. And there was one tank, an M-26. Four heavier M-42's had tried to reach Yudam-ni but skidded off the road because of snow and ice.

Supply seemed to pose the greatest problem. The dumps of the two regiments had three days' supply of food, three of fuel and two of small-arms ammunition in addition to what each unit had on hand and what each individual carried.

CHAPTER 5
YUDAM-NI

November 27, 1950; 2nd Battalion, 5th Regiment, Yudam-ni, 8:00 A.M.:

PFC Robert Johnson waited for the artillery to lift; for three hours it had pounded the hills on both sides of the road in front of him. He took a last look at a puff of black-gray smoke behind him rising from where an errant artillery round had fallen short and exploded among a group of marines. "What a hell of a way to start the day," he thought.

Before the barrage had stopped, Capt. Uel D. Peters told him to move out. Johnson raised an arm and signaled the men of F Company forward toward their first objective, the road junction of Yongnim, twenty-seven miles to the west.

"We didn't stop at Yudam-ni," Roisie said. "We just passed through the 7th Regiment and turned sharply west, to where the Eighth Army was in a hell of a lot of trouble."

Johnson was still excited, as he had been since learning that he would be the "point," that he would be in front of everyone else—in effect, leading the division. He moved slowly, cautiously along the road, which at best could be described as improved dirt. The sun was at his back, which was good. He checked for mines, kept an eye on the hills for a glint of sun off a rifle. Two Corsairs were overhead if he needed help. A spotter plane was about a quarter of a mile in front, gliding slowly from one side of the road to the other, searching for the enemy. Always on his mind was a place to take cover should he run into gunfire. His most pressing concern was his rifle. Would it fire when he needed it? He had stayed up most of the night cleaning it, wiping off the excess oil so it wouldn't freeze. Just about everyone in his company thought they were still heading north, toward the Yalu, and it wasn't until later in the day that they discovered the division had veered west.

As the point, Johnson set the pace for those who followed. He didn't push it. Peters had told him to stop if he ran into trouble and "wait for the Corsairs, let them do the work."

He hadn't gone far when he heard from behind, "Stop! Stop! The road may be mined!" He held up an arm and led the column off the road and waited for the engineers to move up. They were there in a couple of minutes, found no mines, and the marines again headed west. There was always a platoon of engineers near the front of the column, near the action. Often they did as much fighting as a rifle platoon. The only

91

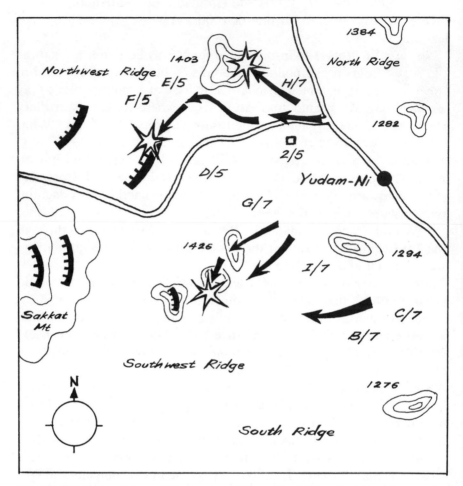

Map 5—Marines attack to the west toward the reeling Eighth Army on the morning of November 27, 1950. Crescent-shaped positions by the Chinese are at the left on both sides of the road high in the mountains, with a commanding view of the road.

difference between the two was that the engineers figured they were learning a trade.

So far, the towering peaks the marines had passed under were in control of the 7th Regiment, but this would end soon.

Hagaru-ri, 8:30 A.M.: Cpl. Marvin E. Pugh was on the way home. Someone had decided his family needed him more than the Marine Corps. He was in the lead truck, beside the driver, in a small convoy heading toward Koto-ri on an ammunition run. As the truck rounded a bend about three miles south, he saw the machine gun in the center of the road, then flashes of orange and pink from the muzzle, and the windshield disintegrated. He ducked, but not before bits of glass dug into his face and through his clothes.

"Hold on, we're going through!" the driver shouted, jamming the accelerator to the floor as he drove the two-and-a-half-ton truck straight toward the still-firing machine gun. The other vehicles had turned around and were racing back to Hagaru.

Pugh raised his head in time to see the gun and the three Chinese who had stayed with it disappear under the front, then heard the grinding of steel. To the left, in a level area that ran from the road about 125 yards to the hills, he saw nothing but Chinese. As far as he could see down the road, there were Chinese.

The driver failed to see a small patch of ice, and the truck skidded into a paddy. "I jumped out, the driver jumped out his side, and we ran for our lives," Pugh said. But Pugh went down with a bullet in his right leg. The Chinese ran past him after the driver. Pugh heard several shots and knew he had been killed. The Chinese returned, stood around him for several minutes, talking. Then one pointed a rifle at Pugh's left knee and pulled the trigger. Now no one would have to guard him. Then they began to take off his clothes. One got his parka. Another got his woolen shirt. Then his pants and boots. Finally, one tried to pull off his underwear, but Pugh pulled it back. They did this several times; then the Chinese laughed and left.

Pugh stayed where he was until dark, then crawled down the bank of a small stream and dug a small hole, knowing that sand did not freeze, yet realizing that he had very little chance of surviving the cold. The Chinese had now cut the road south from Yudam-ni.

* * *

Radio Relay Platoon, Koto-ri, 8:30 A.M.: Lt. Felix Ferranto slipped behind the wheel of his jeep and drove down toward the road, turned right, and headed toward Hagaru. He had made the trip a number of times recently without incident, so he saw no need to have someone ride shotgun.

Two miles north he saw the small house he had passed several times. Beside the road he spotted a bedroll that was not there on previous trips. Nevertheless, he continued up the road. He had a more pressing problem: finding a site to relocate his radio relay station so it would be closer to the 5th and 7th regiments.

He sped around a sharp turn and saw for the first time a group of Chinese. They were about a hundred yards away, so he made a tight U-turn, ran into a paddy, then got back on the road and headed south. He heard the sharp crack-crack-crack of single-shot rifles. He stopped, grabbed his carbine, and began to fire. But it was frozen. He dropped it and got the jeep rolling again. Just then a bullet struck him in his left leg, but he kept moving. As he neared the house, he saw more Chinese and realized the bedroll belonged to one of them. He tried to race through, and the last thing he remembers seeing were Chinese about thirty-five yards away waving potato masher grenades. One exploded, overturned his jeep, and when Ferranto opened his eyes, he was a prisoner.

The Chinese had now cut the road north from Koto-ri.

Hill 1403, Northwest Ridge, 9:30 A.M.: "It was a beautiful sight," Sgt. Gene O'Hara thought as he watched two Corsairs napalm the top of the hill.

"Just beautiful! Just beautiful! If any Chinese are up there, they're gone now," he said to no one in particular.

Before the planes had finished, the men of Capt. Leroy M. Cooke's H Company, 3rd Battalion, 7th Regiment, began the ascent.

"It was one hell of a climb," O'Hara remembers.

But it was a necessary climb, because at midday the 2nd Battalion, 5th Regiment, would be passing on the road below Hill 1403, and Roisie didn't want any Chinese on top.

O'Hara carried a rifle, four grenades, and two bandoliers. His web belt was full. He had two canteens, even though the water had long since turned to ice. He carried his shovel, pack, sleeping bag, an Army blanket he had scrounged, a poncho, and a box of C rations. It was snowing and slippery. The hilltop where they would spend the night was only about five hundred yards high, yet it took them three hours to get there. Then they collapsed into holes the Chinese had already dug, possibly the worst thing they could have done.

B Company, 1st Battalion, 7th Regiment, Yudam-ni, noon: "We went a little farther on patrol then we had the day before," Kiser said, "and, man, there was a mess of them." First Lt. Joseph R. Kurcaba, who was now the company commander—Wilcox had been wounded— reached Kiser's side, saw the great number of Chinese, and told his radioman, Hedrick, "Call for an air strike before we're spotted." There were ten to twenty Chinese in one group, thirty in another. Perhaps fifty alongside some rocks. There were hundreds, perhaps a few thousand, scattered everywhere. They weren't hiding. They didn't seem concerned about marine air. They knew they were in control of the situation.

Hedrick got on the radio and shouted, "Any aircraft . . . any aircraft . . . !" Overhead he saw two Corsairs and heard their familiar call sign, "This is Lovelace . . . this is Lovelace."

"I wasn't as professional as I should have been," Hedrick recalled, "So I shouted into the radio, 'Help! We're surrounded . . . we're surrounded . . . !' " By this time the Chinese had spotted B Company, and the marines were under heavy fire. Hedrick directed the planes to the hillside where the most Chinese seemed to be, and they worked it over pretty well.

Kurcaba and his men were backing slowly down the hill and firing up at the Chinese.

Meanwhile, Davis was in his jeep in Yudam-ni checking his units. Pearl, his radio operator, was riding in back.

"Suddenly I asked Davis if he would pull over and stop for a second," Pearl said. "I was getting a faint signal from a 'Baker Company.' It was very weak and I could hardly hear it: 'Help! We're surrounded . . . we're surrounded . . . !' "

Davis then took Capt. John F. Morris's C Company, 1st Battalion, 7th Regiment, and went back down the road to get B Company out of the tight spot in which it found itself.

"We had to fight our way in," Pearl said, "but we made it, and we got their wounded out, too."

Back on the road, Davis stopped a convoy heading south and put the dead and wounded aboard. He put C Company on a high hill on the right side of the road between Hills 1419 and 1520, about five miles south of Yudam-ni, to guard the supply route.

Davis returned to his command post in Yudam-ni. Kurcaba took B Company back up Hill 1276, where the men built fires, warmed themselves, and heated a few cans of food. Kiser, whose platoon was down to fourteen men, picked up seven replacements. Then they settled in for the night.

Everyone in B Company knew by this time that they were surrounded, that the Chinese had slipped in behind and cut the road south.

"You knew you couldn't send a patrol out a thousand yards and expect it to return," Kiser said.

"We knew there was a complete ring around us, and it really didn't make a hell of a difference which way we went, so long as we went in a group," he said. "The men knew the situation was changing in favor of the Chinese, but I don't think anyone felt it was hopeless."

2nd Battalion, 5th Regiment, 12:30 P.M., enroute west: "We weren't too far out when we ran into rifle and machine-gun fire, and a few roadblocks," Roisie remembers, "but whenever we seemed to run into the Chinese, they would back up."

"I don't know why, exactly, unless they were trying to draw us into a situation where they hoped we couldn't get out."

Johnson was still the point as the marines passed below the last two peaks in their control—Hill 1403 on the right and Hill 1426 on the left. Several hundred yards ahead, Johnson spotted a stream that had turned to ice and a small stone bridge and wondered if it was mined. But he didn't have time to dwell on this.

"As soon as I hit that bridge, I ran into automatic-weapons fire," he said. "I jumped onto the ice and ran to the far side of the bank, where there was some cover." The leader of his four-man fire team, PFC Phil Calvert, was at his side in seconds, and Cpl. J. J. Collins, their squad leader, was a few steps behind. "We talked about where the fire was coming from," Johnson said, "then Calvert took off up to where we thought they [Chinese] were, and we took off after him."

By now others were going up on the right and the left. "We heard a little firing, and by the time we got to the top, the Chinese had fled, a few had given up," Johnson said. There were four prisoners and four wounded marines, so they helped them down.

Capt. Samuel S. Smith's D Company, 2nd Battalion, 5th Regiment, had inched down the road but ran head-on into heavy machine-gun fire from Mount Sakkat on the left, where the Chinese had built two tiers of reinforced fortifications. Then word was received from the spotter plane that several thousand Chinese were just ahead, in the hills, on the road, everywhere. Peters slowed his advance to a crawl. Then mortar rounds began to fall on both rifle companies. Machine guns were firing at the marines from both sides of the road.

"The situation overall didn't look good," Roisie said, "so I thought I'd better stop them and dig in for the night."

At midafternoon D Company was dug in astride the road leading west, just slightly ahead of any other marine unit. Tied in with D Company on the right side of the road was Peters's F Company, which stretched into the heights of Northwest Ridge and tied in with Capt. Samuel Jaskilka's E Company, 2nd Battalion, 5th Regiment. There was a gully, or saddle, between them.

"If we'd continued down that road maybe five or six hundred yards, if we'd gone another two hours, until around four instead of two, we could have been cut off by the way they were coming in," Roisie explained. "They were coming down off the hills to the right."

"I was very concerned about the Chinese," Roisie said. "I know General Smith was. Every time I talked to him he would tell me, 'The Chinese are coming. Be ready for them.' "

"We were all very greatly concerned," Roisie added, "but we were ready for them."

To this day no one who was there can understand why the Chinese failed to cut in behind the 2nd Battalion, 5th Regiment, and isolate yet another segment of the division.

Lt. Ed Deptula had the 1st Platoon in Jaskilka's E Company, which brought up the 2nd Battalion's rear, and the 1st Platoon was the company's rear element.

"I never did care to be all the way back," Deptula said. "I wanted to develop the situation that I was going into rather than be moved up from reserve to take over someone else's mess. I never appreciated that."

Shortly after Roisie halted the 2nd Battalion's advance, Jaskilka called his platoon leaders, his mortar officer, Lt. Bob Uskrat, his forward observer, Lt. Bob Resinger, and R. W. Barnett, his gunnery sergeant, together to give them their orders for the rest of the day, to point out where he wanted each platoon positioned. They were standing in a circle partway up the side of Northwest Ridge when a shot rang out.

"I was talking and pointing to a spot where I figured would be a good place for the 1st and 2nd platoons to tie in," Deptula said. "Next thing I know I'm on the ground, flat on my back, and I remember thinking how damn cold that ground was." A sniper's bullet got him in the right thigh. "I guess he saw me pointing and thought, 'There's a guy in charge of something.' "

"That damn bullet went between all of us and got him," remembered Lt. Jack Nolan, in charge of the 2nd Platoon.

"We all dove for cover," Nolan said, "and I went with Ed. I could see right away he was hit, but I looked down at that damn wound and didn't see a drop of blood."

Deptula was more concerned about the new long johns he'd put on that morning than the bullet hole. He knew it would hurt for a while, become stiff. Nothing serious, though.

But the long underwear, that was different. It kept you from freezing on nights when your sleeping bag was coated with ice, when there was a thin layer of frost on your face.

"Hey, don't chop me up down there! Watch out for my long johns!" Deptula hollered at Nolan.

But it was too late. Nolan had all but butchered his clothing in an effort to check the wound. The bullet hadn't gone through; in fact, it's still in there today.

"He jumped up and shouted, 'So long, you sons of bitches, I've got mine!' " Nolan recalled. But Deptula's leg quickly stiffened and he hit the ground again. His platoon sergeant, Russ Borgomainero, was eight to ten feet away. "He was sort of humped down and I could see tears coming down his cheeks into that fiery red beard and mustache of his," Deptula remembered.

"Right then and there I turned the platoon over to him."

Deptula reached into a pocket and pulled out his map case and compass and gave them to him. "He stood there and took the stuff. I think he was really sad," Deptula said.

Deptula was on a stretcher being carried down the hill. As he passed Jaskilka, Deptula looked up, smiled, and said, "I've got that million-dollar wound. I'll see you back in the States."

98

Jaskilka glanced down at him, checked the small bandage, and told him, "With that little thing, you'll be lucky to get back to Japan."

"As far as I know, Deptula was the last casualty to leave Yudam-ni by ambulance," Nolan said. Those who left later did so either aboard a light plane or a helicopter and were life-or-death cases.

Jaskilka stopped for a moment to look at the towering peaks of Northwest Ridge that rose around him like the quills of an excited porcupine. He was impressed by the rugged high ground, covered with ice and snow, and wondered why the Chinese hadn't bothered to defend it. So far, they had only harassed his men with small-arms fire from long range, then withdrew once the marines started to close with them. So where and when the Chinese would stand and fight was anyone's guess.

He tightened the fur-lined hood of his winter parka against the frigid cold, then moved his company to the top of Northwest Ridge. His men scraped and pawed at the icy ground, then jabbed their shovels at the rock-hard earth, only to have them snap off in their hands. It was around twenty degrees below zero and getting colder.

F Company, 2nd Battalion, 7th Regiment, Toktong Pass, 4:00 P.M.: His orders were specific: Guard the road, the main supply route to Yudam-ni, and the only way back to the sea. "Some smart commander . . . became concerned about the long road between Hagaru and Yudam-ni without any security on it," Capt. William E. Barber said. "We didn't have enough people to get solid security over everything, so somebody made a very good appraisal of the situation and said, 'We ought to at least get somebody halfway between on the high ground.' "

That's where Barber's company was—high atop Toktong Pass at a critical point along the road. The first thing his men did was dig in. Although it was just about dark, fires were built that disclosed his position to the Chinese.

"I considered a long time whether I ought to dig in," Barber said. "The ground was frozen. That's a pretty tough damn job. And the men were pretty tired. But you do whatever you think is going to be the most effective in the long run."

He could have put up warming tents. He could have outposted a large knob of rock not far away that was higher than where he was. It would have made a good observation post. But he had only a certain amount of time and a limited number of things he could do. Digging in, he felt, was the best thing to do.

"There are lots of things to consider," he said. "Once a fire team and a squad establish their territory, they're supposed to stay there. But if there's a poncho on the ground, it becomes a little easier to move back fifteen yards, then another fifteen yards.

Had they not dug in that night?

"We would have been eliminated," Barber said. "By any rationale we could not have survived. I would not have expected by any objective analysis we could have survived."

Once he made the decision, he didn't let it go at that. He checked throughout the rest of the day and into the evening. "I didn't like casual compliance with my orders, whatever the situation," he said, "so we got pretty well dug in."

He wasn't too popular with his men that night, yet his decision should not have surprised anyone. Barber took over the company a few days after the battle of Sudong. "I saw a platoon open fire on three Chinese and not hit any of them," he said. "This was a job for one man."

He decided then and there that his men would get a steady dose of rifle practice. He got some cans, and they began to shoot. By the time they reached Toktong Pass, every man in his company was a much better shot. They worked better as a unit, too. On the way up from Koto-ri they had the opportunity to call in a few air strikes, use their mortars at night, register artillery, all the things that a rifle company has to do well for the men to survive.

Before he left Hagaru, Barber asked for and received two 81mm mortars and additional machine guns. His company was a hefty 222 men, some with combat experience, most without. Many were reservists.

Barber had been a platoon leader on Iwo Jima, later a company commander. In June 1950, when the Korean War began, he was at the Marine Barracks in Philadelphia. In the early days of fighting an unusually high number of company commanders were killed, so a call went out through the corps for anyone with that type of experience.

"They found me in Philly, I went over in October," Barber said.

His three platoons covered a total perimeter of about 340 yards. Lt. Robert C. McCarthy's 3rd Platoon had what Barber felt would be the toughest area to defend: the center of the perimeter. Lt. Elmer Peterson's 2nd Platoon had the left side, and Lt. John Dunne's 1st Platoon had the right side. The top of the hill was bare. There were a few trees and a couple of shabby houses at its base, which was high above the road from Hagaru to Yudam-ni. The 3.5 rockets and company headquarters were back there. The company 60mm mortars were close by. So were the 81s. Capt. Ben Read's H Battery howitzers, back in Hagaru, weren't able to zero in on the area because of heavy truck traffic up and down the road.

Barber didn't like this, so he made certain Sgt. Robert Kohl's 81s were registered on that high rocky area he was so concerned about.

He wasn't too happy with the area he had to defend, and if the Chinese let him alone during the night he planned to do a lot in the morning, adjust his lines in certain areas, and put some men up on those rocks, which were about 125 yards away.

More than anything else, that rock pile worried him.

Most of his men were well up on the crest of the hill, which sloped gently downward and to the rear in the direction of the road.

Below he could see the headlights of the six-bys rumbling north with ammunition, food, fuel, and medical supplies for the big supply dumps they were building at Yudam-ni in anticipation of a long stay in the high country.

Barber spent most of the early evening near the mortars and machine guns. He wanted to set up fields of fire, get the mortars registered on what he thought might be trouble areas. As it got dark and became colder, he kept in close contact with his platoon leaders by sound power phones, which had a range of about one hundred yards and required no batteries.

Hill 1403, Northwest Ridge, 10:00 P.M.: "We had the highest ground around and we didn't think anyone could take it from us," said Sgt. Gene O'Hara of H Company, 3rd Battalion, 7th Regiment. His company was about five hundred very difficult yards to the right of Jaskilka's E Company, 2nd Battalion, 5th Regiment.

"We certainly didn't think the Chinese would be back," he said.

"We were doing all the things you weren't supposed to do in a situation like this," O'Hara said. "We didn't have any trip flares and we probably wouldn't have put them out if we had them. We were just too tired. None of the officers ever came by to inspect our perimeter. My foxhole was a little farther out than the others—on a point, sort of, and someone should have come by if for no other reason than to check our fields of fire. But they didn't. I can understand why. They were just as tired as we were, probably more.

"We were so damn beat up physically, so fatigued, and that makes you very careless. So a lot of little things that we'd normally do, well, we didn't, we just let them slip by."

Cooke's H Company was on a 50 percent alert, but if one third of the men were awake, they were fortunate. There were two others in O'Hara's hole that night. After the fires were put out, O'Hara told one to take the first watch and wake him in two hours. Then he took off his boots and crawled into his bag. So did the other man in their hole. Soon both were fast asleep.

"I found out later that the BAR man did the same thing just after we fell asleep," O'Hara remembers.

Bugles and gunfire woke them just after 10:00 P.M.

E Company, 2nd Battalion, 5th Regiment, Northwest Ridge, 10:00 P.M.: Jaskilka inspected company lines, then returned to his command post, about 125 yards behind his three platoons. He liked the way the machine guns had been placed to ensure an excellent field of fire should the Chinese attack down that alley, which ran perpendicular to the marines' line of attack. And he was pleased with the way Borgomainero had skillfully tied in the 1st Platoon with F Company, 2nd Battalion, 5th Regiment, on the left, or west.

"A splendid platoon sergeant," Jaskilka thought.

He noted, too, that the company's three 60mm mortars were registered on the alley just in front of the 1st and 2nd platoons. So he made his report to Roisie, the battalion commander, then settled down for the night, thinking of tomorrow and hoping he wouldn't freeze.

His men were bedded down, and in the morning the battalion would continue the attack to the west, toward the Eighth Army, which was reeling backward under a Chinese onslaught.

But right now Jaskilka had another thought on his mind. One more night. Just one more night. Then he'd be going home, for he had orders transferring him the very next day to duty in the United States. And, with a little luck, who knows, he just might make it home in time for the birth of the expected baby.

Nolan's men could hear the shuffling of padded feet on snow, then clearly hear the Chinese talking.

Nolan grabbed the field phone.

"Captain, this is Nolan. They're gathering in front of us. The place is crawling with 'em. Request illumination."

Jaskilka called battalion, placed the request, but was told there was a shortage and that they couldn't be spared now.

He called Nolan, passed along the bad news, and instructed him: "Hold your fire until the last moment."

F Company, 2nd Battalion, 5th Regiment, Northwest Ridge, 10:00 P.M.: Johnson, Calvert, Collins, the others in Peters's company were up about a thousand feet on a hilltop that was level for several yards and mostly open. There wasn't much cover on top, or on the way up.

"We thought this was strictly a rearguard action," Johnson said. "We thought they were whipped. We thought that if we met any Chinese at all it would be the remnants of the division the 7th Regiment had whipped earlier at Sudong. We had absolutely no idea we would run into fresh troops, and so many of them."

Yudam-ni and the five great ridges surrounding it were dark and quiet. Once the sun had disappeared, the temperature dropped rapidly, and it was now well below zero. The fires had been out for some time, and the men were beginning to turn numb. It got dark early in winter, usually at about 4:00 P.M., and they had been without warmth since then. A few slept, but most were awake. All knew that something had better happen soon just to get the blood flowing again. Patches of white were appearing on faces, the first sign of frostbite. Fingers were already numb. Toes were turning to ice. Rings of frost began to coat mouths and nostrils.

As the marines lay awake in their mountain bags, weapons ready, the Chinese were beginning to stir.

Although no one knew it at the time, the Chinese strategy was amazingly simple, and effective: Isolate and destroy. Koto-ri was now surrounded by the 60th and 77th Chinese divisions. Hagaru-ri was cut off and surrounded by the 58th and 76th CCF divisions. The peaks around Yudam-ni were swarming with Chinese from the 89th, 79th, and 59th divisions. Chinese had also surrounded Morris's C Company, 1st Battalion, 7th Regiment, on a hilltop five miles south of Yudam-ni.

And Barber's F Company, 2nd Battalion, 7th Regiment was surrounded on top of Toktong Pass, midway between Yudam-ni and Hagaru-ri.

On the night of November 27 and during the early-morning hours of November 28, the Chinese had the Marines' 1st Division cut into five separate parts, much as you would a worm that had stretched itself to the limit.

At 10:00 P.M. the Chinese struck.

2nd Battalion, 5th Regiment, Northwest Ridge, 10:00 P.M.: The first gunfire broke out in the D Company area along the road leading west. It wasn't much, it didn't last long, and the company wasn't hit again that night.

But within minutes the battalion's right flank was aflame.

Peters's F Company was hit hard. So was Jaskilka's E Company. A section of F Company's line was overrun at the point where it tied in with E Company, and Chinese were pouring through the gap. Jaskilka's 1st Platoon was under heavy attack. His machine guns were spitting death. The company mortars lobbed round after round on the Chinese, who now were just yards away from his 1st and 2nd platoons. The battalion 81s were firing in support of F Company.

Nolan had a four-man fire team about forty yards in front of his lines. "We were tied in with a telephone to the fire team leader, a young guy by the name of 'Sharkey'—at least that's what everyone called him . . . I don't think he had a name," Nolan said.

"He called me and said the gooks were out there, that he could hear them moving and talking."

Nolan crawled out to his position behind an old stone foundation to see and hear for himself.

"There's one over there," Sharkey told Nolan, pointing off into the dark. "There's another one over there. And there. Goddamnit, they're everywhere."

"Sharkey, I can't see a goddamn thing out there."

"Goddamnit, Lieutenant, you need glasses."

"I really did, you know," Nolan admitted. "I couldn't see a damn thing that night."

Nevertheless, he pulled his fire team back inside his perimeter and got on the phone to Jaskilka and asked for illumination because he was about to open fire.

Then the high-pitched, shrill sound of bugles pierced the frigid night air. Gunfire, shrieks, and shouting echoed up and down marine positions on all the ridges, in Yudam-ni, on the hilltops where the 7th Regiment rifle companies were under attack.

This is where the Chinese decided to stand and fight, and they brought with them mobility, knowledge of the terrain, great numbers, and the element of surprise.

"We were rapidly becoming aware of the Chinese out there in front of Roisie's battalion," Murray said. "What we really didn't realize was that there were so many of them, and that they would hit [Lt. Col. Robert D.] Taplett's 3rd Battalion in the valley at the same time."

"I wasn't concerned about Roisie," Murray added. "He was in very good defensive positions. But once the Chinese attacked, I was very much concerned about Taplett's battalion. He was in an assembly area and had taken only normal precautions. I know for a fact he wasn't deployed like he would have liked to have been to withstand such an attack."

F Company, 2nd Battalion, 5th Regiment, Northwest Ridge, 10:00 P.M.: The marines used the "buddy" system, so Johnson shared his hole with PFC Tom Jonnel. Johnson had the first watch, 6:00 P.M. until 8:00 P.M. "I woke him in two hours," Johnson said, "and told him with absolutely no knowledge of the situation, 'Tom, the gooks aren't about to attack tonight. Next watch I'll stand in my bag.'"

Johnson took off his parka and put it under his sleeping bag to provide a little more insulation from the frozen ground. Off came his cartridge belt and field jacket, with which he covered the open end of his bag, and fell asleep.

"The next thing I knew, Tom was nudging me and whispering, 'The gooks are coming! The gooks are coming!'"

"No shit, Tom?" Johnson asked, half in jest, half asleep. "I couldn't believe it, but I started to get dressed. That's when I heard the Chinese shouting and firing."

He grabbed his cartridge belt and rifle, fired a couple of shots in the air to see if it was working, then waited for the Chinese to appear.

"We were at the edge of this hill, but not close enough to look over. We had to crawl forward to look down."

Calvert tossed an illumination grenade over the top but didn't see anything.

"There was no firing in our immediate area," Johnson recalled, "but there was an awful lot of shooting on our right, over where Easy Company was. I could hear the machine guns in 'Easy Alley' and see the red and green tracers and explosions everywhere."

"It looked like the Fourth of July," he remembered. "Then the Chinese came at us."

They were on one side of the hill, the marines on the other. If one showed his head, the other shot. Grenades fill the air. To the right on a knoll connecting F and E companies Johnson saw the Chinese rush the top, overwhelm the marines there, then start firing on marines who were perhaps thirty yards away. Then the Chinese raced down toward the low ground.

Collins had thirteen men in his squad. They were about ten yards apart, two to a hole. He was in his sleeping bag, a few yards back of his men. Their line of defense stretched about fifty yards. "We hadn't fired a shot since Seoul," Collins remembered. "That night we were just freezing to death."

The corps was his kind of life and he enjoyed it, thrived on it, and despite some pretty bad moments, he had a lot of fun. "I drank a lot of beer, kicked some asses, lost a few stripes, but it was good and I liked it," he said, so much that he stayed in for twenty-three years, including a few pretty bad ones during World War II. He was, as they say in the corps, a fine breed of ass-kicking marine and one of many who were in the right place at the right time on this bitterly cold night.

Before it got dark he saw the Chinese perhaps three hundred to four hundred yards away, across a gully. For this reason they didn't dig in on the front side of the hill.

"But we didn't expect anything," Collins recalls. "We all thought we were up there where nothing was going on."

One of his men was on top and awake when the Chinese hit.

"He ran down and woke me, shouting, 'The goddamn enemy is coming up the hill by the thousands,'" Collins said. "I didn't believe him and, hell, it was too cold to go out and see."

"You better believe me!" the marine shouted at Collins. "They're here! They're here!" he continued to holler and began shaking Collins.

"So I got out, and that's when I first saw the Chinese," Collins said.

"They were on top of the hill perfectly silhouetted," he said. "It was a full moon and there was lots of snow. It was almost like daylight, and killing them was easy," Collins said. "But there were so many. No matter how many we shot, they kept coming. When one went down it seemed as if two appeared in his place."

Collins checked his right, then his left. He saw four of his men running back down the hill, away from the fighting. "They were following a corporal whose squad was next to mine, and he was flying," Collins remembered.

Collins ran over, caught up with him, and grabbed him by the collar. "I used every four-letter word on him I knew, and I knew quite a few.

"I got his squad turned around, and the guys from my squad headed back to their positions," Collins added. "This running is for the birds!" he shouted at them as he pushed and shoved them back up the hill.

"We're going back up this goddamn hill!" he shouted at them, "and by God we did."

"But I didn't blame them for running," Collins said. "When a leader runs, people follow. Anyway, some of them were new, had never heard a shot fired."

And the corporal who bugged out?

He fell later at the bottom of the hill and broke a leg and was awarded a Purple Heart.

Headquarters, 3rd Battalion, 5th Regiment, Yudam-ni, 10:00 P.M.: Taplett's men were in an assembly area close to the fork in the road where one leg continued north, the other branched west. In the morning his battalion would follow Roisie's 2nd Battalion as it headed west toward the Eighth Army. His men were still digging in, adjusting defenses at various points. Earlier in the day Taplett had taken his jeep and followed Roisie's men until they halted at about 2:00 P.M. He wanted to see the terrain, spot the key features, just to be on the safe side for the next day's march.

"My battalion was in the low ground with no defensive mission whatsoever," Taplett recalled. "I was told that I was completely protected all around with companies of the 7th Regiment on all the hills.

"I started getting very uneasy about everything that was going on," he said. "I got very suspicious. I was finding out that things were not so nice and comfortable as I was led to believe."

He was extremely worried about Hill 1384, a high chunk of land that loomed ahead and just slightly to the right of his command post.

He'd been told by regiment that marines were up there and not to worry.

Nevertheless, Taplett sent Maj. Harold W. Swain up a draw between Hills 1384 and 1282 to see if contact could be made with anyone. Even the Chinese. If Swain drew fire, Taplett would know for certain who was up there.

Swain and his men moved up the draw, then began to climb Hill 1384, shouting,

"Any marines up there?"

No response.

"Anyone up there?"

Silence.

"Hello, up there!"

Not a voice was heard, not a shot was fired. No one was up there. Taplett called regiment again.

"Are you sure somebody is sitting up there?" he asked.

Again he was assured that there were marines on top of 1384.

"You gotta be crazy as hell," Taplett responded testily. "You can't be serious. There's no one up there!" He didn't wait for a reply.

"I started taking additional precautions—protective measures—of my own," Taplett said.

He tried to fill in all the gaps as he saw them. He sent a force up 1384. He repositioned H and I companies so they were now facing Northwest Ridge, particularly Hill 1403. He made a few changes at other locations.

Two platoons from G Company were close to the base of Southwest Ridge. The third was outposted a bit higher on that same ridge.

Taplett's command post was in a small draw between 1384 and 1282. His Headquarters and Service Company was close by. So was his Weapons Company.

Later, one platoon from I Company was moved to a spot about five hundred yards up 1384. A platoon of South Korean police had two heavy machine guns about two hundred yards above the CP.

Taplett was in his tent talking with his executive officer, Maj. John Canney. There was something wrong. Taplett couldn't quite put his finger on it, but he could sense it. "John, I have a feeling something isn't right up there," he said. "Everything is too quiet."

Minutes later, Taplett's phone rang. It was regiment.

"The outpost is not on 1384. It's on 1282."

Taplett did some quick outposting, made a few more shifts here and there, and went from a 25 percent alert to a 50 percent alert.

The first strong indication that things were coming apart in the valley occurred just before 10:00 P.M., when Chinese surprised H Company at the roadblock it had set up at the road junction. The Chinese fired at the marines, the marines fired back. Then Weapons Company reported Chinese prowling around its position.

The phone rang in Taplett's command post. It was the battalion surgeon.

"Will you come on down? I've got casualties here that don't make sense."

Taplett and Canney ran out of their tent and headed for the aid station nearby.

What they saw were marines, wounded, dazed, frozen, no shoes, no clothes, a few with only blankets. He talked to them briefly and found out they were from H Company, 3rd Battalion, 7th Regiment, and that they had been on Hill 1403.

"Let's get the hell out of here!" Taplett shouted as he and Canney ran back to their CP.

"Never once that night did I have any information that the 2nd Battalion was under serious attack," Taplett said. "I didn't know about it until the following day."

But he quickly became aware of the problem H Company, 7th Regiment was having on Hill 1403.

Cooke's three platoons were quickly overwhelmed. The mortars were overrun. Casualties were very heavy. Some men were caught in their sleeping bags. All but one of his officers, Lt. Minard Newton, were wounded. First Lt. H. H. Harris was rushed to the top to replace Cooke. He found the platoons of Lt. Paul E. Denny and Lt. Elmer A. Krieg cut to ribbons. He quickly moved Newton's platoon from the left to the right flank and counterattacked. Enough ground was regained to hold off the Chinese for two hours, but at 4:00 A.M. H Company was pulled off Hill 1403 toward the rear of Jaskilka's E Company, 5th Regiment. There really wasn't much left of H Company, 7th Regiment.

"We were on a 50 percent alert up there," Cpl. James J. Schreiner recalled. "I was fortunate to be in a three-man foxhole so we could get more rest—at least we thought so. It was dark and cold. The other guy was in his bag. I was crawling in mine. Then all hell broke loose."

What followed was mass confusion. The marines were caught almost totally by surprise.

"Throughout the night it seemed we just counterattacked, then they'd counterattack," he said. "Then, much later, we were ordered off the hill. We left with just what we had on our backs and the weapons we carried. Our sleeping bags, food, extra socks, clothing were left on the hill." Before the Chinese were driven from the hill earlier in the day, they had carefully mapped the location of every foxhole. When Cooke's men reached to top of 1403, they plopped into the holes, dead tired. That night, when the Chinese attacked, they knew exactly where the marines were and exacted a terrible toll, virtually eliminating the company as an effective fighting force.

Taplett knew what Chinese control of Hill 1403 meant. They could sweep down behind Roisie's battalion and isolate it. They could attack marine positions on North and Northwest ridges from the rear. They could fire down into the valley and eventually attack the village itself.

Roisie quickly became aware of the danger because a number of men from H Company had wandered, dazed, into areas just behind his F and E companies, 2nd Battalion, 5th Regiment. Roisie shifted some of his men into a blocking position just in case the Chinese did come down 1403, but for some reason they did not.

Now Taplett was getting radio reports of stepped-up enemy activity throughout his entire area. "They were trying to envelop our positions," Taplett said.

V. G. Davis was a three-striper in I Company with a squad of his own, but on the afternoon of November 27 he lost it to another sergeant, who returned from the hospital. So Davis reported to his company and waited for reassignment.

He was given five riflemen and sent to an outpost about a hundred yards from where the 3rd Battalion had a blocking position on the road leading north, at the junction where another road swung sharply west. It was just a small mound of earth, a tree, off to one side in a field of shocked oats about twenty feet away. They got there just after dark. Davis wrote down the names of the five men: Jones, Nolan, Williamson, Doyle, Hand. He didn't know them. Later, a seven-man, two-rocket team arrived at his position, but it was so dark he couldn't see to write down their names.

They didn't have a radio, but they did run a line out there, so he had a phone link with the 3rd Platoon of I Company and Sgt. William Windrich.

"If you see or hear anything out there, let us know right away," Windrich told him.

So they waited. It wasn't long before they heard and saw rifle and machine-gun fire on top of the hills ahead and to their right, where the 7th Regiment was positioned. It went on for an hour, until about 11:00 P.M.; then it became quiet. But at midnight more gunfire erupted on the right but now much closer. The fighting was on the valley floor now, across a frozen stream very close to them. But the Chinese were beaten back, and it became quiet around the outpost and the roadblock.

Then Davis heard noises in the direction of the stream. The Chinese were crossing the ice. He could see vague outlines moving toward him.

"I asked Windrich by phone to have the outpost brought in," Davis recalled, "but he told me to remain until we were sure they were enemy."

By this time Davis could see the Chinese clearly only a few yards away and closing. The thirteen marines were just about surrounded. They were in a horseshoe position and the Chinese were just about to close the gap when Davis decided to move.

"We attempted to fire and move to our left out of the horseshoe," he remembered. He was the last man to leave. He was about ten paces behind the rest, firing, dropping grenades in the path of the advancing Chinese.

But when he reached the road, a hook on one of his boots got caught on the phone wire and he had to stop, go down to one knee to unfasten it. Just then a bullet hit him in the right wrist. He got the wire untangled and took off across the road and was shot in the left thigh. He hit the ground, hard, and lay there in great pain, stunned, bleeding. The Chinese ran past, thinking him dead.

"Then they brought up one of our own .30-caliber machine guns and sat it so close the loader had to straddle my left arm. Then they started firing it in short bursts toward the marines.

"They didn't step on my arm," Davis recalled. "In fact, they went out of their way not to step on it."

But the most difficult part was not breathing. Or breathing very little. "It was so cold that if I was to breathe heavily, they would surely have seen it."

By now the return fire was extremely heavy. Davis could see tracers everywhere. The Chinese fired the machine gun for about thirty minutes, then picked up their belongings, the gun, ammo boxes, and left. Davis hugged the ground for another fifteen minutes until the marines stopped firing.

"I was bleeding badly and I thought I had a broken leg," he said. He stuck his left thumb in the hole in his right wrist to stop the bleeding. Then he heard more Chinese approaching.

One of them stopped, worked the bolt on his rifle, and Davis felt certain his luck had run out. But someone said something in Chinese, and they walked on. Then another soldier came by, stopped, bent down, and gently rolled up Davis's sleeve and felt his left wrist. The marine felt the cold hand on his arm and knew that he was losing his watch.

"I realized that I had to get to a safer place," he recalled. Then he thought of the phone. If he could crawl to it, make contact with his platoon, then he could probably reach his own lines without getting shot at by his own men.

But when he reached the spot where the phone had been, he discovered the Chinese had taken it. Strangely, though, the marines' packs were still where they had left them, and untouched by the Chinese. So he used the bandages in one to bind his wounded wrist. But he was still in a lot of trouble.

"I was in a position well exposed to marine lines now," he explained. "They began shooting flares, and as they came down, they began shooting at shadows. I was flat on my face and they were knocking dirt all over me. But after a while, when they realized there was no return fire, they quit shooting."

By this time Davis realized that as soon as it got light and they saw him, the marines would open fire, so he shouted toward their lines:

"Quit shooting, you dumb bastards!"

Then they really cut loose. So he shouted again:

"Quit shooting! Quit shooting, you assholes!"

Then he heard a friendly voice hollering, "That's that dumb damn Davis out there. Quit shooting! Quit shooting!"

"They held their fire and let me walk in," Davis recalled. He was placed in a jeep and sent to the 7th Regiment's aid station, which was closer than the 5th's. They bandaged his wounds, put a splint on his arm, and gave him morphine. His leg was not broken.

John Yancey is shown at an exhibit of paintings depicting the fighting in Korea. This photo was taken in 1952 in Little Rock, Ark.

Lt. John Yancey is shown at Camp Pendleton, California, in August, 1950, just before he shipped out for Korea.

Sgt. Gene O'Hara is shown with his machine gun in 1948 at Camp LeJeune, North Carolina, in 1948.

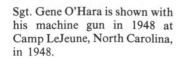

PFC Robert Johnson, who was the "point" when the marines attacked to the west on November 27, 1950, is shown in Japan in 1950.

Photograph shows former marine Gene O'Hara in 1968. He was one of the few survivors of Hill 1403 when the Chinese struck the night of November 27, 1950.

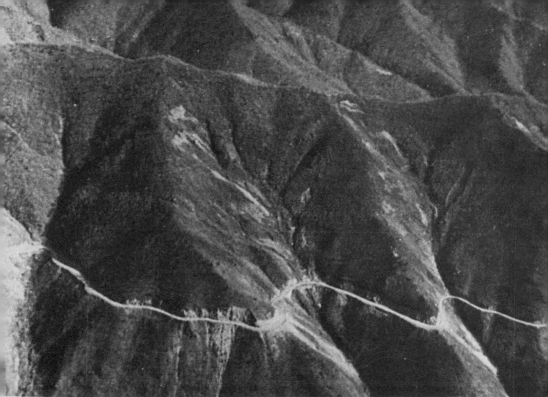

Photo by Gen. Edward A. Craig, USMC.

Photo by Jim Wilson.

Retired Gen. Edward A. Craig at his home in El Cajon, California, in 1987.

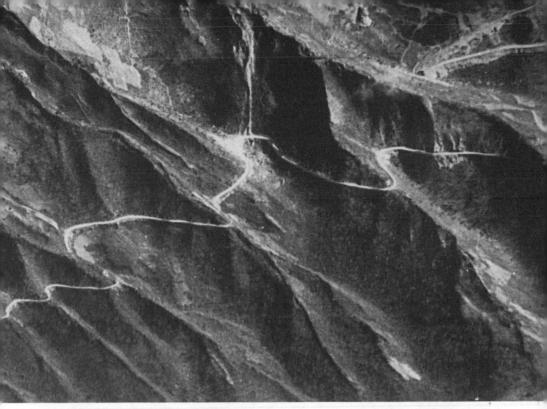

Aerial photographs taken by Gen. Edward A. Craig in early November, 1950, show the narrow, winding road that the marines would later take to reach the Chosin Reservoir and Yudam-ni. In many areas the road was too narrow for tanks and trucks and had to be widened by engineers.

Photo by Jim Wilson.

John F. Morris is shown in Oceanside, California, in 1987. He was the commanding officer of C Company, 1st Battalion, 7th Regiment.

Dave Brady, a police officer in London, is shown at an awards ceremony before his recent retirement. Brady is a former Royal Marine and one of the few survivors of the fighting in Hell Fire Valley.

Don Saunchegrow, who drove the ton-and-a-half Personnel Carrier No. 10426 through Hell Fire Valley with twenty-five British Royal Marines aboard. He is shown at his home in San Marcos, California, in 1987.

Survivors of the fighting in Hell Fire Valley are shown at a reunion in 1970. From left to right and numbered, they are: 1, Jerry Maill; 2, Don Saunchegrow; 3, Sgt. Lance Rice; 4, Lt. Col. Peter Thomas; 5, Sgt. Eric Blyth.

Photo by Jim Wilson.

Former British Royal Marines, survivors of the fighting in Hell Fire Valley, are shown at a reunion in England in 1975. From left to right and numbered, they are: 1, Dick Twigg; 2, Bert Toogood; 3, Jan Stock; 4, Arthur Derby; 5, Fred Hayhurst. Sitting is Douglas Drysdale, who as a lieutenant colonel was in charge of the Royal Marines in Korea.

PFC Richard N. Walker, nineteen, was a jeep driver in Headquarters and Service Company, 3rd Battalion, 5th Regiment. He drove the commanding officer, Taplett, around. He did some driving for S-2, intelligence. He picked up POWs at the front and brought them back for interrogation. It was better than life in the trenches. But then one afternoon in October he forgot to take his rifle when he drove Taplett to a meeting at regiment. The next morning he was carrying ammunition for a machine gun in I Company.

And life in a foxhole, he quickly found out, is a lot more precarious than life at battalion.

When the Chinese attacked, I Company was on 100 percent alert. Taplett's men were ready. No one surprised him. But no one had counted on the overwhelming number of Chinese.

Walker thought he was in an area where there wouldn't be hard contact with the enemy. Most of the troops felt this way, but their world exploded just after 10:00 P.M., when Chinese raced through the command post area, and Walker remembers thinking, "I sure didn't expect to see Chinese back here."

I Company foxholes were about fifteen yards apart, two men in each. Capt. Harold G. Schrier's machine guns had a good field of fire, and none of the Chinese who tried to cross in front survived.

Behind Walker the Chinese were on both sides of the road, running into the company area. Three jeeps from battalion were racing down the road with ammunition. The Chinese opened fire from both sides, but the jeeps drove through.

Later, word was passed that "friendlies" would be coming through, so be careful with your fire.

"Some of them straggled in throughout the night from the hills in front of us," Walker remembered.

He spent the rest of the night fighting the Chinese off with his rifle, shagging ammo for the .30, then feeding it. Overhead the faded yellow flares of the Chinese and the blue-white flares of the marines exploded.

Taplett and Canney were in and out of the battalion CP until 1:00 A.M., when the Chinese overran the I Company outpost on Hill 1384. Two marines slid down the hillside from the outpost and told Taplett that a large force of Chinese had attacked them.

Minutes later, the Chinese were knocking on Taplett's front door. Grenades ripped away part of his tent.

121

"I tried to call Murray but could only talk to the operator," Taplett said.

"Suddenly I have this strange feeling that I'm sitting here in no-man's-land all by myself." He told his staff to get away. Only his S-3, Maj. Thomas N. Durham, and his radio operator, PFC Louis (Swede) Swinson, remained. Grenades had destroyed his switchboard, and most of his tent was in tatters.

Swinson worked frantically on the switchboard when he wasn't firing. The phones were of no use. A few radios worked. Most had been destroyed by the cold. So communications were virtually nonexistent.

Murray was in his tent when he heard gunfire coming from Taplett's area, about three hundred to four hundred yards away. Although Taplett didn't recall talking to Murray the entire night, the 5th Regiment commander recalled "calling Bob several times to ask what was going on up there."

"He said they'd been hit and were in a helluva fight up there," Murray said. "One time when I was talking to him on the phone, it suddenly went dead and I thought that maybe he had been hit."

Everywhere you looked there were Chinese, and Taplett was sitting in the middle of a no-man's-land. Canney ran to Taplett's CP under heavy fire, exploding grenades dogging his every step, and breathlessly told him that Headquarters and Service Company had pulled back across the road and set up a new perimeter.

"How can you let them do that?" Taplett asked. "I don't think the pressure is that heavy."

The battalion commander told Canney to go back across and "get them back here."

Canney left, crossed the road, started to rally the troops, but was shot in the head and killed.

Taplett sent his S-3, Durham, up to G Company with orders for it to attack back through the command post area, where the Chinese were rampaging.

"It was that counterattack of George Company that saved the day for us all," Taplett remembered.

Charles D. Mize, a first lieutenant, got the company organized, and Lts. Dana B. Cashion and John J. Cahill led their platoons back through the CP area at about 3:00 P.M., routed the Chinese around Taplett's tent, cleared the enemy out of the draw, then started up Hill 1384.

"It was one of the best things I have ever seen," Taplett said. "It was brilliantly and successfully executed."

Attacking abreast with marching fire, they quickly reached the area where the South Korean police had been. They continued for several hundred yards, then halted until daylight. Several survivors of the I Company outpost joined them at daybreak, and the two young officers pressed upward. Then they radioed Taplett that they were close to the top of 1384.

An almost incredible feat. With little or no knowledge in night attack, Cahill and Cashion, without a lost step and very few casualties, had surprised the Chinese and thrown them off balance, giving the marines in the valley a chance to catch their breath, to reorganize. And it gave the few remaining men in H Company, 7th, a chance to get off Hill 1403 and reach Taplett's perimeter.

"We were able to move up and take it [Hill 1384] without too much trouble," Cahill said. They didn't encounter much rifle or machine-gun fire, but they did run into one of the heaviest barrages of concussion grenades any man would ever want to experience. The Chinese were big on them. That was their game plan. Their theory of attack. Get close, toss them in. Create confusion, then follow in and, hopefully, not get hurt. But it didn't always work this way. In this instance, the Chinese did get hurt.

They came down partway to meet the marines but were just about all killed. The rest turned and ran.

"Dana and I started moving after the Chinese then, but we were called back," Cahill recalled. "We were hot to trot because we really had them on the run."

But Taplett said, "No. Come back and consolidate your positions." Which they did, reluctantly.

"As far as we were concerned, they were there, we had them on the run, and we wanted to pursue them," Cahill added. "We thought we could have gone all the way.

"Again, we didn't know we had a tiger by the tail."

They stayed up there throughout the night and very early morning, then came down.

Before they started to pull back, they built a fire and tossed a large box of ammunition in, hoping it soon would explode. It did. It sounded as if the marines were keeping up a steady fire, and the Chinese kept their heads down.

"It almost sounded like the Fourth of July," Cahill remembered, "but we got everybody off that hill without a scratch."

Cahill wasn't surprised that everything worked as well as it did. He had a good bunch of men—and boys. Most were professionals with World War II experience. They were a tough bunch. When he got his first replacements—reservists—there were enough old hands around to show the newcomers the right way to do things. Unlike a lot of professionals, Cahill had a high regard for marine reserve forces. "They were more careful," he explained. "It wasn't that they wouldn't take a chance, or do the things they had to do. They just didn't rush into it, and as a result I think it paid off . . . as a result, they were around much longer."

"It was like a stampede when they came over the top of us," remembered Tom Malmo, a corpsman of H Company, 3rd Battalion, 5th Regiment. "It was like they didn't see us."

They ran over and around the marines in the north end of the valley and got all the way to the aid tents far to the rear. Three Chinese burst into one of the tents.

"We're operating," a Navy doctor said, and the Chinese bowed and backed out.

2nd Battalion, 5th Regiment, Northwest Ridge, 10:30 P.M.: Chinese were everywhere. You couldn't turn in any direction and not see enemy soldiers. "My immediate concern was the boundary between Companies F and E, since the Company F platoon tying in with me was reported overrun," Jaskilka said. He talked with Borgomainero and learned that the Chinese thrust had missed his platoon but that several men had wandered into his command post without shoes.

"Why these men left their shoes behind was never explained to me," Jaskilka said, but he sent them immediately to the battalion aid station to keep them from freezing.

Jaskilka then sent Borgomainero one squad from his 3rd Platoon and a .30 machine gun, then covered the battalion's rear to reinforce his left flank, where the breakthrough was, between F and E companies.

"When next I talked with the battalion commander to report Company E's position," Jaskilka said, "he ordered that I send a patrol to the left to regain contact with Company F."

But this proved futile because the Chinese had completely taken over the knoll, which wasn't regained until 6:00 A.M.

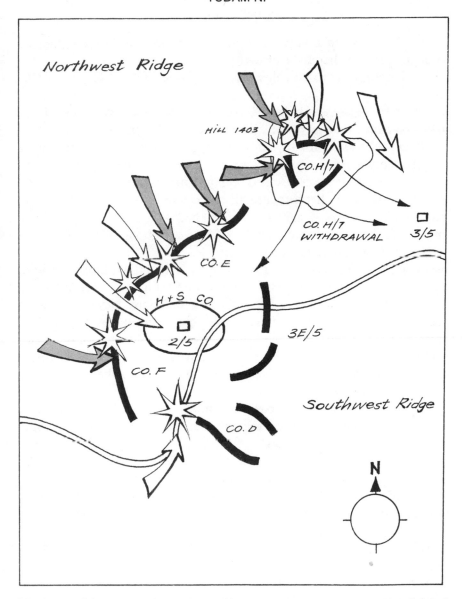

Map 5A—Light arrows show where Chinese attacked at 10:00 P.M. the night of November 27, 1950. Dark arrows indicate where Chinese struck the second time the night of November 27 and the early hours of November 28.

The gap between F and E companies had become so great that the company mortars had to be moved. Two of the tubes were out of action. Chinese continued to run down the backside of the hill toward the valley.

"We didn't have any holes," Collins said, "and that was a big advantage for them. But they were still perfectly silhouetted on top and that was a big advantage for us, and we killed plenty." The Chinese were about twenty yards away and closing fast. It was already bayonets and rifle butts in some spots. Collins was moving back up toward the top of the hill when a bullet tore into his collarbone and lodged in his lower back. Corpsman Les Arnatz dug swiftly through several layers of clothing, patched him up temporarily, put him on a poncho, and began to slide him down the hill on the ice.

Jonnel saw Collins on the ground, the corpsman working over him, calmly, coolly, under fire, and remembered a night not too long ago when they were in reserve. "J.J. and I were on guard duty and we were freezing to death. I had an extra woolen shirt, and it was beautiful. It was lined with yellow silk, with dragons on the cuffs. But he was cold, so I loaned it to him. I told him I wanted it back. Then I looked down, and there he was, bleeding all over the place. I remember cussing the shit out of him about that."

"As they carried Collins past us," Johnson remembered, "his eyes were open and he looked at several of us and said, 'Don't let them come through. Hold them . . . don't let them come through.' "

But it was too late. The Chinese were in charge on the knoll, on the top of the hill, and were still running into the valley.

"All of a sudden they started coming over the top and down at us," Jonnel said. "Mortars were dropping on the top between them and us, but they kept coming."

He fired his Thompson until it was empty. He had no time to reload. He grabbed an M-1 that was partly frozen and cranked each shot off one at a time. Chinese raced past him but he couldn't turn. He was too busy firing straight ahead. Chinese were about ten yards in front. He dropped the rifle that wouldn't fire at all now, picked up a BAR and had it on full automatic, but it didn't work well, either. It was one shot at a time from the twenty-round magazine. He was on one knee, no cover. He stuck his K-bar in a chest, then swung the BAR at another. Ammunition was gone.

"We finally pushed them back over the top," Jonnel said. "Then we went up and fired down at them."

The breakthrough between F and E companies was still a major problem, so Roisie ordered the two remaining squads from the 3rd Platoon over there on the double. It worked. The Chinese were slowly contained. Although they still held the top of the knoll, they were no longer running down toward the valley.

Nolan's platoon had the responsibility for the ravine, or alley, with a hill on the right, another on the left.

"We were down there in that draw tryin' to dig in but that was like tryin' to piss up a rope," Nolan remembered. "It was frozen."

A streambed, some rocks, and washed-out ground ran through his position.

"All we could do was spread out and try to take advantage of whatever natural cover we could find," he said. "Our machine guns were set up on the ground."

There was some small shrubs and trees out about two hundred yards, and another hundred yards beyond that there was an old abandoned house. He set up a light and a heavy machine gun on the right side of the stream, the same on the left side, with interlocking fields of fire. No one could come down that alley into those bands of fire and survive.

The hill on the right rose sharply. On top there were other marines. At least that's what Nolan had been told. "I wasn't concerned about the right," Nolan said. "I was told there were some marines up there, so I assumed there was. But I never saw any, though.

"In fact, if the Chinese had gone about seventy-five yards to my right we never would have seen them," Nolan said. The nearest marines on the right were several hundred yards away.

On the left of the streambed Nolan's platoon tied in with the 1st Platoon, now run by Sergeant Borgomainero. "He was a professional, a real teacher, all the men respected him," Nolan said. "He had more time as a platoon leader than any second lieutenant I knew of."

Did Nolan think the Chinese would attack that night?

"No, not really. And when they did, I didn't realize that there were so many of the bastards out there."

When the Chinese attacked, they came in a column of twos all the way up that alley right into Nolan's machine guns.

"I think they knew we were there," he said. "What I think happened is that after they made the initial contact and found us out there, waiting, they didn't have the authority to go around my right flank. I attribute that to their lack of communication."

The Chinese were gunned down before they could reach E Company's lines. They tried to pull back their wounded but couldn't.

The Chinese withdrew and began to dig in about eight hundred yards away from Nolan's still-warm machine guns. He called Jaskilka, told him where the Chinese were, and almost immediately mortar fire descended on them. It was midnight. It had been a slaughter. Chinese bodies covered the ground like a carpet. There were piles in front of the machine guns. The Chinese never came close to cracking what the marines called "Easy Alley." But the outcome was no surprise to Nolan, who said of his men, "They were hired killers, really."

The problem now was to get warm or at least not freeze. The temperature was well below zero. No one crawled back into his bag. A few tucked their feet in. A few others went back to the warming tents at the battalion command post.

Most checked their weapons and filled empty clips, which was difficult to do wearing heavy mittens.

"We opened up boxes of what we thought were eight-round clips for our M-1s," Nolan remembered, "and damned if we didn't find five-round clips for the World War I Springfields.

"Just imagine a bunch of marines scramblin' 'round in the dark on their hands and knees, cursin', lookin' for eight-round clips. Well, that's what we did, and damned fast," Nolan said.

The Chinese tried the alley again a few hours later. Small-arms fire hit Nolan's men first. Then a grenade attack. But it didn't last as long as the first—about forty-five minutes at most—and was much weaker. The turning point came when tracers set the old house on fire and turned night into day. With the fire behind the Chinese, it was like a turkey shoot. "The old house lighted up the entire area and afforded beautiful observation of the enemy," Jaskilka said. "The rest was duck soup."

"I didn't comprehend the magnitude or the scope of the attack until I saw the bodies in the morning," Nolan said. He counted 201 Chinese dead in front of his machine guns, the closest five feet away. There were no dead or wounded in his platoon and only a few cases of frostbite.

At dawn he tried to give his men a little rest, some warm food, a little warmth around a fire because he knew that very soon the attack west was scheduled to resume and his platoon would lead.

Peters's men were still fighting. Lt. Gerald J. McLaughlin was standing by a tree near the skyline. A Chinese soldier darted by. McLaughlin shot him with his .45, then picked up his Thompson and dropped his carbine that no longer fired on full automatic.

They could see the knoll where the first breakthrough had occurred. It was littered with dead and dying. In some places you couldn't see the ground. Johnson crawled forward to get a better look at that old two-wheeled machine gun, but rifle fire drove him back. Then McLaughlin passed the word that the platoon had to help get back some lost ground.

"We were walking in a column just below the crest of the hill when someone heard something on the other side and shouted at McLaughlin, "Are those marines over there?"

"The lieutenant poked his head over the top, fired a quick burst, then leaped backward as three grenades sailed over his head," Johnson said.

All three landed in the snow just in front of Johnson, perhaps four or five yards away. He turned to hit the deck but instead bumped into PFC Walt Iverson.

Wham!

Wham!

Wham!

"I didn't get a scratch," Johnson said. Neither did Iverson.

A little ways farther they ran into two Chinese huddled over a captured .30. One was dead. The other was holding a bandage over a gaping wound in his stomach. McLaughlin helped him to his feet, spoke to him in Chinese, but saw that he was dying. So he gently put him back on the ground, and the column moved on.

But the situation was deteriorating so rapidly that instead of recapturing lost ground, the company was told to pull back into the valley.

"When we got off that hill and into the narrow end of the valley, I'd never seen anything like it before," Johnson said.

"I couldn't believe the number of bodies that were there. There were Chinese as far as the eye could see, just nothing but frozen bodies. I guess when the Chinese broke through, they ran into a lot of machine guns. It was grotesque."

When it was light, Jaskilka went up to check the casualties. From about a hundred yards out all the way up to fifteen feet in front of his machine guns he counted three hundred Chinese dead. He noted two enemy groups of ten men each and remarked:

"These men were in a tight squad column formation and were apparently cut down by our first burst of fire. Their positions further indicated to me that we achieved complete tactical surprise, for I don't believe they knew we were quite so far up the alley.

"Perhaps they expected to find us closer to the road. Of further interest was that many of the enemy carried the Thompson submachine gun. Judging from what I saw later, these enemy troops were well clothed and well armed."

The casualties for Jaskilka's company: one killed, fourteen wounded, and twenty-four cases of frostbite.

November 28, 1950; F Company, 2nd Battalion, 7th Regiment, Toktong Pass, 2:00 A.M.: Barber's men were on a 50 percent alert, which meant that in a two-man hole, one was awake, the other asleep, if that was possible. They had taken their boots off, massaged frozen feet, and put on dry socks each man kept under his armpits to keep them from freezing. "For what we were doing, you didn't need to move around," Barber said. "You could fight in your sleeping bag."

Barber was asleep, one of those infrequent five-minute naps he was able to catch. Then his sound power phone rang. It was Peterson.

"He said he could hear noises in front of his lines, that people were talking out there. So we talked for a while. I tried to find out what was happening," Barber said.

"I'm coming over to take a look, so if you see a figure, I want you to challenge," Barber told Peterson.

"At that moment, based on the truck traffic going up and down that road, I didn't think we were under attack," Barber said.

"It didn't seem very logical, it just wasn't very smart tactically to attack us when they could have bypassed us," Barber said. "So putting all those things together, I didn't in my own mind consider it to be very probable that this was any heavy attack."

"Before I could get to Peterson's platoon to talk with him, my people started firing all along the line," he said.

"Here they come!" Cpl. Thomas Ashdale shouted.

"We got the flares out and then we saw we had a battalion out there —five to six hundred Chinese—moving against us," Barber said. They were coming down from that high rocky area that Barber had wanted to outpost. The attack hit McCarthy's platoon the hardest, as Barber had anticipated.

McCarthy was in his sleeping bag at the time. Two of his rifle squads were stretched across the top of the hill in a quarter-moon perimeter. The squad on the right tied in with Dunne's platoon, which in turn circled around to the rear and down to the lower part of the hill overlooking the road. The squad on the left tied in with Peterson's platoon, which also circled around to the rear and down to the lower part of the hill overlooking the road.

McCarthy's 3rd Squad was stretched thin in an almost straight line and tied in at both ends with the 1st and 2nd platoons. McCarthy's position perhaps could best be described as a shallow oval.

There was a full moon. It was a clear night. And terribly cold. Half the company was on alert, the other half in their bags, resting, if that were possible.

McCarthy inspected his lines at 1:15 A.M. and didn't like what he saw. His men were too lax. Challenges were halfhearted. So he raised some hell. "I got the squad leaders and the machine-gun section leaders together and informed them of the laxity of the watch," McCarthy said. When he checked the holes again at 1:30 A.M. he found everyone a lot more alert. He crawled into his bag a few minutes later.

Heavy firing on three sides woke him at 2:00 A.M.

"They were probably about a hundred yards from us when we got our first inkling they were coming," Barber remembers. His men began firing when the enemy troops were about fifty yards away in a skirmish line in groups of ten to twelve.

The mortars were hit first. Lt. Joe Brady and his gunnery sergeant, Al Phillips, were downed by shrapnel. Seven other mortarmen were wounded and two more were killed. One tube was destroyed. PFC Lloyd O'Leary was now directing the fire of the company 60s. The 81s were not in action yet.

The front two squads of McCarthy's platoon and one machine gun were quickly overrun. Of the thirty-five men in these units, fifteen were killed, nine wounded, and three missing a short time after the Chinese struck. McCarthy had only eight men on the line who could fight, and the Chinese attack hadn't peaked. One marine shot six with his pistol after his rifle jammed.

Grenades were everywhere. Three exploded near PFC Harrison

Pommers. Another went off just above his helmet, knocking him sense-less for several minutes, but he continued to lead his fire team the rest of the night. Ashdale's squad was in the thick of it. Marines were dropping everywhere. Chinese bodies were piling up in front of the marine machine guns.

PFC Kenneth Benson, Pvt. Hector Cafferatta, and two others were out about twenty-five yards in front of McCarthy's platoon. They were his eyes and ears. It was late when they got to their position. The ground was like concrete. So they just dug through the snow, tossed some pine branches in there, then threw in their gear and set-tled in for the night. Supper was cold biscuits. They were in voice contact with their squad leader, Sgt. John Komoroski.

"Keep your eyes open," he warned them.

"There was no way we ever thought we'd encounter what we did," Benson remembers. "I had no idea we'd see any Chinese. It was still like a game. We hadn't seen anything or done anything since we'd joined the company."

"We really didn't know anything," he added. "What do you know when you're only nineteen? We spent most of our time eating and keeping warm."

Rumors were flying through the company that everyone would be home for Christmas. "I never expected to be back by then, but I did expect the war to be over by then," Benson said.

Benson and another marine were awake, looking, listening. It was too cold to talk, even whisper. Cafferatta was in his bag with his boots off, his socks on. The fourth man in their fire team was trying to sleep.

They were kids trying to cope with the battlefield. If they lived, they'd be men. Already they had learned a lot since that first night with F Company, the night they took off their boots and left them out in the cold. Next morning they were chunks of ice. "We had a heck of a time getting them on," Benson remembers.

"Dummies!" Komoroski shouted at them. "Next time bring them in the bag with you!"

They were comfortable with their squad leader. He was older, in his late twenties, and had fought in World War II. "It was a good feeling he was with us," Benson said. "He told us what to do, how to stay warm, what to do with weapons so they wouldn't freeze. The whole bit."

132

What they were concerned with was the terrible cold. You just couldn't wear enough clothing to keep warm.

"Then, all of a sudden, bugles were blowing," Benson said. "That was it. Then the noise started. Rifles and machine-gun fire, slow at first, then it picked up." Now it was everywhere. In front, to the right, the left. The sky was bright with tracers.

"I was trying to sleep when I heard some pretty heavy shooting," Cafferatta said. "To hell with it. I didn't want to open my eyes. But there was more shooting, and heavier, so I opened my eyes and I saw these gooks coming in the snow."

"We must have been right among them, but they didn't do anything to us," he recalled.

Cafferatta came out of his bag firing, and didn't stop until daybreak. He saw Benson. "I checked to see how the other two were, but they were dead," Cafferatta said.

Both men remembered what their squad leader had told them: "Don't stay out there by yourselves if anything starts. Pull back to the lines." They grabbed all the ammunition they could carry and started back.

"I knew we had to get the hell out of there," Cafferatta said, "so we started crawling back, shooting all the way."

"Get your boots!" Benson shouted.

"We don't have time!" Cafferatta hollered back.

"Gooks were running everywhere, here, there. You couldn't miss hitting something if you just kept shooting," Cafferatta said. They got back to the perimeter and jumped into the nearest hole.

Two Chinese reached the top of their hole but Cafferatta jumped up and clubbed them with a shovel. Then he picked up a Thompson submachine gun one of them dropped and emptied it to his right at Chinese who were running by. A grenade landed in the hole, but he threw it out. It went off just after he let it go and tore the meat off one finger. Another grenade landed beside Benson, who picked it up and threw it out. It blew his glasses off and temporarily blinded him. His BAR was empty. Everyone around them was either dead or wounded except for Cafferatta.

"I looked at Benson and thought he was gone," Cafferatta said.

The rest of the night Benson and another man who was wounded loaded the weapons and Cafferatta did the firing. Dead piled up in front of his position at a remarkable rate. To the onrushing enemy he must have looked like a giant—he was well over six feet tall and weighed 215 pounds.

"Hector was standing up and firing at anything that moved," Benson said. "He wasn't touched. It was unbelievable." Bodies covered the ground in front of him like a carpet. Chinese reached the front of his hole, but they never ran over him.

"How are you?" Cafferatta shouted. "Can you see yet?"

"No!" Benson said, handing him another loaded rifle.

They were kids, but they were tough kids.

Just before the company left Hagaru for the pass, one of them, a corporal, twenty, received a "Dear John" letter from his girlfriend, telling him she had found someone else. He was distraught. He wanted to get home in the worst way, but the only way to do that was to suffer a serious injury. So he turned to a friend and asked:

"Will you break my arm?"

"Sure. Get down on the ground."

The corporal lay down, one arm stretched straight out.

"I used a big log and hit him as hard as I could," the friend said, "but nothing happened." However, the pain was so intense the corporal passed out.

"Jesus, you didn't break it," he said when he regained consciousness.

"Goddamn it, we'll do it again," his friend said.

"I hit him again, and again it didn't break."

"Then we decided to prop it up on a rock so it would break for sure," the friend said.

The corporal took three deep breaths, his friend grabbed him from behind around the chest and squeezed as hard as he could, and the corporal fell to the ground, unconscious. The arm was propped up on a rock and his friend was just about to pick up the log when an officer came by.

"What's wrong with him?"

"He fainted, he's sick. He just passed out."

"As soon as the officer left, we slapped him around, slapped the shit out of his face, and brought him around," the friend said.

"This takes a lot of nerve, you know," the corporal said.

Later, after they'd reached Toktong Pass, they had a couple of minutes to talk during a lull in the fighting.

"How's the arm?"

"Sore as hell, but I'm glad you didn't break it. I wouldn't want to miss this."

The fighting went on until daybreak. It was a steady rumble that wouldn't go away. At times the hill seemed to shake. When the firing slowed, as it did from time to time, Benson and Cafferatta squeezed their hands through layers of clothing, trying to find a warm spot and bring back some circulation.

Peterson's 2nd Platoon was in trouble. Gunfire was heavy on the left. Barber pulled a squad from Dunne's 1st Platoon on the right and shifted it to patch a hole between Peterson's men and those of McCarthy. A bullet hit Peterson in the shoulder while he was trying to get part of his line together. He fell to the ground and a corpsman was over him in seconds, found the hole, stopped the bleeding, and Peterson was back in action.

Dunne's platoon hadn't been too heavily involved up to this point.

"We arrived after dark and were told to dig in—shallow—and that we would consolidate our positions and improve them in the morning," PFC James C. Kanouse said.

"We didn't do much digging at that point that night. Fortunately, when the attack came, it didn't come at our positions. If it had," Kanouse said, "I'm sure we would have been very unprepared as far as the 1st Platoon was concerned."

He heard a lot of machine gun fire, then it became very intense, and Chinese seemed to be everywhere.

"We were surrounded quite rapidly," Kanouse recalled.

"Gunfire seemed to be coming into our positions from through the other platoons," he said. Then the 2nd Platoon, on the left, fell back. They were pushed off the top of the hill and bent backward into the 1st Platoon's rear area and partly into the 3rd Platoon's area," Kanouse said.

But Barber reached the 2nd Platoon in time to rally the men, shift some, get them just about back to where they were. Barber was busy throughout the night. When the firing began, he was headed toward Peterson's platoon. Then he ran to McCarthy's. He never stopped. Two of his runners were dropped by enemy fire.

But his perimeter was slowly shrinking. Chinese were everywhere, inside the perimeter, then shoved out. At one point they were thirty feet away. Close by, marines and Chinese were in hand-to-hand combat.

The fighting at Fox Hill continued until daybreak, when the Chinese began to pull back in fear of marine air.

It was deathly still at first light, one of those moments on a battlefield when you can hear a snowflake falling.

"How's everyone?" Komoroski asked as he crawled from hole to hole. "Who's been hit? Keep your eyes open! We'll be all right. The Corsairs will be overhead in a minute or two."

Northwest Ridge, 2:30 A.M.: John G. Fulop, an engineer sergeant, crouched in his hole well behind Jaskilka's E Company, 5th Regiment, watching the fireworks display overhead—red and green tracers, differently colored flares, mortar and artillery explosions on the hilltops.

"It looks like Christmas, goddamn if it doesn't," he remembered thinking.

At midafternoon on the twenty-seventh, when Roisie's 2nd Battalion was digging in on Northwest Ridge, Fulop went up there to blow some holes for the men. He had some C-2, C-3, and C-4 plastic explosives with him, which did the job very nicely. He favored C-3. It was pliant and powerful. "Funny thing about it, though. As you would mold it in your hands, then perhaps touch your brow, you'd get a terrific headache. But if you'd break off a small bit and eat it, you'd never get a headache."

Headquarters Company, 1st Battalion, 5th Regiment, Yudam-ni, 4:00 A.M.: PFC LeRoy R. Hintsa was in a tent, resting, in the valley when the fighting erupted in the hills. "We heard explosions and then a piece of shrapnel came through and hit a water can. From here on, all hell broke loose that night," he said. "We didn't know what was going on until early morning."

Hintsa jumped into the nearest foxhole and stayed there the rest of the night. Just before dawn the wounded began slipping, sliding down the hillsides toward the aid tents. Many couldn't get out of their holes and were freezing. So Hintsa and others started toward the top with stretchers to help out. He made several trips, then rested briefly. A marine staggered by toward the aid tent. "His lower jaw was missing. All he had was frozen red icicles on his face," Hintsa said.

A corpsman came over, told the wounded marine there was nothing he could do, that when he thawed, he would die. Then he handed him a pencil and a piece of paper and told him to write a letter home.

136

"The last time I saw him," Hintsa remembers, "he was sitting outside the aid tent writing a letter."

F Company, 2nd Battalion, 7th Regiment, Toktong Pass, 6:00 A.M.: When daylight finally came, the marines realized just how badly off they were. They had taken a lot of casualties, more than many had suspected or expected. Cafferatta nudged Benson, still unable to see, and tried to describe the carnage: "Everywhere around us there are dead Chinese."

Then he saw a hand move out a ways from his hole. "I went out to help one of them, but he just lay there and didn't acknowledge anything, so I walked away," Cafferatta said.

"That's when he threw a grenade at me. I heard it hit the ground and then I hit the ground. It went off, but I wasn't hit, but I was so goddamn mad I went back and shot him in both shoulders and the belly."

Then Cafferatta told Benson, "I'm going back down to our hole and get our gear and bring it up here." He climbed out and started down. Almost immediately, shots rang out. Then Benson heard Cafferatta's voice, soft, in pain.

"Hey, Bense . . ."

"What?"

"I'm hit. . . ."

"I'll come down after you. . . ."

"No. You can't see. Stay where you are. . . ."

"You keep talking and I'll come down. . . ."

Cafferatta was already crawling back and tumbled into their hole before Benson could get out.

"I don't know if it was a wounded Chinese up close or one firing from a distance that got him," Benson said.

"I got hit in the right arm and once in the chest, but I didn't know I was hit in the chest until three days later," Cafferatta said.

Soon corpsmen were carrying wounded back to the aid station and warming tents, Cafferatta among them. Walking wounded guided Benson to the rear, where fires were already going. He could smell the hot coffee long before he ever got close to it.

"It tasted like a million dollars," he remembers, "and I didn't know whether to drink it or put my hands in it."

After he'd warmed his body, inside and out, he had someone take him to the aid tent to visit Cafferatta. "His feet were frostbitten and he was in a lot of pain," Benson said. Benson still couldn't see, so he moved into a hole full of wounded close to the warming tents.

Early on the morning of the twenty-eighth the marines spotted a flight of Corsairs approaching from the direction of Hagaru. "We were not sure where they were going," McCarthy said, "but we hoped they were coming to our assistance."

They flew on to Yudam-ni, where the need for their firepower was much greater. Nevertheless, just the sight of them stirred the marines on top of Fox Hill, and they all cheered as the planes roared overhead. It was quite a boost to everyone's morale just seeing them in the sky.

"When it got light we were ordered to get back some of the ground we had lost, as we moved out early in the morning and, after some hard fighting, got back everything," Kanouse recalls.

In the process, they moved six hundred to seven hundred yards beyond the area that had been lost, killed a lot of Chinese, and retrieved a machine gun that had been taken the previous night.

Now the Chinese were on the receiving end. They were caught in the open trying to get to the top of a hill. "It was daylight, we had good targets," Kanouse recalls. "At one time there were ten of us standing up and firing at them. It was as if we were qualifying on a rifle range, only the targets were live."

The range was great but the firing was deadly, and the enemy troops were dropping everywhere. That rifle practice was paying off. The marines were moving out now at a brisk pace. They shot a few more Chinese, captured a few, then slowed down. They didn't want to get too far out. So Kanouse and another marine went back to ask Dunne what they should do—consolidate where they were, continue to advance, or return. He told them to return. The trip back to Fox's perimeter was just about as rough as the advance had been. A lot of Chinese they had shot on the way out were waiting for them on the way back, so they were shot a second time. Once back inside the company lines they tried to get warm, eat what they could heat, take care of the wounded, and collect and clean all Chinese weapons. It looked like they might be needing everything that could fire as soon as it got dark.

By this time the fight was just about out of the Chinese. A few made isolated runs at marine lines to hurl grenades, but they were quickly eliminated.

138

It had been a hell of a night, but it was over.

Barber was out among his men early, sizing up the situation. He was very low on ammunition. Grenades were almost nonexistent. The mortars were down to less than ten rounds a tube. He'd get an airdrop later in the day, he was told. Everything that could fly was heading for Yudam-ni, where it was a life-or-death situation for the marines.

At about 10:30 A.M. eight P-51 Mustangs arrived on station overhead. They were directed to their target—that rocky ridge to the northwest of Fox Hill—by radio via Hagaru, then to the planes. Barber had nothing that could put him in direct contact with the flight commander. But his SCR-300 gave him good communications with Hagaru, and the strike order was then relayed upstairs to the planes.

"We were a bit surprised to have someone other than marine pilots coming to our assistance," McCarthy said. "The P-51s were from an Australian squadron, and they turned out to be a red-hot outfit. When they made their runs on the ridge, several passed Fox Hill much lower than the hill itself. They bombed and rocketed the ridge very effectively. Then they strafed the valley along the Yudam-ni road. Some of the Aussie pilots appeared to be low enough to chop kindling with their propellers. After the air strike there was very little activity."

Caring for the wounded was a major problem. Corpsmen spent all their time moving them in and out of sleeping bags, changing bandages, warming their food. Morphine Syrettes had to be warmed in their mouths before they could be used. Men died because plasma had frozen.

How Battery in Hagaru finally got registered on Fox Hill and fired just enough rounds throughout the day to let the Chinese know what they could expect later. It kept their heads down, too, and cut down on sniper fire.

The airdrop arrived at midday. Ammunition, food, and medical supplies floated down in a near-perfect drop. Nothing was scattered. However, two marines were shot trying to bring in the supplies.

"I hadn't anticipated difficulties of resupply," Barber said. "The road was open when we went up there, and from my viewpoint we had everything under control." But in wartime, situations that are under control at one moment have a way of becoming out of control very quickly. Such was the case at Fox Hill. No one there expected to run into so many Chinese.

In summing up the night of November 27–28 Barber said: "I didn't do anything at all that night. The platoon leaders did it all."

The casualties after the first night of fighting? There were 350 dead in front of the first platoon and down toward the base of the hill. In front of Cafferatta's position and slightly to the right the dead were roughly the equivalent of two platoons. Barber's company had twenty dead, fifty-four wounded, and three missing.

The perimeter on Fox Hill had shrunk but little despite the ferocity of the attack. What was left of McCarthy's platoon—twenty-two men —was now repositioned in a straight line near the top of the hill. How Battery continued to pound the Chinese from Hagaru just enough to give warning that the marines would exact a deadly toll should the Chinese attack again. O'Leary's 81s continued to smash onto that rocky ridge. They didn't do much damage, but the pounding kept the Chinese underground long enough to give Barber's men a rest.

"A lot of shots came through here," Murray said in the early hours of November 28, referring to his command post. "It sounded like they were going through the top of the tent." It was too hot to remain where he was, in the forward part of the village. He remembered seeing a small hump not too far away and close to the road.

"I think we better go over and get behind that thing," he told his executive officer, Lt. Col. Joseph L. Stewart. "We can get a telephone line in and set up over there and we can operate with a little bit of cover."

Murray took a runner and a radio operator with him and Stewart, and the four remained there the rest of the night, directing his units, taking messages, trying to get a better grasp of what was happening out there.

Murray didn't know if this was just another Chinese counterattack or if it was where the Chinese had decided to make a stand. Nor did he realize the broad sweep of the attack.

"I really didn't know at that point what it was," he said. "I knew that we were being attacked. I knew that we had not been able to get back to Hagaru, that we had sent a patrol out to try and recover one of the trucks stopped up there on the road and they couldn't get through. So I figured we were surrounded by something. I knew that we had Chinese pretty much on all sides of us, but I didn't know how many."

But he wasn't concerned to the extent that he thought the marines might be wiped out. He was surprised at the strength of the Chinese attack. "I was shocked to discover that there were as many as there were," he said.

Litzenberg was in a substantially built small stone house with glass windows and a wooden floor. Close by, in the southwestern corner of the village, his staff worked in tents as first light approached on November 28.

Litzenberg was aware of the fighting; he heard the gunfire. You couldn't miss it. He knew his rifle companies were in trouble. But he knew little else at this time.

"We started to get reports from every part of the perimeter of the 7th Regiment," his operations officer, Woessner, said. "We didn't know specifically until next day or even into that night what the 5th Regiment's situation was."

Davis had a feeling there might be trouble. "My patrols had run into increasing resistance all afternoon," he said. His radio, which had been silent in the early morning, began to crackle at about 10:00 P.M. with reports from his rifle companies in the hills. He also received reports from two key companies in the 2nd Battalion.

"I did receive direct reports from Phillips on 1282 and I knew he was in real trouble and I was greatly concerned," Davis said.

"I knew, too, that Hull on 1240 had been kicked off but that he had gone back up," Davis added. "I could see that there was a pattern of heavy combat developing all around us now," Davis said.

Then the order spread through the valley for all available men who could squeeze a trigger to man the lines and prepare to go up into the hills.

"The radio calls never stopped that night," Pearl remembered.

General Smith was quartered in a small house on the northern edge of Hagaru when the Chinese struck on the night of the twenty-seventh. An operations trailer was close by. So were several blackout tents in which his staff worked.

They had no phone lines to Yudam-ni that night, and the amount of traffic that can be handled by radio relay is very limited.

"So all we got were sort of fragmentary reports that they [the 5th and 7th regiments] were under attack," said Col. Alpha Bowser, General Smith's operations officer.

Division was on instruments that very critical night.

The fighting that began twenty-two hundred yards down the road leading west had now spread like a grass fire in a windstorm into the valley, the village of Yudam-ni, and up to the hilltops of the five ridges, most importantly Hills 1282 and 1240.

What took place up there the night of November 27–28 could well determine the fate of more than ten thousand marines.

CHAPTER 6
NORTH RIDGE

ord spread quietly along the line: "Mr. Yancey wants to see bayonets on the ends of those rifles."

"Jesus Christ! What does he know that I don't?" wondered Pvt. John Kelly, "and I'm right up here on top, lookin' down."

Phillips's E Company, 2nd Battalion, 7th Regiment, was strung out across the top of the hill. Yancey's 2nd Platoon covered an area of about fifty yards in a crescent-shaped perimeter. He had two machine guns on the left—one of them was Gallagher's—where he felt the Chinese would sweep down from a high ridge and slam into his flank, and another on the right, where his men tied in with Bey's 3rd Platoon.

Phillips's command post was in a large shell-like crater near some rocks, brush, and small trees about forty yards to the rear. Close by were the company mortars, his radioman, and two runners. Ball, the executive officer, was about thirty yards away. Both were between Yancey's men and Clements' 1st Platoon on the backside of the hill.

"It was the usual Korean hill," remembers Clements, "straight up and straight down, and always a tough climb. More than anything else, the climbing wore my people out."

From time to time patrols from E Company made contact with patrols from D Company on Hill 1240, about a thousand yards south.

It was well below zero as the men waited in their holes for something to happen. It was too cold and too dangerous to sleep.

At about 9:45 P.M., McCann, Yancey's radio operator, picked up a warning call from Hull's D Company: "Watch out! One of our men was just bayoneted in his foxhole."

"It was around ten o'clock when the shooting started," Kelly said. "There were bugles, yelling, shouting, gunfire all over the damn place."

"I could see the Chinese, rather what I thought were Chinese," he added. "Because of the moon behind us, all the snow and the white clothing they wore, all I could really see were shadows."

But the shadows were firing. Then the shadows were running toward him. Machine-gun fire began to kick up the frozen ground. He heard the short bursts from Gallagher's .30 on the left. To the right he could hear the slow, steady tat-tat-tat of the other .30 firing down at the onrushing Chinese. Their sound was music to his ears. He had worried that they might have frozen.

145

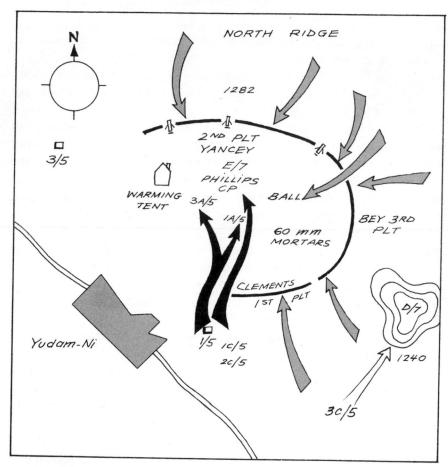

Map 6—Chinese attack Hill 1282 the night of November 27, 1950. Arrows leading up from the south show the route that relief forces took to reach the top of the hill.

The shadows were beginning to stumble and fall in the snow a few yards away.

"Mr. Yancey was behind us, shouting to keep firing, encouraging us. He was firing his carbine and throwing grenades," Kelly said.

"I was trying to get some sleep when they attacked," Clements said. "They tried to come up through Mr. Yancey's position. I was surprised. I thought they'd come from another direction. Instead, they tried to come up just about the same way we did."

Then, as suddenly as they had appeared, the Chinese withdrew. But this was the way they fought. Light, probing attacks along the perimeter until they found a weak spot, usually where one unit tied in with another. The marines learned this at Sudong, and they remembered the lesson at Yudam-ni.

The Chinese would be back.

"Come on over, Lieutenant, I want to show you something!" Gallagher shouted.

"Damn it, I can't now, I'm too busy." But Gallagher persisted.

"So, against my better judgment, I went."

But before he did, he put his men to work. "Dig your holes a little deeper," he told them. "Pull in the Chinese dead and use them for sandbags. Take some ration tins, put pebbles in them, and string them on communications wire out about thirty yards."

And he had them put out trip flares and grenades with the pins half pulled.

Only then did he head for Gallagher's position.

"Look, skip," Gallagher said, pointing to a long string of bodies that stretched right up to the muzzle of his gun, the last one touching it. He was proud. On one of the bodies they found a plotting board and a tape measure. "Probably a scout," Yancey said. "Pretty damn thorough," he thought.

Yancey started back to his CP, a shallow hole in the center of his platoon, talking to each man as he passed.

"Dig it a little deeper," he told a replacement. Others he tried to calm. "They'll be back, but we can hold. Just do what I tell you."

Then a shot rang out at long range and a spent bullet grazed his right cheek and went down into his nose. Blood streamed down his face and into his mouth and froze.

It was quiet on the hilltop now and remained so for about two hours, until about 1:00 A.M.

November 28, 1950: Yancey heard them first, moving slowly up the hill, but he couldn't see them. He grabbed the phone and shouted for illumination, but Ball told him there was a shortage of those shells that turn night into day.

"Shit!" Yancey slammed the phone to the ground. Now they would have to depend on the trip flares. Minutes later the approaching Chinese tripped the flares, and the attack was under way.

They smashed into Yancey's platoon with a ferocity the marines didn't think possible. One wave after another. Bugles, whistles, shouting, each sound telling the Chinese what to do.

They tried to get around Phillips's company on the right but ran into Bey's machine guns and were cut down. As rapidly as they were killed, others filled the void.

Yancey was in the center of his men, his platoon sergeant, Alan Madding, close by.

Yancey heard a "swisssh" zip past his head. "It was a horrible sound. It was like a freight train going by," he said. Then he heard an explosion about twenty yards behind his hole. Then another "swisssh" whizzed by. He dove to the bottom of his hole and began to dig. Then another "swisssh."

"I got down in that hole as far as I could and said to no one in particular, 'Shit! Someone's shooting at me with a bazooka or recoilless rifle. Is this really fair? They're for tanks!

"That was when my hair started to turn white at the temples."

Chinese were everywhere. They were almost into Bey's platoon. They were crawling up the hill in front of Yancey's men. They were swarming down from the high ground on the left in front of Gallagher's flaming machine gun.

Yancey was on the phone to Phillips, asking for the 60s. "Lay them on the saddle on the left and walk them back to me!" he shouted over the din of battle.

Madding remembered a radio broadcast he had heard at Sudong that had described the division as having been "surrounded by hordes of Chinese." He turned to Yancey and asked, "Skipper, how many damn Chinese in a horde?"

"My God, there were lots of them," Kelly said. "I didn't expect to see that many. I didn't expect to see anything until they told us to fix bayonets. We stopped them, though. The closest they got to me that time was about thirty-five yards."

Chinese dead began to pile up around the perimeter. When one group was cut down, others appeared.

"They kept coming and we kept stopping them," Kelly said. "They came at us again, we stopped them again. And again. I couldn't believe the firing around us."

Then it was hand grenades as the Chinese got close to the top of the hill. "They looked like big raindrops falling," Kelly said.

"I was shooting as fast as I could and tossing grenades," Kelly said. "I remember reaching down for one, pulling the pin, and throwing it at some Chinese who were just a few yards away. Then the whole sky lit up. It was an illumination grenade. Someone had brought up the wrong box, but it turned out okay because now we could see them."

Gallagher's machine gun was firing in long bursts now. So were the BARs. Forget those short bursts of four or five you heard about in boot camp. Machine-gun barrels were red-hot. BARs caught fire.

Yancey was running behind his men, firing from the hip, shouting, encouraging, "Keep firing! Don't let them get through!"

Breathing was difficult. Frozen blood covered his face. He could see the 60s exploding among the Chinese. The 81s from the valley dug huge gaps in the advancing Chinese.

Arms, legs, torn bodies flew through the air. Madding ran from hole to hole, passing out ammunition and grenades. Phillips was behind his men, urging them on, shouting, "You're doing well! Keep it up!" Then he helped carry the dead and wounded to the rear.

Sgt. Robert S. Kennemore ran down the hill toward one of the machine-gun bunkers. Phillips saw him and shouted, "Don't go down there, you damn fool, they've taken it!"

Kennemore dropped to the ground and crawled to another hole. The men were all firing. The gunner was on his knees holding the weapon in his hands and spraying everything that moved in front of him.

Then Kennemore crawled from body to body, Chinese and American, gathering ammunition and grenades and passing them out. Chinese were everywhere, so close he could hear the tap-tap as they armed their potato-masher grenades by tapping the handle twice on the frozen ground. It had been rifles, carbines and machine guns. Now it was bayonets, rifle butts, and knives. A grenade landed in a foxhole. No one in there saw it. Kennemore did, but it was too far away for him to get there and toss it out. He put his foot on it and pushed it into the snow as deep as he could.

Wham!

Chinese bodies were everywhere. Soon the 1st Special Company ceased to exist. Marine casualties were very heavy.

"I could hear Mr. Yancey over the guns," Kelly said. "He just didn't stop. Even in the midst of all that killing, I can remember thinking, 'Damn it, if he can stand there, so can I.' "

To his right Yancey saw that the Chinese had broken into Bey's position and were fighting hand to hand. Casualties over there were heavy on both sides. Finally the Chinese were shoved back down the hill.

"There were so many grenades in the air that night, it looked like a flock of big blackbirds overhead," Yancey said.

A great puff of black, acrid smoke rose from where a Chinese grenade had exploded. A young marine, a replacement, saw it, panicked, shouted "gas!" and turned and ran. Four others followed. Yancey and a sergeant close by, swinging their carbines by the barrel, beat them back into their holes.

The intensity of the Chinese attack began to slow at 2:30 A.M. Then, on a signal by a bugler, they began to pull back, and all was quiet except for the moans of the wounded, who soon froze.

Yancey was checking casualties, handing out ammunition and grenades. Then he dropped into his hole to rest, his face covered with frozen blood.

Robinson, who had left Yancey at Hagaru to ride shotgun for Litzenberg, lay on a stretcher in the battalion aid tent in the valley. His feet were severely frostbitten. He could hear the gunfire up on the hilltops. He knew it must be hell up there. And he knew, too, from the wounded coming down, that his company, Yancey, friends, were in the thick of it, were getting pounded.

He got off his stretcher, pulled on his boots over painfully swollen feet, picked up a rifle and ammunition from a pile of weapons outside the tent, and trudged up 1282 in the dark.

Yancey was hunched in his hole when he felt a tap on a foot.

"I looked down and saw Robinson," he said.

"What the shit are you doing up here?"

"Thought you might need some help, skipper," he said.

"I sure as hell do. Get on down to the right flank and organize that situation."

Robinson nodded and crawled off to the right. Yancey wondered if there were anything down there to organize.

Phillips, now twice wounded, was on the phone to the 1st Battalion, asking for replacements. "We've got a lot of wounded," he told Davis. Because of the tactical situation that night, both Phillips and Hull were reporting to Davis. Lt. Col. Randolph S. D. Lockwood, the commanding officer of the 2nd Battalion, 7th Regiment, was still in Hagaru, fourteen miles south, along with most of his staff.

It was about 3:30 A.M. now. The 1st Battalion, 5th Regiment, was positioned slightly to the right, or east, of Yudam-ni and very close to Hills 1282 and 1240, just in case the Chinese did break through, overwhelm the two rifle companies up there, and attack down toward the valley. To the right of the road and just south of the 1st Battalion, 5th Regiment, were the relatively unguarded 105 and 155 howitzers.

Davis called Litzenberg and Murray, explained the rapidly deteriorating situation on 1282, and was told to send two platoons from the 1st Battalion, 5th Regiment, to the top immediately.

He quickly dispatched Lt. Nicholas Trapnell's 1st Platoon, A Company. A short time later he sent Lt. Robert Snyder's 3rd Platoon through ice and snow to the top. It was a tough climb in light. At night it was an almost impossible climb. Yet both officers led their men to the top with no casualties.

Yancey heard feet crunching in the snow. He called for illumination and this time got it. About 150 yards out he saw a long line of Chinese walking slowly toward his platoon. Behind them, about fifty yards, was another line. And another. Still another. He guessed there was about a hundred men in each line.

McCann was with Yancey in his foxhole when the Chinese struck. The other runner, PFC Rick Marion, was alone in another hole.

"Get over with Rick," Yancey said.

McCann crawled out of his hole, got up, and started to run just as a concussion grenade went off near him, blowing him off his feet. He landed on his side, rolled twice and into Marion's hole. As he did, what sounded like an artillery round whizzed over his head. "If there was

151

one, we knew there would be another, so we just kept our heads down," he said. "Sure enough, another whizzed over our heads and exploded about six feet away."

As the Chinese closed, Yancey heard an officer—he was waving a pistol and leading the others—shouting, "Thank God, nobody lives forever. . . . Thank God, nobody lives forever."

"I couldn't believe what I was hearing. I thought my mind had gone," he said.

He turned to Madding. "Sarge, do you hear what I hear?"

"What do you hear, skipper?"

"Listen."

"Thank God, nobody lives forever. Thank God, nobody lives forever," the Chinese officer said again and again in near-perfect English.

"That's what I hear, too," Madding said.

"Hold your fire. Nobody shoot until I do. He's my meat. He's mine," Yancey said.

"I called him a goddamn renegade missionary Chinese and shot him at seventy-five to a hundred yards before they could get into grenade range."

"And that's when the shit really hit the fan," Yancey said.

The Chinese struck with a fury the marines hadn't believed possible. Machine guns blazed on both sides. Mortar fire plastered the hilltop, driving the marines to cover. Every weapon was firing. "It was like the grandest Fourth of July celebration ever, many times over," Yancey said.

Chinese had now broken into Yancey's right flank and again were running through Bey's platoon. Others charged down the hill on the left straight into Gallagher's machine gun. It was as if they had a death wish. Mounds of Chinese dead lay in front of his foxhole. Bodies were piled so high it was difficult to fire over them.

Yancey was on the left, near Gallagher, when he heard someone shouting, "Skipper, over here. Someone's coming up the hill—they might be ours—but they don't answer the password."

Yancey ran over to where his third machine gun was dug in, about twenty yards to Gallagher's left and facing slightly toward the valley.

"Give 'em the password!" he shouted.

"Lua, lua, lua, lea!" one of the marines shouted.

"Rua, rua, rua, rea," came the response a few minutes later from someone coming up the hill.

"Fire! Fire that son of a bitch!" Yancey shouted as he turned and headed for the right flank where the Chinese were streaming through. Behind him he could hear the rat-tat-tat-tat-tat of the machine guns.

By now Chinese were on top and firing down into the valley, raking the headquarters area of several units with rifle and machine-gun fire.

Yancey was behind his men, rallying them, shouting, cursing. He was firing his carbine one shot at a time. It hadn't worked on automatic for some time.

Fighting had slowed on the right before he could get there, and Yancey thought that Bey's platoon had been overrun for sure. He couldn't hear the machine gun that had anchored his platoon down there.

"That must be where they penetrated," he thought. So he took eight to ten men and headed in that direction with bayonets fixed. He had just about reached the breakthrough when he turned and saw that he was the only one still on his feet. The others had all been killed or wounded.

He turned toward the Chinese just in time to see a grenade coming at him. "I tried to ward it off but I didn't do a good job and it landed about fifteen yards away and went off," he said. A piece of shrapnel went through his open mouth and lodged in the roof. Blood poured from the wound, nearly choking him. Around him rifle and machine-gun fire had reached a crescendo he'd never thought possible.

Shrapnel buzzed through the air, cutting down everyone in its path.

Then another grenade exploded and blew Yancey through the air. He wasn't wounded, but it dazed him for a few moments. Then he got up and, blood streaming from his mouth and nose, ran back to Clements's platoon, shouting, "Gimme a squad, Clem, I gotta get those damn Chinamen out of my right flank!"

"He gave me a squad and I was turning to go when a bullet hit him dead center in the forehead. It went through his helmet and he fell in the snow," Yancey said.

"I was about two feet away when he got hit. He was bleeding bad. It was gushing out. I thought he was dead . . . I knew he was dead. So I took his men and headed for the breakthrough."

But Clements wasn't dead. The bullet went through his helmet at an angle and then spun around his head between the steel pot and the liner, tearing them both up and ripping open the right side of his head.

"It felt like someone hit me with a ball bat. I was afraid to touch it.

I didn't know how much of my head was left. And I really didn't want to know," Clements recalled.

"I didn't feel anything for a long time, and when the feeling did come back, it was just one big ache."

But he never lost consciousness and he was back on his feet a short time later.

Yancey told Clements's squad to fix bayonets and "follow me" and started toward the breakthrough in the 3rd Platoon. But no one followed him. "Hell, I don't blame them. They saw what happened to the first counterattack," Yancey said. But he went back and in a few minutes had them moving forward.

At the breakthrough Yancey spotted a Chinese soldier on his left and shot him. Another jumped up in front of him, pointed his burp gun at him, and fired. Bullets were flying everywhere. Yancey raised his carbine, pulled the trigger, and nothing happened. It wouldn't fire.

"That Chinaman was only a few yards away now so I went after him with my bayonet. He emptied his magazine at me . . . about twenty or more shots. One of them hit me under my right eye. I went down and dropped my carbine.

"It felt like half my face had been blown away," he said. "I looked up and that damn Chinaman was almost on top of me. He was reloading. I had an old pistol in a shoulder holster so I pulled it out and gut-shot him before he could get the magazine in."

Behind him he could hear Phillips shouting, "Yancey! Yancey!" "I guess he needed help in the CP, but I couldn't give him any. I had enough trouble of my own.

"I saw Ball, too. He was about twenty yards away. He was wounded. He was sitting there, cross-legged, just like they taught us at Quantico. Chinese were all around him . . . right on top of him. Ray was just sitting there, squeezing 'em off. He couldn't have gotten out. He wasn't going anywhere. . . ."

Just about everyone on 1282 had been hit at least once. Many of those had frozen hands or toes. The aid tent was full. Dead and wounded were laying in the snow twenty yards behind the holes. That was the rear area now. Many were still where they had fallen. Corpsmen couldn't reach them because of the heavy fighting. Those who could still fight, did so. Only the critically wounded were removed from the line.

Yancey could hear the cries of the wounded. "I'm hit, I'm hit. . . ." "My God, I'm bleeding. . . ."

"At daybreak we figured it would let up, but instead it got worse," Yancey said. But the marines could see them clearly now, hundreds and hundreds rushing toward them.

"We shot everything we had at them. Rifles, carbines, machine guns, grenades," Yancey said.

Then he led his men—those who could still move—out of their holes to meet the Chinese. Some of the wounded even crawled out.

"How we killed that bunch of men I'll never know," Yancey said.

"It was like Custer's Last Stand," Yancey remembered. "I kept wondering where did all those fucking Chinese come from."

Phillips jabbed a bayonet-tipped rifle in the snow behind his men and said: "This line will stand. We don't move back one goddamn inch."

They couldn't have backed up, even if they had wanted to. The dead and wounded were behind them on the ground. They couldn't get them out, and they weren't going to leave them.

Phillips' 1st and 2nd platoons had dwindled to a few tired, wounded, frozen men. They were very short of ammunition and grenades. Just as they were about to go under, Trapnell's platoon reached the top. He couldn't find Yancey's men, so he joined Bey's platoon on the right, where his men were needed the most.

Snyder arrived on top a short time later with his platoon. He looked for Bey and Trapnell but couldn't find them so he used his men to beef up what was left of Clements's and Yancey's platoons.

The Chinese had now pushed a wedge between Yancey's men and those of Trapnell and Bey. And from his position on the far right Bey could see that the top of the hill was engulfed in explosions and gunfire. By this time nothing could be heard on the phone in the command post but Chinese. They fought for more than an hour there. Dead and wounded from both sides covered the ground like a red carpet.

Yancey had been bleeding badly for some time. The blood had frozen on his mustache and around his nose, forcing him to breathe through his mouth, and the inside of his throat felt as though it had been sandpapered.

Phillips was dead. A burst from a burp gun caught him as he was throwing grenades. Clements was hit twice. "He died like a marine should," Yancey said. Lt. William Schreier of the mortar section was wounded. So was Snyder. Ball, wounded several times, had died in the aid tent.

McCann had been with Yancey most of the night, but now he couldn't find him. So he ran over to Gallagher's machine-gun position on the left. He was just about out of ammunition, but still firing. Between bursts he was looking for stray rounds on the ground. "Don't fire until they're right in front of you!" McCann shouted, then ran back toward the company command post.

"They were right in front of me the whole damn night," Gallagher said. "It was a nightmare."

"Everyone in the CP was dead when I got there," McCann said. He remembered a radio operator once telling him if you ever need the artillery, use Channel 23.

"So I grabbed the company radio, switched to 23, and shouted, 'Is there anybody there that can hear me?'"

"Some guy in the valley answered, 'Yeah, go ahead.'"

"We're on 1282. The gooks are right on top of us. We're damn near out of ammo. If there's anybody that can come up and give us a hand, we sure can use it."

While he was talking he saw a hand appear over a small rise in front of him, then spotted a grenade sailing toward him. It went off about twenty feet in front of him. "I tossed one back and blew him to hell."

By now McCann could see the Chinese running between the foxholes on top of the hill. He tried to find Yancey but couldn't. He looked for the other runner, Marion, who had been shot in the leg, but couldn't find him, either, so he ran back to Gallagher. The machine gunner had found some ammo, and the gun was still blazing.

Close by, two marines were firing over the top of their foxhole at the charging Chinese. A grenade went off in front of the marines. One died instantly. The other died a few minutes later as he tried to pull the five-inch wooden handle from the grenade that had been blown between his eyes.

By now the Chinese had sliced through the remnants of Yancey's platoon, leaving Sgt. Kenneth Keith on one side with four men, and Yancey on the other with nine. They were almost out of ammo and grenades.

There was no shortage of Chinese, living or dead.

"There was no way to count how many we killed. Chinese were stacked like cordwood," Yancey recalled. "Down the hill for a hundred yards or so you couldn't walk without stepping on a dead Chinaman."

"When they attacked us, some of 'em even stumbled over their own dead."

"I went back to try to find some grenades," Kelly said. "Then someone shouted, 'We need every man back on top!' So I headed back to the top. So did every man that could walk."

He'd gone only a few yards when he saw a marine with a gaping hole where his stomach had been stagger down from the top, stumble, then fall. Kelly ran to him, got him up, and turned him over to a corpsman. "The only thing he said was, 'My goddamn carbine froze. My goddamn carbine froze.' "

Kelly started toward the top again but saw that the marines were now backing down from the crest. The Chinese were up there now and firing down at them.

Bey ran over and stopped the retreat.

"He really raised hell with us," Kelly said.

"We're going to stand here. No more coming down off that hill!" Bey shouted at the men.

"So we stopped," Kelly said. "We gave no more ground."

"I thought Bey was a candy-ass when I first met him, but I changed my opinion of him that night," Kelly said.

Then someone shouted, "We have to take the hill!"

"I guess it was Bey," Kelly said. "So back up we went. The Chinese were firing at us, and a lot of the men were hit. But we had some reinforcements now and we continued up toward the crest, slipping, crawling, grabbing a bush.

"We were just about up there when we saw some marines were near the top on the right. So I and another guy shoved off to the left up a draw. We thought we'd try to get up from that side.

"He ran past the body of a marine, looked down at him hurriedly, shouted to me, 'He's dead, leave him alone!' and ran on up the side of the hill. At that moment his eyes opened. I shouted for the other guy, then took off my parka and covered him with it. Then we started to carry him down the hill."

The Chinese had spotted them by now, and bullets were kicking up the ground. A grenade went off behind Kelly's head, and he thought,

"My God, I'm hit." But it was a concussion grenade, and it only knocked him silly for a few minutes.

The other marine was bending over him when he came to. "I wanted to get the hell out of there in a hurry," Kelly remembered. "So we picked up the parka and slid, dragged, and pulled him down the hill."

They'd gone only a few yards when a Chinese soldier appeared out of nowhere and ran straight for them.

"He was only about fifteen or twenty feet away. He didn't have a rifle," Kelly remembered. "I got a quick look at his face and he had a sort of doped . . . crazed look. So I dropped the parka, grabbed the rifle on my shoulder, and pointed it at him. Before I could pull the trigger he jumped . . . he threw himself on the bayonet. I didn't have time to move. He just flew through the air and landed on the bayonet."

They finally got to the aid tent, turned the wounded marine in, and started back toward the top.

But the Chinese were up there now, in force, and massing for one final sweep that would clear 1282 of the few marines still alive up there. Then there would be nothing to stand between the Chinese and the valley below.

They would sweep down from the heights, eliminate the artillery, wreak havoc in the headquarters area and out the road to Hagaru-ri in yet another location, and close tightly the marines' only escape route.

CHAPTER 7
CHARLIE ARRIVES

November 27, 1950; C Company, 1st Battalion, 5th Regiment, Yudam-ni, 10:00 P.M.:

Capt. Jack Jones's men were in a bivouac area in the southeastern corner of the village and, since the 3rd Battalion, 5th Regiment, was in front, and other friendly units were scattered around them, they put up their shelter halves, crawled into their bags, and tried to get a little sleep.

It had been a long day for them. They were up at 3:00 A.M. and on patrol on the far side of the reservoir. At midday Jones was told to get his men aboard trucks and "hurry back."

"I didn't have any idea where we were going," he said. "No one seemed to know." They ate cold rations, tossed their gear aboard, and were off. Only the driver of the lead truck seemed to know where they were headed.

Once the convoy was rolling, the men tried to get some rest, but as one complained, "Who ever got any sleep in a goddamn six-by?" Some tried to clean their weapons. There was the usual cursing about everything. Others took their boots off and massaged very cold toes, then put on dry socks. Everyone in the company had a dry pair. Jones knew the value of fresh socks after a day's march through knee-deep snow. He'd spent a year with the Army in Colorado learning how to survive in weather such as this.

"Put boughs on the ground before you put your sleeping bag down," he stressed continually. "Wear several layers of light clothing as opposed to two layers of heavy clothing. Take your shoes off in your sleeping bag no matter how cold it is, and rub those toes.

"I think we saved a lot of toes. If they didn't take their shoes off for eight to ten days, when they did pull them off, well, they took the meat off with them."

He showed them how to build concealed fires, to prepare food better in subzero temperatures.

"Most of us were just trying to stay warm that night," recalled Lt. Max Merritt. "It was very, very cold, and we had no fires."

Jones's company was in a minimum-security situation—just a perimeter watch, a sentry here and there.

Gunfire erupted minutes after they crawled into their tents. Rifle fire at first. Then the machine guns and grenades. Now mortars and artillery. By this time everyone was up and alert. At about 10:30 P.M. they

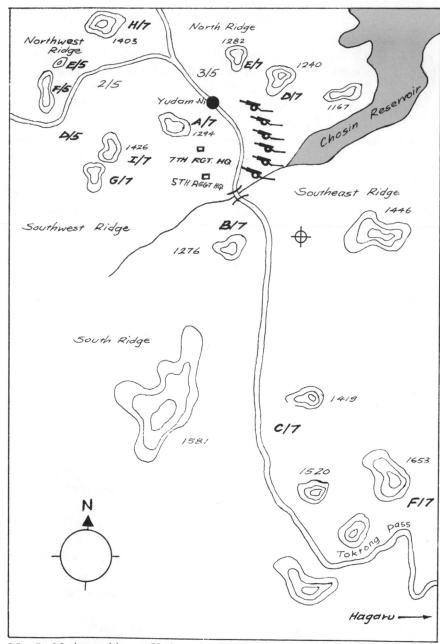

Map 7—Marine positions at Yudam-ni and around the Chosin Reservoir on the morning of November 28, 1950, are shown.

could see what was happening on the hilltops and hear gunfire in the valley ahead of them. Then the rumors began: "They're kicking the hell out of Easy"; "Dog 7 has been kicked off 1240"; "Fox is in big trouble."

The first wounded were filtering down the trails—a trickle at first, then a stream—and into the aid tents, and a picture of what was happening on top began to take shape.

November 28, 1950: Lt. Col. John Stevens, commanding officer of the 1st Battalion, 5th Regiment, sent a runner after Jones at about 1:00 A.M. The situation, Jones was told, was this: E Company of the 7th was on Hill 1282 and just about finished. Casualties were very heavy. Two relief platoons had already gone up, and they'd lost most of their men. But they were holding. D Company, 7th, was on Hill 1240 and in worse shape. It had been shoved off the hill shortly after 10:00 P.M. but had gone back up.

"I was told to go up and hold Hill 1282," Jones said. "I had no orders to report to anyone. We didn't know if anyone would be alive when we got to the top."

"We could hear the firefight. The bugles. We could see the flashes," Jones said. "It was heavy. I mean really heavy . . . everything was busting loose up there."

He hurried back to his company and briefed his platoon leaders. He said he didn't know what to expect once they got to the top other than "We'll be involved in one terrific fight."

C Company—three rifle platoons, a machine-gun platoon, four 60mm mortars, headquarters personnel, an assault squad—was above strength, about 250 men. Jones had great confidence in his three platoon lieutenants, Merritt, Byron Magness, and Harold Dawe. He had a fine executive officer in Lt. Loren Smith. Of Sgt. Roger Wallingford of the company mortar section, Jones said: "He was outstanding. He could—and did—walk the 60s to within ten to fifteen yards of our lines."

Just before starting up Hill 1282 Jones was told to send Dawe's platoon up Hill 1240, where everyone could see and hear the fighting going on up there.

This didn't sit too well with Jones. He had counted on his full-strength platoon. But he also knew that a lot of wounded were coming down 1240.

It was tough going up 1282. "There were easier routes to the top,"

Jones said, "but we would have been silhouetted against the snow, so we took the harder ones."

"We just started working our way up the best we could," Merritt said. "There wasn't much of a trail."

It took C Company more than two hours just to get within two hundred yards of the top. Along the way, Jones and Merritt talked to wounded coming down. "We wanted to get a picture of what was going on up there before we walked into it," Jones said. The picture they got was this: The Chinese were up there, in force, and there weren't enough marines alive to do anything about it.

Those coming down were numb, stumbling, falling, sliding down a trail of red ice. Weapons were used as crutches. Medical supplies had run out on top. Ammunition was just about gone.

"I didn't know anything about the area," Jones said. "The maps we had weren't very good."

They worked their way toward the top in columns until they reached a point that from the sound of gunfire and explosions Jones felt was fairly close to the top.

"Then we formed a line with fixed bayonets and moved on up," he said. "It was very touchy. We didn't know what the situation was up there. If we saw people, would they be Chinese or marines? We didn't want to go up there firing into our own people."

About 150 yards from the top the company came under fire. Mortar rounds fell in front of Merritt's platoon. As they got closer to the top, rifle and machine-gun fire buzzed through the night air. About a hundred yards from the top, Jones found Sgt. Daniel Murphy of E Company's 3rd Platoon. "The Chinese are on top," Murphy said. "They've overrun the command post." He told Jones there were a few survivors on a spur out of sight along with what was left of Trapnell's relief platoon. What was left of Bey's platoon was there, too, he said. The rest of the survivors of E Company and what was left of Snyder's relief platoon were on the reverse slope near where the command post had been.

"We were hit awful hard," Murphy told Wallingford. "He told me there were only twelve to fifteen men left in Bey's platoon."

As Jones's men were just about to the top they were hit with a grenade attack, but they were concussion, not fragmentation. "They didn't hurt you much," Merritt said. "They just knocked you silly for a while."

Jones and Smith led the men over the top as the marines shot, clubbed, and bayoneted the Chinese and drove the 3rd Company, 1st Battalion, 235th CCF Regiment, from their holes. Then they fought their way into the command post area and a sea of bodies. Close by were a few survivors. Snyder was the only officer. His platoon had been hurt badly.

"There wasn't much left up there," Wallingford said, "only bodies." Because of the heavy fighting, he hadn't had time to set up his mortars.

When PFC Winston Keating Scott, nineteen, got to the top, he was exhausted. He'd lugged four cans of .30 ammunition and extra water up the hill in addition to several clips for his carbine. Gunfire dug up the ground at his feet, and he wondered why he wasn't hit. Bodies were everywhere. Chinese. Marines. Were the marines dead? Alive? There was no way to reach them without getting killed.

As it got light, Merritt could see marine bodies not too far away, but a captured .30 was spraying his men from about seventy-five yards to the left of where he was. "That damn thing just kept raking the top of the hill. Six of my men were hit," he said. To the right of Merritt's position the hill rose another fifty to seventy-five feet. A few of E Company survivors and what was left of Snyder's platoon were up there. "But we couldn't get to them," Merritt recalls. "All we could do was hold what we had on that ridge line."

Like Merritt's 1st Platoon, Magness's 2nd Platoon came under fire from that same captured machine gun as soon as his men reached the top and were pinned down.

Magness looked around, spotted Merritt, ran over, and dropped in the snow. "We gotta do somethin' about that damn gun," Merritt said. But first they had to locate it.

"I got to my knees to try and find out where it was," Merritt said. "I heard it, then I felt it. I got hit in the right shoulder and fell forward in the snow."

"I'll get a corpsman," Magness said, and crawled toward his platoon. "I didn't see him again until we were both back in the hospital," Merritt said.

"When we got to the top, we were ready to go," Scott said. "We wanted to take the Chinese on right then and there and settle this thing. We were so keyed up, the blood was really flowing."

He was tossing grenades and firing his carbine, when it would fire.

The other men in his machine-gun section were firing their weapons, too, and hurling grenades. They hadn't had time to set up the machine gun. The Chinese were returning the fire, round for round, and giving a good account of themselves. A lot of marines were dropping.

Then, from one of the foxholes, the marines heard someone shout, "Hey, knock it off, knock it off! You'll get ten for every one you throw!"

"So we knocked it off," Scott said. Now they had time to set up their machine gun, set their fields of fire, distribute water and ammunition. Yet all around them the fighting raged.

"It was eerie," Scott recalled.

He and a few others then crawled forward to look into the nearest holes to see if any marines were alive. "First, we went through the bodies collecting ammo, rations, first-aid packets. We left the dead and started to drag some wounded back to our lines," he said. Then he heard someone shout from a foxhole about forty yards away, "Hey, anybody got any water? How about some ammo?"

Scott grabbed several bandoliers and a canteen and zigzagged to where he heard the shouting. He dropped to the ground, crawled forward, then peered over the edge as rifle fire dug up the earth around him.

"I saw two men reading a comic book," Scott said, "and I was really pissed. I risked my life to get to them and they didn't even cover me. I dropped the ammo and the canteen on their heads and ran back to the machine gun."

Fighting was so heavy and casualties so high that Jones's men couldn't do anything for the wounded. As it got light, his men were able to locate a few survivors. One over there. Two out there. A few in another foxhole. There weren't many.

Jones passed this word to them: Go down to the valley and help take the wounded. This was important. Get the injured to the aid tents before they froze.

Clements was on his feet, bloody, the right side of his helmet shattered. His head felt five times its normal size, as if someone had put it in a vise and spun the handle tight.

But he knew where he was, what was happening. "I saw this captain —I didn't know who he was—leading his men toward me. So I went out to meet him and turn over what was left of the company," Clements said.

"He took one look at me—my helmet, the blood—and told me to get down to the valley," he added. Clements showed Jones where his people were, the original company position, and pointed out some wounded. Then he started down.

Yancey spotted Jones's men as they reached the top of the hill, but just barely. One eye was closed, the other was just a narrow slit. His face was covered with blood. He was still groggy from a concussion grenade that had exploded close by several minutes earlier. Because of the gunfire, he couldn't reach Jones for another hour. Then he heard someone shouting at him. "A sergeant yelled at me, 'This is the way down!' and handed me a long stick. I held one end, he held the other, and he guided me down." Yancey was bleeding when he reached the bottom, so a corpsman tied him to a tent pole in a sitting position with a piece of torn blanket so he wouldn't choke on his blood.

"I fell asleep but woke up in a few hours. Chinese were running around outside shooting up the place," he said. "They'd broken through on the valley floor and were tossing grenades everywhere. I looked up at the top of the tent and could see the sky and there were so many holes it looked like a fishnet. And I didn't have a gun. I thought sure as hell this was the end of me." A few hours later he flew out of Yudam-ni strapped in a litter basket, one of two attached to the outside of a helicopter. He was on his way to a hospital at Hagaru-ri and from there to the Army's 121st Evacuation Hospital at Hungnam. From there he would go to the giant Navy base at Yokosuka, Japan, where he would be reunited with other survivors of E Company.

As he lay in the basket and gazed at the sky, all purple and hazy, he thought how beautiful it was. But even up there he couldn't escape the shooting.

"I could see tracers coming up at us and feel the 'copter swaying gently from side to side trying to dodge the bullets, and thought, 'Jesus Christ! They're still trying to kill me.'"

For Mr. Yancey, the war was over.

Kennemore lapsed in and out of consciousness through the early morning of November 28. He knew he was hurt badly. One leg was shattered. The other hung by a shred. He didn't bleed to death because the blood had frozen. As it got light he heard the fighting raging around him. He lay in the snow where the exploding grenade had hurled him. As Jones's men fought their way past him, he moaned, cried out feebly.

"Hey, this one's alive!" someone shouted. A corpsman dropped beside him, yelled for a stretcher, and Kennemore was carried to the valley.

Gallagher, bloody from shrapnel wounds, was helped down the hill.

"Getting the wounded out of there was my prime concern," Jones said, "because I didn't know how long we'd be up there." So cooks, clerks, engineers, artillerymen, anyone who could climb to the top made their way up the hill to help bring down the dead and wounded.

There was no letup in the fighting. Magness's platoon was still heavily engaged. So was Merritt's. To the left of where Jones had set up a temporary command post about thirty Chinese were firing down at the wounded and the litter bearers. Smith shouted for Wallingford to grab six or seven men from his mortar section, fix bayonets, and together they drove the Chinese back. Once the dead and wounded were off the top, Jones set up a perimeter of about two hundred yards. Then he counterattacked to the left, to where the captured machine gun was still firing, and drove the Chinese from the top of Hill 1282.

The rest of Capt. James B. Heater's A Company, 5th Regiment, arrived to strengthen the defenses, and Jones knew that he was there to stay. But he also knew that the Chinese would be back. "There was some nice fortifications up there and we dug them a little deeper, improved them, then just waited," Jones said.

Jones spotted Merritt, blood running down his arm, ordered him to the valley, then gave his platoon to Lt. Robert H. Corbett of the mortar section.

Then the Chinese struck again, violently, furiously. They wanted that hilltop back in the worst way and were willing to pay any price. Jones heard the bugles first. Then the shouting. Then the Chinese attacked in waves. Grenades and small-arms fire cut them down. Others tried to attack C Company's rear, but this didn't work, either. Jones always had the backside covered, no matter what the situation.

Six times Jones ran forward to help bring back wounded. Grenade fragments hit him in a leg. A squad of Chinese charged into one of his machine-gun positions, and all were killed. Two other Chinese squads fell, side by side, before rifle fire and grenades. Still another squad tried to assault the summit and was cut to pieces. Marine air couldn't help. The Chinese and marines were much too close.

"We fought all day long," Scott recalled. "The machine guns never stopped. Some of them burned out."

Again, Hill 1282 lay under a blanket of dead and wounded.

Scott still had his carbine, but now it didn't fire at all.

"There was a failure to fire, a failure to feed, and all the malfunctions that could occur, did occur," he said. "I remember to this day what it said on the side: General Motors Inland Division. It was a very damn long time before I ever bought a General Motors car."

At about midday a signalman came crawling through stringing wire. He had an M-1 on his back but it was too bulky, always snagging on brush, rocks, branches.

"Anyone wanna trade a pistol for an M-1?" He asked.

"You're crazy, asshole. Who'd give up a pistol for a rifle?"

"Do you want a carbine?"

"Yeah."

So they swapped, a move that later in the day would save Scott's life.

"Most of the men were resigned we'd die on that hill," Scott said. "We never thought we'd get off.

"We fired at them, they fired back at us. It just never stopped.

"We just tried to stay alive. A lot of us took out all our rations, all our sugar, and ate everything we had. Then we smoked all our cigarettes. If the Chinese did take that hill back, we didn't want them to find anything on us that would help them in any way."

Then, late in the afternoon, Jones was ordered back down to the valley. He was replaced by Capt. Harold B. Williamson's H Company, 5th Regiment.

"Pack up and get ready to go down," the men were told.

The dead and wounded were removed first, then the men started to file down the trails, grimy, weary, but not beaten.

Keating had his M-1 slung over his shoulder and a burned-out machine gun in his arms. There were still a lot of parts on it that could be used, and he thought they'd need every gun that could fire before this was over. He carefully picked his way down when he heard the spine-tingling whine of incoming fire. And it was close, too close. There was a deafening explosion just behind him. Minutes later he came to, his face buried in the snow. Then he felt the warm flow of blood on his left hand. It wasn't too bad. Just a scratch. He tried to rise but couldn't. There was a sharp pain in the center of his back. He put his hand inside his clothes. It was wet, sticky. He pulled his hand out and it was covered with blood. Suddenly he was scared. He looked around, but there was no one near him.

"Corpsman, corpsman," he called out weakly. Then he lost consciousness.

The stock of his rifle, much heavier than that of a carbine, was shattered, split in two by a piece of shrapnel the size of a joint on his little finger. It had torn a hole in his back, missing his lungs by a fraction of an inch.

When he came to, another marine had reached him. A corpsman was on the way. After receiving a shot of morphine, he was carried to the valley on a parka rigged between two rifles.

The corpsman was killed along the way. "He didn't have time to mark the big red 'M' on my forehead to show that I'd already had one shot of morphine. So when I got to the bottom, they gave me another," Scott said, "so I wasn't feeling much pain.

"There was a heater in the aid tent and they placed us with our feet toward the stove. That was the first time I'd been warm in some time. It was really nice."

There was a lot of fighting going on nearby. Scott could hear it. But he wasn't as scared of the Chinese as he was of getting hit by the supplies that were being dropped all around them.

"They carried us outside the tent and put us in the sun. Just then a C-119 came over and started to drop its load. I could see the doors open, the guy standing in the rear kicking out the packages, then watch the chutes open. Sometimes they didn't open, the planes flew so low."

The Chinese paid dearly for trying to take Hill 1282. In addition to the more than four hundred dead who covered its slopes, there were many hundreds of dead and wounded on top. Captured Chinese documents indicated that only six survived Jones's assault against the 3rd Company, 1st Battalion, 235th CCF Regiment. Of 116 officers and men in the 2nd Company, ninety-four were killed.

The price for holding the hill was high, too. E Company was reduced to less than thirty men, some wounded, most suffering from frostbite. The two relief platoons were badly hurt, suffering forty dead and wounded. Only six men could still fight in Snyder's platoon. Jones's C Company suffered fifteen dead and sixty-seven wounded.

After eighteen hours of fighting as savage as any in the history of small-unit warfare, Hill 1282 belonged to the marines.

But control of vital Hill 1240 was very much in doubt during the night of November 27 and the early-morning hours of November 28.

CHAPTER 8
RETREAT, HELL!

As his men crawled into their holes well after dark following a day-long patrol, Hull remembered what Davis had told him earlier: "Get on up to the top of Hill 1240 and hold it." He could see the gunfire breaking out on nearby Hill 1282 and wondered what lay ahead for him.

D Company, 2nd Battalion, 7th Regiment, had a fine combat record. Its previous commanding officer, Dick Breen, had turned it into a sturdy, feisty outfit. "Actually, the men were downright vicious," Hull said, "and my runner, Walter Menard, was one of the coldest killers I ever saw in my life. He could walk through machine-gun fire and never get a scratch.

"He could cope with a battlefield," Hull said.

D Company was in the middle of a losing streak as far as commanding officers were concerned. The last three had been gunned down.

"When I joined the company, I was introduced to Menard, the company clerk and runner for the other company commanders," Hull said.

"Right away I noticed that he was avoiding me, he just didn't want to get near me," Hull said, "so I called his hand.

"I asked him what his problem was.

"He told me he didn't want anything to do with me, that he was bad luck for company commanders.

"Don't worry about it," Hull told him. "You just go where I go. I'll last longer than you."

The hilltops were exploding by this time. There was gunfire in the northern end of the valley. Tracers arched lazily from one peak to another.

Just after 10:00 P.M. the Chinese slammed into Hull's perimeter. "They came right up the front," Hull said. "They didn't try to fool anyone. No need to. There were so damn many of them.

"If they'd ever hit us at one time, there was no way in the world we could have held that hill for a minute," Hull said. But they didn't. They hit the center of the line, stopped, then hit the right flank, stopped, then hit the left flank. Then they'd start over again.

After four hours of this, the Chinese did what Hull feared: They struck in force at one point and drove his men from their holes.

"They hit us with such force they knocked us off that hill," Hull said. Hull caught a round in the left shoulder. In and out. He could still fight.

175

"The Chinese were an arm's length away. We were being overrun," Hull remembered. "They were running right through my CP. I was in the center of the position, so that meant the lines were gone.

"I got Davis on the phone and told him we had been overrun and that we were falling back," Hull said.

"You've got to hold that position!" Davis shouted back. "You're the only thing between the Chinese and the artillery!"

"Hell, by this time we'd lost it," Hull said. "The last order I can remember giving was for all members of the company to pull back down to the south base of the hill."

Just about everyone in the company had been hit at least once. As his men began to straggle toward the south base of the hill, it was obvious that there was no D Company. In a few minutes there were about forty survivors on hand, many wounded, bleeding, but all eager to go back up.

Hull organized them into one platoon, put Lt. Anthony Sota in charge, and they went back up in a skirmish line. Hull was a few yards behind with a radioman and his runner, Menard, who was bleeding.

"The survivors estimated we were off that hill no more than twenty minutes," Hull said. "It was pitch dark, but we attacked straight back up in a northward direction," he said.

Sota's platoon went up with such force that momentum carried them right through Hull's old command post all the way to the top of the position.

The Chinese were so busy pilfering, trying to find something warm to wear, boots to replace their tennis shoes, sleeping bags, food, that they didn't see the marines coming. When they did, it was too late.

"We mustered around a case of grenades Davis had given me and put up a little perimeter," Hull said. "They were doled out one at a time, whenever someone heard Chinese coming up the hill."

Hull was lying in a small hole he had scraped out of the ice and snow. His first sergeant was beside him on the left, Menard on his right. Chinese were everywhere. The head and arm of a Chinese soldier appeared over the hilltop several yards away. A grenade sailed through the air and landed to the left of Hull. The sergeant rolled his body over it and took the full blast and died. Menard literally shot Chinese off Hull's back.

Hull called Davis but was told, "We don't have any help now, but we'll try to get some up there as quickly as possible."

"That meant we were on our own and had to hold no matter what," Hull said.

"We were prepared to stay there and die," he said. "We'd hold at all costs."

An exploding grenade peppered his face with bits of steel, and blood ran from a dozen tiny wounds. They fought and died until first light of November 28, when Dawe's 3rd Platoon, C Company, 5th Regiment, fought its way up.

Until he neared the top Dawe didn't run into much trouble—just some scattered rifle fire, a few grenades. "Then it started getting quite hot," he said.

Dawe had twenty-six men split into three squads, one on his left, another on his right, and the third behind as a reserve. Each man carried from twenty-five to fifty extra rounds of ammunition. When Dawe reached the top he immediately saw the Chinese and what was left of Hull's company. About twenty yards separated them. Dawe's men then came under very heavy fire and he became "greatly concerned because some of my men were wearing dynamite."

Amazingly, his platoon wasn't taking any casualties. "The Chinese were in close, yet their fire wasn't dropping any of my men. Either the Chinese were the world's worst shots, or every man in the 3rd Platoon led a charmed life," Dawe said.

"There was a lot going on up there," Dawe remembered. "Hull was firing, giving orders to the few men he had left. He told me where the enemy was, what the situation was. About a half hour later, he started down. He was covered with blood."

Dawe lost two men on the way up, then didn't lose another until the afternoon of the twenty-eighth. During the twelve hours he was up there, he lost a total of nine men.

Before Hull left, he turned around for one last look.

"On my word of honor, it looked like the ground was paved with Chinese bodies all the way down to the foot of the hill," he said.

Two hundred marines had gone up Hill 1240; seventeen came down. "Everyone had at least one hole in him, and some had more," Hull said.

Hull and his runner, Menard, were carried to the aid station, bloody, both twice wounded.

In the last afternoon hours of the twenty-eighth, the marines still held Hill 1240. The artillery was safe. The valley still belonged to the marines.

For now, all they wanted to do was hold the ground they had. It wasn't going to be easy. Fighting was still raging on the hilltops, in parts of the valley, which was unlike the Chinese, who preferred to fight only at night, when the planes were grounded by darkness and the artillery spotters couldn't see too well. But this was different. The Chinese were in so close neither the planes nor the artillery could be used effectively without killing marines as well.

"We discussed staying where we were, what we'd do to stabilize the situation and hold the area," Murray said. "We'd say, 'I'll send you this unit to help you here, and you send this unit to help me!' "

Did he think the marines would continue the attack west?

"Those are still our orders as far as I was concerned. If it turned out that this was a temporary thing and we beat it back, we would go on. Certainly it wasn't in my mind that we'd come back at this time.

"Nor was it in my mind that we'd sit there forever," he said.

November 28, 1950; headquarters, 7th Regiment, Yudam-ni, 7:00 A.M.: Murray and Litzenberg were together at first light in the 7th Regiment commander's tent amid the echo of gunfire from the surrounding hills. Both knew two things for certain: They were surrounded; and there were an awful lot of Chinese out there, more than they ever thought possible.

The first thing they did was combine, for the time being, the headquarters units of both regiments into one. Then they set about consolidating positions of the various regimental units.

"It was weird, watching the fighting going on up in the hills," Murray said. He had his glasses on the marines, watched the fighting swing back and forth. First the Chinese were on top, then the marines. It went on and on.

"I'd sit there watching, thinking that this was sort of a dreamlike thing . . . that I'm just there as a spectator watching this damn war go on. Like I bought a ticket to a football game."

Headquarters, marines' 1st Division, Hagaru-ri, 8:00 A.M.: Bowser became aware of the intensity of the Chinese assault early. "I tried to convince General Smith that I should fly up to Yudam-ni to case the situation . . . that I should go up there and talk to Murray and Litzenberg and get a firsthand report on just what the hell was going on and how bad things really were, because they were sounding really bad."

General Smith, however, had his own thoughts on this. He had already talked to the two colonels on the radio and had a fair idea of what was happening, of just what the marines had run into. So he told Bowscr:

"No. I don't want you to go up there because it's fourteen miles of bad weather, of snow and ice, and a helicopter's reliability is questionable. You might not get back."

"Can I send somebody?"

"Okay."

Bowser sent his executive officer, Lt. Col. Joe (Buzz) Winecoff. His helicopter came under fire dozens of times, and he was fortunate to make it back. "He was very lucky to get out of there at all," Bowser said.

Winecoff talked with Murray and Litzenberg, together and separately, to their battalion commanders when possible, and got to see what actually was going on up there.

"His reports to us later that afternoon when he got back were invaluable in making up our minds that we were going to initiate a withdrawal whether a withdrawal order came from X Corps or not," Bowser said.

"So our withdrawal actually was initiated as a reconciliation or whatever you want to call it to make it look like it wasn't a disobedience of orders twenty-four hours ahead of the time corps told us to withdraw."

Headquarters, 7th Regiment, Yudam-ni, 9:00 A.M.: "Any idea of our continuing the attack west to cut off the Chinese attacking the Eighth Army was absolutely out of the question and ridiculous to the extent that if we had carried out such an order, that would have been the end of us," Woessner explained.

He talked with Winecoff and told him: "The only thing that would allow us to survive would be for the 5th and 7th to combine and attack south and rejoin the division."

"Murray and Litzenberg got together early, and from that point on the two staffs worked together, planned together," Woessner said. But he added: "We made no plans to do anything but hold until we got orders from division to return to Hagaru."

179

Murray and Litzenberg were now feeling the full impact of the Chinese onslaught. "We were getting reports that Fox Company was surrounded [at Toktong Pass], and although they were managing to hold on, it was apparent that they needed help," Woessner said.

Litzenberg was becoming increasingly concerned with casualty reports. "I knew he was pretty shaken up by the fact that Phillips [E Company, 2nd Battalion, 7th Regiment] was killed," Woessner said. "So was I. He had been a friend of mine."

"He [Litzenberg] was concerned particularly in connection with the wounding or death of somebody he knew or had been a company commander for him. He showed a lot of emotion," Woessner remembered.

Headquarters, 1st Battalion, 7th Regiment, Yudam-ni, 11:00 A.M.: Morris's C Company was perched out on a limb about four miles south, between Hills 1419 and 1520. At 2:30 A.M. the Chinese swooped down from higher elevations and attacked his perimeter, which was manned by two rifle platoons. They shot it out until daybreak, when the Chinese pulled back. His company suffered forty casualties, and the situation was anything but encouraging. He was surrounded, vastly outnumbered, and clinging to a perimeter that had shrunk. The only reason the Chinese had withdrawn was their fear of marine air power. They'd be back after dark.

Davis was concerned. He wanted C Company back inside the perimeter at Yudam-ni. He knew that the company couldn't break out, so he sent a force from the village and, after five hours of marching and fighting, C Company returned to Yudam-ni.

Gunfire could be heard throughout the rest of the day and into the evening. It picked up after dark, but with far less intensity than on the previous night.

November 29, 1950; F Company, 2nd Battalion, 7th Regiment, Toktong Pass, 2:30 A.M.: It was a replica of the first night. The Chinese came down off that rocky hill in great strength. Fighting was bitter, but not as bad as on the previous night. And they ran into marines who had dug their holes deeper, changed their lines slightly, pulled in Chinese dead and used them as sandbags. It paid off.

Chinese mortar rounds exploded on Barber's men, killing a few,

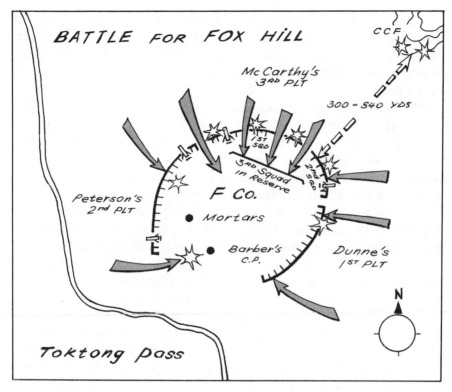

Map 8—Chinese attack F Company at Toktong Pass in the early-morning hours of November 28, 1950. At top right is the high rocky area from where Chinese fired down on Fox Company.

wounding many. In response, Read's How Battery in Hagaru stepped up its pounding of Chinese positions. O'Leary had the company 60s now as well as the two heavy 81s. The 60s killed many Chinese assembled in front of Barber's perimeter. He had the 81s zeroed in on that rocky hill.

"He was a marvelous man," Barber said. "As far as I knew, he was just another PFC when he came to us with his two 81s. But when you're looking around for people who can do things, you see people like O'Leary, who was a good mortarman. A guy like that can do a lot—acquire targets, take care of ammo, make advance plans, get you on target in a hurry. You recognize these people in a crisis."

The Chinese again slammed into the 3rd Platoon head-on. More Chinese hit the two flank platoons, and after fifteen minutes of fighting broke through and cut in behind the 3rd Platoon. But McCarthy turned a .30 around and took care of most of them. Peterson brought a lot of rifle and machine-gun fire in on them and killed just about all of the forty who were running around behind marine lines.

When they got that situation cleaned up, Barber found that there were gaps of twenty to twenty-five yards where his flank platoons tied in with the 3rd Platoon, so he had the 3rd Platoon drop back just far enough so the perimeter was once again intact and tight. While this was going on, PFC Richard Bonelli carried a .30 from one position to another, firing at the Chinese just enough to prevent them from taking advantage of the two gaps.

The Chinese tried to crack through the 1st Platoon a couple of times but were beaten back. Several men in Dunne's platoon suffered shrapnel wounds but all were able to fight, to squeeze off a round. That was the difference. If you could squeeze, you fought. If not, you were moved back to the aid tent.

"It was mass confusion that night," Kanouse recalls.

McCarthy was on the phone trying to raise the 1st Platoon when machine-gun fire hit him in the legs. Barber, who just got there, was wounded, too.

"There was a gap between McCarthy's platoon and the platoon on the left," Barber said, "and it looked like that might be where the main attack would come from. So we were moving some machine guns and some men over there, and that's when I got hit in the groin. I didn't go down, but it sure hurt."

H Battery's deadly fire from seven miles away kept the Chinese at bay as they tried to break through Peterson's men. Peterson, moving back and forth behind his lines, was hit for the second time. A corpsman stopped the bleeding, and he stayed where he was.

Barber was down on his hands and knees now, crawling from position to position. "The reason for this was simply that it was a hell of a lot easier to stay down low than to get up and then have to go down again. I was okay as long as I was either down or up, but I couldn't get down or up very well. And you don't stand up in a foxhole in the front lines. So I stayed down."

Down the line Barber heard someone shouting and using his name. "We're from the 11th Marines, Captain Barber. Will you surrender?" This was coming from somewhere below Peterson's men. The voices were all different. The English was pretty good. But Barber ignored it. As for surrendering, ridiculous.

The 1st Platoon was still taking light fire from the Chinese, who, for some reason, never hit Dunne's men hard. Just glancing blows. But one squad wishes it had never wandered into Dunne's area. They strayed across the path of a .30 and were killed in seconds. Machine guns don't take prisoners.

Sgt. Frank Pitts was one of those men Barber liked, the ones who when a crisis occurs, stand out. Until then they just don't come to your attention.

"He was hit two or three times and he continued to fight," Barber remembered. "He had a bullet hole through his helmet. It went through the first night but didn't hurt him.

"He continued to wear that damn helmet with the hole in it like it was a badge of courage. So I finally had to tell someone to tell Pitts to take it off, to get rid of that damn thing and we'll get him another one.

"I think he was just damn proud of that helmet and wanted to wear it to show that he was invincible," the captain said. "He was just an unbelievable man."

But he wasn't invincible.

He was killed later on a patrol.

Barber expected the Chinese to pull back at daybreak, as they had done the previous morning. But they didn't. They stayed around and fought for another hour and a half.

"We could see them good," Barber said. "We had plenty of ammunition, and they made good targets. And we had pretty good mortar support, so we inflicted very heavy casualties on them."

When the marines went out to check casualties, they discovered why the Chinese hadn't pulled back. They found a dead bugler not far from their lines.

"Apparently the bugler was supposed to have blown retreat," Barber explained, "but he'd been shot." So they stayed and fought until all were eliminated.

Just after sunup, Sgt. John Audis, who had taken over the 3rd Platoon after McCarthy was shot, led his men back up to the top of the hill to reoccupy their original line. The Chinese were in no mood for a fight, so there wasn't much gunfire, and only two marines were wounded. But one of them was Pommers, who had survived the grenade attack the first night. He was seriously wounded but stayed with his fire team until he was no longer needed.

He was taken back to one of the warming tents, then worked over by the corpsmen, then the surgeon. The marines took their dead, wrapped them in ponchos, put a tent flap over them, then they were buried later. The Chinese suffered about 150 dead and wounded the second night, and the marines could hear the cries of many until they froze. Twenty-nine marines were wounded.

By now so many of them had been hit it was impossible to find two men in the same foxhole who could fight. So Barber paired one healthy marine with one who was wounded but could still fight.

Those who could walk did the chores—cut firewood, helped the wounded who couldn't help themselves, dragged in supplies. The planes were overhead at about 7:00 A.M. Corsairs kept the Chinese back while the transports dropped the much-needed supplies.

The first drop was excellent. Everything landed on or close to the big "X" marked on the drop zone. Recovery was no problem. Kanouse liked that. You couldn't beat a good drop, particularly if you were a PFC. A lot of the drops fell outside marine lines, which meant the lowest ranks usually had to go out and bring everything back, often under intense enemy fire.

"The Air Force C-119s flew overhead in a straight line," he recalled, "and a lot of their supplies fell outside our lines. But the marine R4FD's flew in a circle overhead, and their drops were more accurate."

Shortly after the day's first drop, a helicopter flew in with batteries for the radios. Tracers flew past the helicopter as the pilot coolly brought the craft down. "They had the batteries aboard, which we needed very bad, so I took one and started to run to the CP," Kanouse recalled. "Just then a bullet zinged through the canopy, and the pilot became very upset and wanted to leave. Of course, bullets were zinging by us all day and we weren't too upset about it, and we sure couldn't leave."

Kanouse was cutting wood nearby when the helicopter touched down. "Sergeant [Charles C.] Dana, the first sergeant, wanted to hold the pilot at gunpoint until we loaded some badly wounded men aboard, but Captain Barber said, 'No, we can't do that. If we do, they'll never come back.'

"I always felt sorry he didn't take some of the fellas out. I always felt maybe we could have saved a couple of lives had we been able to place them in that helicopter," Kanouse remarked.

The pilot took off amid a hail of bullets.

Then the phone rang in Barber's CP.

"I got an order to move back to Hagaru," he said. "Well, hell, you're conditioned to obeying orders, so I started looking around trying to figure out how I was going to do this. I had some wounded. They certainly couldn't walk. I didn't have any way of getting them out of there."

At this point Barber didn't know what the situation was at Yudam-ni. He knew it was bad, but he didn't know the severity of the situation.

"But if the situation there was that critical, and the Chinese wanted my hill that much, it just might be damned important to us," Barber said.

He knew that he held a very important hilltop.

"So I thought, 'Well, hell, we're here . . . if we're ever going to get our forces together in either direction, we're probably going to have to fight for this damned hill sometime. It's probably better to hold on to it while we got it.' "

Morale was high. His men had been in one pretty tough fight and so far they had come out of it in fairly good shape. He had a lot of confidence in them.

"I sent back a message and requested to stay where we were, citing what reasons I could without the enemy getting too much information should they intercept it," Barber said. "I told them I could comply with it with some difficulty. I had wounded. Lots. But I said I think we can stay here and that we can do a good job."

When his message reached regiment, Litzenberg read it, then radioed back to Barber, "Well, hell, if you can hold out and we can get you some airdrops, by all means we'll stay."

Another big drop came in that afternoon, but it was way off. Supplies landed as much as six hundred yards outside the perimeter. Now marines would have to dodge a lot of ground fire before everything was safely inside their lines.

Peterson, twice wounded, took some men from the 1st Platoon and ran out to try to retrieve what they could. It didn't work. Heavy fire from that rocky ridge pinned them down. O'Leary started to pump round after round from the 81s on top of the ridge. Rifle and carbine fire peppered the area as Peterson started sending the men back, each with a bundle, on a one-man-at-a-time basis. Brady was first. He'd been hit in the hand the first night, but he was running like a halfback with two mortar rounds under his good arm, dodging everything the Chinese sent his way. Sgt. David Smith, the company supply sergeant, quickly put together a detail to help get the ammo back behind their lines. A bullet broke a leg. Lt. Lawrence Schmitt ran out to get him. The sniper's rifle barked once more. One of Schmitt's legs was shattered. Then a fire team went out and took care of the sniper.

Slowly, each man made it back with something the marines needed. Still, there was a lot of badly needed ammo out there, but because of the heavy fire, Barber decided to wait until dark.

What they did bring back was vitally important. Now each wounded man could lay on a stretcher off the frozen ground. And there were plenty of blankets to cover them. And C rations that hadn't had time to freeze were recovered so everyone had a good meal—good in the sense that no one had to eat food that was partly frozen, partly thawed.

A marine, hit in one hand, brewed coffee with the other, and all hands had something warm in their stomachs. Patrols fanned out to eliminate snipers. All things considered, it was a pretty good day so far for F Company.

Benson's sight returned and he rejoined his platoon on top of the hill. "As soon as it became daylight I realized I could see, so I joined the squad again," he said. "There were only four out of the original thirteen left," he recalled. "Now we were scared. The realization was sinking in. This is for real. The shock was beginning to wear off, and the real feelings of fright came."

He loaded magazines, cut wood, and brought in Chinese bodies to use as sandbags.

"Why don't you go down and see how Hector is?" Komoroski said.

"Thanks, I will."

". . . and have a cup of coffee while you're there."

When Benson walked in, Cafferatta was awake and still in a lot of pain. You could see it etched on his face, hear it in his voice.

"Bense, my feet are terrible. . . ."

"I rubbed them with my hands until they were warm," Benson remembered. He couldn't help but notice the empty stretchers here and there, which meant that marines had died during the night.

Barber's wounds were bandaged by a corpsman. Barber was weary. "I was really worn out physically, mentally," he said, "and this worried me. I didn't want to do stupid things." So he went back to his CP to rest for a few hours. He thought about turning over the command to his exec, Lt. C. B. Wright, but later decided against it. Marine casualties were extremely heavy. Chinese casualties were tenfold.

"By this time some of us began to think this was probably our grave that we were sitting on," Kanouse remembered. "The able-bodied could have moved out of there, but we couldn't have taken our wounded, so moving out of our position was unthinkable."

"We had been told that reinforcements were coming on two or three different occasions, but they never appeared," he said. "It was kind of discouraging."

Barber got his officers together at dusk and laid it on the line. There would be no replacements. Worse, he'd just learned that the 5th and 7th regiments at Yudam-ni and the marines surrounded at Hagaru were under very heavy assault by the Chinese. "They're completely surrounded," he said. "They're going to have to fight their way out."

Then he pointed to the road below and said, "That's the only way out. If we don't hold this hill, they haven't got a chance."

Most of the men now carried Thompsons that had been liberated from the enemy. Just about everyone had an M-1, too. And a sidearm. Some carried .45s. Most wore .38s in a shoulder holster that had been sent from home.

It was dark now, and several marines were preparing to go after the rest of the airdrop. No one carried a weapon. You could carry more with both hands free.

Artillery fire from Hagaru and O'Leary's mortars kept the Chinese down. Each man made two trips to get everything back: mortar shells, grenades, rifles, and machine-gun bullets.

It was a great feeling to sit in a hole with all the grenades you could use. With more bandoliers than you could carry. Let the Chinese come.

Their holes were a little deeper now. Whenever anyone had a few minutes with nothing to do, he dug. You just couldn't get deep enough. Chinese sandbags were everywhere.

It was bitter cold. Hands and feet were numb. Wounded who could shoot slipped quietly into the foxholes to pair up with the few who were still in one piece. There weren't many of the latter. No need to check the perimeter. Every man who could fight was there, hoping, praying that the Chinese wouldn't hit them once again, yet knowing that this kind of thinking was unrealistic. The Chinese wanted Fox Hill in the worst way. They had sacrificed too much flesh to back away now.

So the marines huddled in their holes and waited.

Headquarters, Marines' 1st Division, Hagaru-ri, 6:00 A.M.: General Smith's orders to Litzenberg left no doubt about the gravity of the situation: "Clear the road to Hagaru . . . break through without delay using the entire regiment."

The order went out to all commanders to be prepared to withdraw to Hagaru and to be prepared for further withdrawal south. Each was instructed to destroy any supplies and equipment that must be abandoned.

Late the following afternoon, X Corps made it official by instructing General Smith to pull back all marine units north and northwest of Hagaru.

"General Smith was not a guy to tell regimental commanders 'how to,' " Bowser said. "He said, 'Here's what you'll do.' He never said, 'Here's how you'll do it.' " So General Smith told Bowser:

"Hell, if we attempt from here [Hagaru] to draw up some operations orders for those two guys [Murray and Litzenberg] knowing as little as we do about what they're faced with and what they have to do, they may not be able to execute it. So there's no use giving them an order they can't execute."

General Smith contacted his two regimental commanders in their radio van and said, "You guys get your heads together and we'll hang on to Hagaru as your return point and you just move back on down the road. When we all get together here, we'll put our heads together and see what we do from here on."

"So he left them the greatest of latitude in how they would do this," Bowser said, "which was a damn good thing he did."

Hagaru was now becoming a major problem, perhaps even greater than Yudam-ni. The Chinese had it surrounded and were slowly shrinking the perimeter. It had to be held if the division was to survive and, as Bowser said, "We weren't sure we could."

Did he think the two regiments might not be able to break through the ring of Chinese at Yudam-ni?

"Yes. We considered that a great possibility."

But there was one note of optimism.

"We began to realize that Chinese communications was so bad they never really knew how well off they were, or how bad off we were," Bowser said. "Had they known this and been able to react to it, there were several cases in which they could have cut us to ribbons."

Headquarters, 7th Regiment, Yudam-ni, 9:00 A.M.: Once Murray and Litzenberg were told to fight their way south to Hagaru, they set about turning the two regiments around, not an easy task in the face of Chinese gunfire.

The marines were in a valley that ran east and west. Their positions ran about five thousand yards along the hills on the north and south sides of the valley. Yudam-ni was in the center. The width, from crest to crest, was perhaps two thousand yards.

"Before we could start back to Hagaru, we had to turn around from the east–west valley through ninety degrees into a valley that ran south from Yudam-ni," Litzenberg said. "The flanks were now the hills on the east and west, each flank being about thirty-five hundred yards. From crest to crest the distance was about twenty-five hundred yards. The total perimeter now was eleven thousand yards."

The turnaround movement was executed battalion by battalion, company by company. As one battalion or company came off a position in the east–west valley, it was assigned a position in the north–south valley. The major question was when to make the change—after dark or in daylight. Since the Chinese liked to fight at night, it was done during the day so air power and artillery could keep the Chinese at a distance.

Taplett's 3rd Battalion, 5th Regiment, would be the point. His men would clear the road, knock out the roadblocks, and keep the hilltops clear. A makeshift Dog/Easy Company was put together comprised of survivors of Hills 1282 and 1240 and attached to Taplett's battalion. Close behind were engineers and one tank. Then came a battalion of artillery. Just before Toktong Pass, halfway between Yudam-ni and Hagaru, the howitzers would set up along the road and cover the withdrawal of the last marines out of the village. Roisie's 2nd Battalion would be the rear guard. Just ahead of his men were the rest of the artillery. They were placed close to the rear intentionally. Should any of the vehicles that towed them become disabled, they would either be destroyed or shoved over the side and not hold up the convoy.

Every vehicle would carry wounded. If you were sit-up wounded, you rode shotgun. If you were wounded but could drive, then the regular driver walked and helped the walking wounded. In between were assorted units—medical detachments, supply, communications.

The dead would all be buried in a marked cemetery before they left.

The howitzers at the end of the column would fire all but ten rounds for each gun; then the gun crews were organized to guard wounded and protect the big guns.

"We also decided which rifle companies would be up in the hills, which ones would come down, what each would do," Murray explained.

"Then Litzenberg said he wanted Ray Davis's 1st Battalion to cut across the hills and get to Fox Company," Murray added.

General Smith, at Hagaru, was worried about Barber's men. Smith had tried to send a rescue force from Hagaru north to Toktong Pass, but it couldn't get out of sight of the perimeter.

"I had a long conversation with Litzenberg about Fox," Davis remembered. "He told me he wanted me to go across the hills and relieve Barber's men."

The two regimental commanders then divided their staffs.

"We decided that some of my assistant staff officers would go with some of his, and some of his would go with some of mine," Murray said. "That way, if either one of us was wiped out, we would still have a functioning unit."

Murray told Taplett that he would be pulling back closer to the village, if not inside the perimeter. His 2nd Battalion, 5th Regiment, was still on North Ridge, about two thousand yards down the road leading west. After the furious assault by the Chinese the night of November 27–28, his men were not hit again. They remained where they were until midday, then came down to the road and headed back toward Yudam-ni. Taplett spoke with both Murray and Litzenberg. "They were in tents close together and near the road on the far side of Yudam-ni," Taplett said. "All their tents were shot up."

"They said we'd turn around and fight our way back to Hagaru and that I would have the rear guard all the way back," Roisie said. "We'd have patrols, company-size, in the hills to try and keep the tops clear of Chinese."

It wasn't a retreat, General Smith stressed to his commanders. "We are simply attacking in a different direction," he explained.

Engineers began to scrape out a landing strip for light planes so the critically wounded could be flown out, but this didn't work. Only a few were evacuated before the strip came under Chinese fire.

"At times they [the Chinese] were so close you could almost touch them," said engineer Wendell N. Blodgett, who helped scrape the airstrip with his bulldozer as bullets ricocheted off the front blade. "Around the perimeter that night you could hear 'em moving. They were that close. They'd shout, 'We're coming to get you tonight!' "

Huge supply dumps were appearing everywhere. Boots, gloves, weapons, ammunition, fuel, vehicles, everything that the marines couldn't take with them were piled high. Before the engineers left, they would destroy everything. The Chinese would find only ashes.

The Chinese knew what was happening, that the marines were getting ready to leave. That's why it was so difficult for some of the rifle companies to break off contact and be repositioned in the north–south valley. With each passing hour the Chinese were becoming more aggressive.

Fighting was light throughout the day and into the early evening. Gunfire could be heard in the hills and around the perimeter as the marines settled in for the night.

November 30, 1950; F Company, 2nd Battalion, 7th Regiment, Toktong Pass, 2:00 A.M.: "Send up a flare, O'Leary," someone shouted at the mortarman, "there's something out there!"

It burst a few hundred yards overhead, then floated downward lazily.

The Chinese were there, coming in from the south, bayonets fixed. There were so many it was like a huge stampede of cattle; they were running into each other.

"Mortars! Mortars!" a marine shouted.

"Incoming! Incoming!" another hollered. No need for this. Everyone knew which way the rounds were going.

Boom!

Boom!

Boom!

Bits of steel flew through the air, dug through several layers of clothing to reach skin. It stung, hurt, blood flowed, then froze. A lot of men didn't know they'd been hit until the next day. A few died on the spot.

The Chinese attacked one area, pulled back, slid down the line and hit another area, trying to see if a weak spot had developed. Barber's machine guns were taking a terrible toll. O'Leary's mortars were devastating. How Battery brought in time fire, the shells exploding over the heads of the Chinese. Dead and wounded were piling up at an incredible rate. But they couldn't overrun Fox Company. Barber's marines had held for another night. No one knew quite how they did it, but the enemy didn't find a weak spot.

At dawn fires began to appear inside the perimeter. Again, the aroma of hot coffee wafted through the area. C rations were warmed, somewhat, and eaten slowly, thoughtfully, as if each bit might be the last.

The dead were taken back to the CP and lined up in a neat row alongside those from the previous nights. Wounded were carried to the aid tent, patched up, then moved to the warming tent.

In the holes the men joked about the night's fighting and the fact that no one got his rifle hot enough to warm his hands. Morale was going up fast. The men were elated. They'd beaten hell out of the Chinese for three days and nights.

"Everyone agreed that if the Chinese Communists couldn't take us in three days, they were never going to take us," McCarthy recalled.

Barber, hobbling, crawling, walking with the help of others, at times carried on a stretcher from position to position, checked his lines. He couldn't help but notice the gaps, the foxholes that were empty, the holes with only one man in them and many of them wounded.

He called for an air strike at 9:30 A.M., and everyone on the hilltop was elated when they saw the black and white squares painted on the engine cowlings of the F4U's. This was the Checkerboard Squadron, a red-hot outfit known throughout the division. They flew on station overhead for a few minutes, received their instructions, then went to work on that rocky ridge. They strafed, bombed, and rocketed it, then baked it black with napalm. As a parting gesture they used their remaining ammunition on a large group of Chinese spotted running away just west of Fox Hill. They didn't get far. Then the Checkerboards turned, flew over the hill, dipped their wings in salute to those on the ground, and disappeared. Everyone cheered until they were out of sight.

Then they were alone again. On their own. Marines vs. Chinese. But the odds were getting better. There were an awful lot of dead Chinese out there, the better part of a regiment.

Chores were piling up now simply because there weren't enough able-bodied men to do them.

Life meant very little. Death was everywhere.

PFC L. D. Wilson, a slight, quiet marine, walked down toward the bottom of the hill close to the road. There was a spring there, and a small house not too far away. He had a canteen, a rifle, and six grenades. "Don't go out there!" a marine shouted. "Snipers! They're in the house!" He ignored the warning, moved around to the blind side, and kicked the door in.

Several shots rang out.

Wilson walked out, went down to the spring, filled his canteen with fresh water, and went back up to the top of the hill. He walked over to where a friend lay with a stomach wound and gave him a drink of water. He might die before it's over, but it wouldn't be of thirst. The price for a canteen of water: ten dead Chinese.

Another airdrop came in toward dusk, some of the chutes landing inside the perimeter, some outside, but the marines pulled in all the supplies and suffered no casualties. Things were looking up.

It was snowing now, so hard that visibility was down to nothing. You couldn't see past the end of a rifle. But it worked in two ways. The marines couldn't tell where the Chinese were, and the Chinese couldn't tell if they were rushing a machine gun or a gap in the lines.

Fire was heavy from the rocky ridge, where four Chinese machine guns peppered the marines for hours. It didn't cause much trouble, but Barber decided that he would put an end to it, once and for all.

It was dark as pitch now. Doing what Barber wanted to do would most certainly be difficult—bring in How Battery's howitzers on top of the rock and destroy four machine guns. At a distance of seven miles.

Barber's forward observer, Lt. Donald Campbell, got on the radio to Hagaru and talked to Read, the battery commander, and told him what Barber wanted.

O'Leary was ready with his heavy mortars. The moment he was told the artillery fire was on the way, he'd loft two illumination shells to make it easier for the forward observer to adjust the howitzer fire.

"Four guns on your command," How Battery radioed F Company.

O'Leary was ready with the 81s.

Sgt. Frank Pitts, who would adjust the artillery fire, had his eyes pinned on the knoll, waiting for the illumination shells to explode.

"Fire!"

"Four rounds on the way."

O'Leary's illumination rounds lit up the sky just as How Battery shells exploded on the knoll. There were six shells altogether fired from the 81s, and the entire area was as bright as day.

Pitts, at the very top of Fox Hill, had his glasses on the knoll and saw the four artillery rounds explode. He watched in astonishment as the men and guns were blown to bits.

He couldn't believe it. All four rounds had landed right on target. No adjustment was necessary. And from seven miles.

"Wonderful!"

"Lovely!"

"Beautiful!" Pitts hollered into the radio.

"What about those machine guns?" Barber shouted back.

"Oh, they're gone! Beautiful shooting!" said Pitts.

Word was quickly passed to How Battery: "Cease fire. Target destroyed. Mission accomplished."

Read couldn't believe it. He radioed Fox, "Say again all after 'cease fire.' "

". . . Target destroyed. Mission accomplished."

That was it for the night.

Headquarters, 7th Regiment, Yudam-ni, 6:00 A.M.: The order from General Smith was loud and clear: "The attack will start at 8:00 A.M. on December 1—objective, Hagaru."

194

The shifting of units continued throughout the day. After leaving the east–west valley, each company, each battalion passed by the huge dumps that were springing up everywhere. The men would take what food they needed, ammunition, clothing, then discard what they didn't want to carry. Then the men would move into their new position in the north–south valley. Some were sent into the hills, others began moving down the road south. Still other units fell in alongside the still-forming convoy to provide close-in flank protection.

Disengaging was becoming a problem, though. The Chinese didn't want to let the marines withdraw without a fight. In a few instances it looked as if the enemy might just follow the marines right on through the perimeter.

Barber's F Company at Toktong was a major concern. Litzenberg wanted that critical pass to be in marine hands when the convoy passed below.

F Company, 2nd Battalion, 7th Regiment, Toktong Pass, 10:30 A.M.: Barber's men spent the day cleaning up the area, bringing in more Chinese sandbags, cutting firewood. Taking care of the wounded took more time each day. By this time the wounded and frostbitten outnumbered the healthy.

The men were again taking fire from that rocky knoll. But another red-hot outfit appeared overhead at midmorning and began to plaster that area. It was the LD or Love-Dog Squadron. Each plane had a large LD painted on its tail, and the eight pilots were more daring than those in the Checkerboards.

It was a great sight, and in minutes the knoll was covered with flames. The marines on the ground loved it and gave the squadron a mighty cheer. Then the LDs backed off and flew cover while the C-119 Flying Boxcars dropped more supplies. This time most hit the big "X" in the drop zone.

Then the LD's took a parting shot at the knoll and roared away.

Patrols went out to try to make contact with the Chinese, to get enough information for Barber so he might be able to anticipate the next move.

By this time all hands knew that the 5th and 7th regiments were in a fight to the death and that the pass had to be in marine hands if the two regiments were to stand a chance of survival.

Most of the patrols focused on that knoll. The air strikes had done great damage, killing a lot of Chinese and forcing hundreds more to keep their heads down. But before the planes were out of sight, the Chinese were again firing down on F Company. One patrol reported seeing about fifty Chinese popping in and out of one cave.

There was a little gunfire the rest of the day and into the night but no major probes. When dawn came Fox Company still had the hill and controlled the pass. Its lines were a little thinner, overall the company was a bit weaker, yet those who still could fight were more determined than ever to stay there until the two regiments shot their way south.

December 1, 1950; Breakout from Yudam-ni, 7:00 A.M.: Cahill's men of G Company, 3rd Battalion, 5th Regiment, shot their way through the ring of Chinese who surrounded the valley, and headed south. His platoon was the "point" all the way to Toktong Pass, half-way to Hagaru.

"This was great," Cahill said. "If you'd want to be anyplace, that's where you'd want to be."

"Going out, it was take one hill, come down on the road and take a roadblock, then go back up," he said.

"We pretty much decided if the Chinese were out there, we might as well move by fire, so I said, 'If you can't see anything, just shoot where you think somebody is.' "

The only tank the marines at Yudam-ni had, an M-26, was just behind Cahill's men should his platoon run into a stubborn roadblock.

Just behind the tank was Blodgett and his bulldozer. If the tank was disabled, he would shove it over the side.

"It was hell getting out of there," Blodgett remembered. "We had to fight our way out, and it [the fighting] never stopped all the way to Hagaru. We napalmed the hillsides, but I don't think it did any good. I saw Chinese run out of their caves just to get warm."

He kept the front blade high to shield himself from gunfire. Even so, a stray round blew away the stock of his carbine. Even this was okay, just so the firing didn't disturb the can of beans he had warming on the engine.

"We're pulling out," McLaughlin told his men. "We're to be the rear guard." So F Company, 2nd Battalion, 5th Regiment, moved to the south end of the north–south valley, near a food dump.

"We ate some peaches and other fruit," Johnson remembered, "and waited for the Chinese. They were at the far end of the valley and advancing slowly in a long skirmish line."

A South Korean marine, pointing to the north, was on the road with Johnson. Johnson borrowed his glasses, squinted into them as wind and snow bit his face, then shouted for McLaughlin. "Take a look," Johnson said, and handed him the glasses. McLaughlin watched the Chinese for a few minutes, then ordered his men into a skirmish line. A few shots were exchanged at a range too far to cause any damage.

The Chinese stopped as soon as they reached the first burning supply dump. They were hungry and freezing, and anything they could save from the flames was welcome.

Peters's F Company then moved into the hills on the right and waited for the last of the convoy to quit the village.

"Get the hell out of here, Doc!" an artilleryman shouted at Tom Schaub, a corpsman who was with C Battery, 4th Battalion, 11th Artillery Regiment.

"At that time we didn't think anyone would get out, much less those guys," Schaub remembered. "They acted as if nothing was wrong. They just loaded their guns and kept firing point-blank.

"We picked up the last stretcher and started running down the road," Schaub said. He took a last look and saw the Chinese a few hundred yards away, moving in a wave into the exploding howitzers.

Fulop was one of the last men out of the village. His job as an engineer was to torch everything that could be used by the enemy.

Only superb close air support and the point-blank fire of the cannon kept the Chinese off the engineers' backs. Fulop poured the last of the gasoline on a huge pile of expendable gear, touched it off, then took off as fast as he could past two water-cooled machine guns that were firing at the Chinese.

"They pissed on those .30s just to keep them from freezing," he remembered, "and the smell was terrible."

Withdrawing was difficult emotionally for many of the men.

"I could not accept the fact that we, the men of the United States Marine Corps, were going to throw in the towel and call it quits," MP

Sgt. Kenneth E. Corbin said. "I was one of those who had seen worse days at Iwo Jima, where gains every now and then were measured in inches."

Nevertheless, he followed orders and told his men to destroy all their excess equipment. "I even made every man destroy all papers so that the Chinese would not have anything to use against us in the event we were captured."

Jones's C Company, 1st Battalion, 5th Regiment, was in the valley off Hill 1282, each man pleased that he was alive, sad that others were less fortunate. He learned that the two regiments were returning to Hagaru and that his company would have to go back up in the hills almost immediately and help keep the peaks clear of Chinese.

"Wear all the warm clothing you can comfortably wear, burn the rest, because we're moving out," he told his men. They moved high on the left, screening the convoy as it lumbered out of Yudam-ni. He had a good defensive position and felt certain the Chinese would not attack. To do so would be folly, he felt. Nevertheless, they did attack, and it was folly. They attacked head-on in great strength and quickly overran the front of his position.

"The guys called and told us they'd gotten through," Jones said. "We just told them to lay in their holes and we were going to shoot right back over their heads. We killed twenty-five or thirty on two different occasions."

But the fighting and the cold were taking a toll. "We took casualties consistently," Jones said. "The cold, frostbite, were a drain on personnel, too."

C Company was absorbing engineers, cooks, bakers, company clerks to fill out its depleted ranks. Jones still had a good nucleus of veterans, and the newcomers followed their directions. Every man was dependable. No one ran.

Taplett was just behind the lead elements and the tank at 9:00 A.M. He had a jeep, but he walked most of the way. One moment he was up front with the point, then he dropped back to direct fire into the hills. He didn't sleep for three days.

Murray's jeep was about a mile behind Taplett's. He had a radio operator and was in close contact with the front and rear battalions and the rifle companies in the hills on both sides of the road. He walked most of the time. It kept the blood flowing, kept him warm.

"We started out fairly early in the morning," Woessner said. "As we moved out you could see the Chinese physically moving into the positions we were evacuating. They were looking for rations that we left behind. They were starving and freezing. They were in pretty bad shape."

Litzenberg was just behind Taplett's 3rd Battalion, 5th Regiment. He had a jeep, a radio operator, and a driver, and was in touch with Taplett at the front, Roisie at the rear, various artillery units, and the rifle companies.

The weather was terrible, even for this part of the world—heavy snow, bitter winds, low ceiling—not the kind of sky for close air support. Litzenberg walked much of the way and helped the wounded.

Milt Hull was walking.

"He had a patch over one eye," Woessner remembered. "He was bloody, limping, but walking.

"It was a ragtag-looking bunch. It looked like the Spirit of '76," Woessner said.

The front two thirds of the convoy was under constant attack from the moment it left Yudam-ni. Rifle and machine-gun fire peppered the road. Few bothered to seek cover. A body hit the ground here and there. Wounded in the backs of vehicles were hit a second and third time. Drivers stiffened, then sagged over their wheel.

A few miles outside Yudam-ni, Murray turned for one last look at the small village, a finger of the reservoir off to the right, the tall columns of smoke billowing skyward that told all who could see that the Chinese had won a major victory.

"There was a lot of stuff burning, tents, fuel, ammo, everything we didn't need, we couldn't carry," Murray said of the fires, the exploding ammunition, at a place on the map no one had ever heard of five days earlier, a place that marines would never forget.

"Once we started, we never really stopped," Murray said. "We just kept going. We didn't sleep, stop, or do anything but move toward Hagaru for three days and nights."

The convoy slowed at about 10:30 A.M.

The frozen body of a marine lay by the side of the road.

"Pick him up and put him in back," a sergeant told a frightened, frostbitten young marine sitting up front with the driver.

No response. He didn't want to do it.

The sergeant reached up and yanked him out head first, then slammed him up against the side of the truck.

"We don't leave no one up here," he said, snarling. "We're takin' everybody out, dead or alive."

The youngster reached down and picked up the body and, with the help of the sergeant, put him in back with the other dead.

It's difficult to imagine fighting and surviving under worse conditions.

Each marine had to wear several layers of clothing. To expose skin to the elements was to have it freeze. If you did any strenuous moving about, such as digging a foxhole, there was the sweat factor. Once you stopped moving, you froze. The hood of the parka obscured vision, impaired hearing. Feet and hands ached constantly. Boots were useless. If your feet were not encased in ice as a result of perspiration freezing, they were like two ovens. You couldn't simply warm them near a fire, you baked them. Water froze eight feet from a fire, which restricted liquid intake. Food could never be cooked properly. As a result, stomach pains and diarrhea were constant companions. When this occurred, relieving oneself became a major problem, since it was almost impossible to remove the many layers of clothing in time.

There was no such thing as hours in a day. The only time frame was day and night, daylight and darkness. Few men had any idea what day it was, or the date. They remembered Thanksgiving and knew that Christmas was approaching.

The front of the convoy was four miles south of Yudam-ni and moving at a snail's pace when Davis split off and led his men up the foreboding face of Hill 1419 on the way to Toktong Pass and Barber's surrounded F Company.

The Chinese were well dug in, and the going was extremely tough. Each man carried at least a hundred pounds of equipment, including an extra mortar round for the 60s, all the grenades he could possibly hold, plus his regular ammo, sleeping bag, and food.

"When my platoon passed through the assault platoon there were only four or five men left," Kiser said. "The hill was frozen, icy, covered with snow. It was goddamn cold. You had to drag yourself up the 70 percent grade, clinging to anything you could find, a rock here, a shrub there, a tree stump. It was slow, and the Chinese were firing at us. . . ."

"There were so many Chinese, you couldn't believe it," he added.

Once they reached the top, it was fairly level.

In some places snow was two to three feet deep. In others, just a few inches. But it was always cold. There was no cover from the wind, the driving snow that lashed at their faces and turned their skin raw.

"The first guy broke the snow and it was so tough that we rotated him frequently," Kiser said. They also rotated the lead platoon. When Kiser's platoon was there, he lost four men to snipers.

They moved out in single file with a sense of urgency that they had best get to the pass as quickly as possible or there might not be a Fox Company.

"We just took off and moved," Davis said. The pace at first was pretty good. They weren't slowed by wounded. They had all been sent down the hill to the convoy.

Using the stars as a guide, Davis led his battalion south across the mountains at a pace much too demanding for the terrain, the arctic temperature, the heavy snow.

Davis drove his men relentlessly. He wouldn't let them rest, even slow down. Had they done so, they might have frozen, for each man was perspiring heavily.

B Company had the point. Davis's command group was next, followed by A, C, and H companies in that order.

Davis ranged from the front to the rear, always running beside his men, breaking snow. There was no one for him to alternate with.

"He was remarkable, incredibly tough and strong," Kiser said. "I don't see how anyone else could have done it."

Still, Kiser hated to see him at the front when his platoon was the point.

"He had this radioman [Pearl] who carried a sixty- to seventy-pound radio with an eighteen-foot whip antenna," Kiser recalled. "You think that didn't bring down enemy fire?

"When Davis was there, small-arms fire was pitiful," Kiser added.

201

"An incredible amount of bullets were zinging the ice all around us. I don't see how Davis wasn't hit."

They walked fast, and they hoped, prayed the Chinese wouldn't find the range.

With each passing hour the trail became more treacherous. Those up front had to break the snow, but that same snow-covered path had turned to ice by the time the middle of the column reached there, and the footing was disastrous. It was close to impossible for those at the rear to regain their footing once they had slipped.

Worse, Davis noted the column was slowly drifting west, in the direction of the road, getting closer with each step to an area where artillery fire from Hagaru could be expected to fall at any minute.

Davis tried to reach the point, B Company, by radio but couldn't. He tried word of mouth, but this didn't work. A howling wind didn't help. Nor did muffled ears. So he and his radio operator raced alongside the column until they reached the lead unit just in time to correct its drift.

But their off-course march had taken Davis's men dangerously close to enemy-held Hill 1520, and they came under small-arms fire. This awakened the Chinese on a few hills farther along, and they chipped in with long-range fire.

But Davis's men had the situation under control by 1:00 A.M. of December 2, and for the first time in twenty hours he let them rest, at 3:00 A.M. First they formed a tight perimeter, then they hit the ground like dominoes, weary, completely exhausted, and climbed into their sleeping bags. "We took off our boots, changed socks, put the wet ones underneath our shirts, and put our dry socks on. It was nice to be able to wiggle our toes, to get the circulation going again," said Cpl. Walter H. O'Keefe.

Davis walked among the men, encouraging everyone, pointing out that although they were surrounded by Chinese, this was not a retreat. "We're just attacking in a different direction," he stressed, echoing the words of General Smith. "Fox Company is down the road. They were left there to keep the road open. They're surrounded now, and they need help. That's where we're going—to relieve Fox Company."

They rested until just before dawn, when the order to saddle up was quietly passed.

"I remember telling [Cpl. Richard] Frankas I was really pooped, that

I was tired, that I didn't feel that I could make it any farther," O'Keefe said.

O'Keefe was twenty-seven at the time, not exactly an old-timer, yet the younger marines were already calling him "Pop."

"That wasn't exactly what I thought I ought to be called," he remembered.

As he tried to lift his aching bones off the frozen ground, he overheard a marine nearby say, "I'm going to give up. I'm not going any farther."

O'Keefe didn't know what to say at this point.

"Well," said another youngster close by, "I'm watching that old guy up there, and if he gets up and goes, if that old bastard goes, then I'm gonna go."

"I knew he was talking about me," O'Keefe said. "So when word came to move out, regardless of how I felt, in the old Marine Corps tradition, I got up on my feet and put one foot forward and started moving, and the kids were right behind me.

"I realized then that I didn't mind being called 'Pop' because there was a little bit of leadership there and they were looking for me to set the pace, and I did."

Pearl couldn't reach Fox on the radio. He'd tried everything. Davis was concerned that his men might come under fire because he was sure they were within range of Barber's heavy mortars. That's why he let his men rest until dawn.

C Company took the first ridge that morning, then covered the rest of the battalion as they shoved off. It was slow going. They were drawing light fire.

Davis and Pearl were just about to the top of a ridge, about three quarters of a mile from Toktong Pass, although at the time they didn't realize it.

Then it happened.

"I've got Fox Company!" Pearl shouted at Davis, who was about ten feet away.

They were elated.

"I'd been trying to call them for some time," Pearl recalled, "and I was very concerned. Finally I got a clear five-by-five and shouted to Colonel Davis.

"We were close to the head of the column," Pearl said, "and when we went over that hill we could see them waving their arms and shouting. Then we were shouting back and forth."

Murray rode in a jeep up to the lead elements to see if there was a problem, if there was anything he could do. No problems. The situation was fine, for the moment.

He found Taplett, the 3rd Battalion commander, in a shack back a short distance from the road, enjoying the simple radiant heating system the Koreans had perfected centuries earlier.

"Ah, you've come to visit Dante's Inferno," Taplett said when Murray entered.

"He had his socks off," Murray remembered, "and he was picking the ice out from between his toes. I watched him throw little chinks away, then put his shoes and socks back on."

Later the convoy ran into trouble. Elements of the 7th Regiment could not take Hill 1520, and fire from the top was holding up the vehicles. "I found out that the 3rd Battalion, 7th, was making no progress whatsoever," Taplett said. He tried to get Murray on the phone but couldn't reach him. So he talked instead with Lt. Col. Frederick R. Dowsett, Litzenberg's executive officer.

"The 7th unit is not meeting its objective," Taplett told him. "They're having trouble. What are my instructions?"

"That's your problem," Taplett recalled Dowsett telling him. "Figure it out the best you can."

"I was so goddamn mad," Taplett remembered.

"I'd like to talk to the regimental commanding officer," he told Dowsett.

"He's not here."

"Tell him I'm passing through the 7th at this point," Taplett said as he told Dowsett the coordinates.

By this time his men were taking heavy fire from both sides of the road—mortars, machine guns, rifles.

Taplett sent I Company up the left on Hill 1520, H Company on the right. The fire was heavy; so were the casualties.

"We attacked until dark," Taplett said. "Item was hit stronger and stronger. How met moderate resistance."

"We had to slow How on the right so the convoy could be protected.

We had no artillery support. I was told the priority effort was to protect the rear." Still, his troops got the Chinese off Hill 1520, and the convoy moved slowly past, drawing only light fire.

"I tried to clean off the sides from five hundred to a thousand yards," Taplett said. His jeep was right behind the tank. Swede Swinson was with him, his backpack radio in use constantly as Taplett kept in close touch with regiment and his rifle companies in the hills. It was late in the afternoon now, very cold, and snowing. The men were weary. They had been under fire for many hours, and as night fell, it became heavier.

"I asked permission from Murray to hold up for the night," Taplett said, "but my orders were to continue to attack."

"I'm in good defensive position," Capt. Harold G. Schrier, I Company commander, radioed Taplett, requesting permission to stop for the night.

"No!" Taplett replied. "I've got my orders. Do the best you can."

Schrier did, but it was very costly.

"He ran into a withering crossfire that made his company ineffective until we got to Hagaru," Taplett said. "He had one lieutenant and twenty-five to twenty-eight men left."

Schrier was wounded in the neck that night. To hold the high ground on the left that night Taplett had to send up a composite platoon of clerks, engineers, cooks, and anyone else he could find under command of Lt. Wayne Richardson to support what was left of Schrier's company. The marines really didn't get control of Hill 1520 until about 1:00 A.M. on December 2, when the march south was resumed.

There was no letup in the fighting along the main supply route throughout the early-morning hours of December 2.

The Chinese did not want the marines to break away. The cost in dead meant nothing to them. At first light the marines counted 342 Chinese dead in the I Company area.

Taplett was again behind the tank, weary, alternately riding and walking, when they ran into a giant roadblock at midday. There was a small stream—it was flowing too fast to freeze—and a bridge that had been destroyed. Beyond, behind a mound of logs and dirt, a heavy machine gun sprayed the area and drove the marines to cover. Bullets bounded off the tank, which ineffectively returned the fire. Taplett's G Company cleaned that mess up, then kept the Chinese at bay until the engineers repaired the bridge. The tank crossed, then the bulldozer,

Taplett, and the rest of the convoy. The men were well into their second day of fighting after the breakout, not yet to Toktong Pass, but farther south than many ever thought they'd get.

The situation still was not one to cheer about, yet they were in better shape than twelve hours earlier. At the snail's pace they were moving, it would take another day and a half of fighting to reach Hagaru—a total of seventy-two hours of no rest, not much in their stomachs, dead and wounded mounting.

Hagaru had to be in marine hands when they arrived. Word had reached the convoy that the Chinese were closing on the village, where General Smith had his headquarters, where there were far too few men for defense.

There were vast quantities of supplies stored there, ammunition, medicine, food. Many more warming tents had been erected in anticipation of the arrival of the 5th and 7th regiments. A landing field was under construction for the evacuation of casualties.

All the marines had to do was hold Hagaru for another thirty-six hours.

F Company, 2nd Battalion, 7th Regiment, Toktong Pass, 10:00 A.M.: Barber was elated that Davis's 1st Battalion had fought its way across the mountains. He was extremely happy that they had arrived in daylight because, "We were concerned they wouldn't know exactly where we were, and my people were getting pretty trigger-happy by this time.

"If they came close to us at night, we'd almost sure as hell shoot," Barber added.

"I offered to send out a patrol to help guide them in," Barber said, "but by this time they could see us."

"We'd been up on that hill for maybe five days and out of touch with everyone," Kanouse recalls, "so it was great when we looked out and saw marine helmets on the ridge.

"But we really didn't know what was happening," he said. "We didn't know that Hagaru was surrounded and under attack. We didn't know that the two regiments were coming out of Yudam-ni."

He watched as Davis's 1st Battalion moved in at 11:30 A.M., deposited their wounded at the aid station, then moved on through to take up defensive positions on F Company's perimeter, on nearby hilltops, and wait for the column to come into sight.

"As they passed by, I caught a glimpse of a captain who looked familiar," Kanouse remembered. "I asked a guy who he was, then pinched myself when I found out it was Capt. John Morris, my commanding officer back in the 21st Infantry in New Jersey.

"We talked for a few minutes, and he was very, very upset over the loss of so many of his men the last four or five days," Kanouse said.

Kanouse spotted a few others he knew, thought were dead, but they didn't have but a few minutes to talk. "Before you knew it, they were gone, on to other duties with their units, but it was nice to see them." A lot of his friends had been wounded, though, and it would be some time before he saw them again. Others he would never see.

"We saw a column of marines straggling in toward us," Benson remembered, "but when they got here we realized that they were in just as bad shape as we were. They had a lot of wounded on stretchers— maybe twenty or more.

"But we were glad to see them, and they were glad to see us," he added, "and we were cheering and yelling."

"Dead Chinese were piled everywhere," Hedrick recalled. "Dead marines were neatly piled to one side of the aid tent, wounded on the other side.

"Going into Fox Company, I passed two marines in a hole," he said. "Their eyes told what they had been through. We looked at them. They looked at us. We knew they were thankful that we had arrived, but they couldn't talk.

"Fox Company looked like death," he added.

"My first reaction when I saw his [Barber's] position was, 'Some goddamn dumb reserve officer picked this spot,' " Kiser said. "But after I saw his dead and wounded, I realized he probably couldn't get them off the hill and was forced to stay there.

"When I got there I could see how the men who could still move had taken the bodies of the dead Chinese and stacked them around their positions to use as sandbags," Kiser said. "There were about seventy-five in this one position, all frozen stiff. I imagine they made pretty good sandbags."

Kiser was there only a short while, then moved out and kicked the Chinese off nearby Baker Hill, the same hill he had taken on the way up and that was named after the company. Davis was like this. He remembered that Kiser's platoon had taken the hill going up, that he was familiar with it, so he had him take it on the way back. It was about six hundred to seven hundred yards distant and slightly higher than Fox Hill. It was one of four areas from where plunging fire in varying degrees had peppered F Company.

PFC's Gerald Couture, Tom Marron, and Elbert Englebretson were with Kiser's men as they went up Baker Hill. There were just a few Chinese on top, and they were driven away. Couture spotted the beginning of a small foxhole and started to dig, to make it large enough for three. He also spotted a Chinese machine gun about two hundred yards away and a flock of Chinese who were digging just as frantically as the marines. "We could see them, they could see us," he remembered. "We dug faster, they dug faster. We looked at them, they looked at us, but no one fired.

"It was sort of like, 'Let's get our holes dug, we'll fight tomorrow.' "

The Chinese machine gun later opened fire and pinned everyone down until two Corsairs bombed and strafed the hill. "It was a short but bitter fight. In my squad, I was the only one who walked down," Couture said.

A Company followed B Company beyond Toktong Pass and took another of the hills. Both set up separate perimeters and stayed the night. The rest of Davis's battalion filled out the depleted ranks of Barber's company and waited. Would the Chinese hit Fox once again? When would the convoy arrive below? It snowed heavily that night. And it was terribly cold. But there was no fighting.

At dawn on December 3 a sniper killed the battalion surgeon as he was treating the wounded.

Barber was up at first light, hobbling from position to position, in obvious pain.

A helicopter arrived a short time later, hovered overhead for a few moments, then fell like a rock to the ground. The sniper got the pilot.

"I looked straight up, saw it coming down, tried to guess where it would land, then ran like hell," Pearl said.

Cahill and the twenty-two men in his platoon were still the point as they rounded a bend in the road and came into sight of Toktong Pass. "We saw men with leggings on the skyline," Cahill remembered.

"We figured if they wore leggings and were on the skyline, well, they must be marines, and they were."

"A few of Barber's men came down, made contact, identified themselves. We shook hands, then kept going," Cahill said.

The convoy itself hadn't come into sight yet. There was a problem just short of the pass, and the column was stalled.

The tank was stopped. No one was moving. Taplett moved toward the front. About a hundred yards from the tank he saw that it was taking heavy fire from the hills. He tried to reach it by radio. There was no answer. He crawled forward, used the tank phone to talk to the crew inside, and ordered them forward. Nothing happened.

"There's nobody ahead of you!" Taplett shouted into the phone.

The tank remained where it was.

"To hell with the tank," he thought, then crawled back to his jeep and did what he should have done in the first place: He put Mize in charge of the situation. Then the two young lieutenants, Cahill and Cashion, blasted the Chinese off the hill. The tank started to roll, the convoy close behind.

F Company, 2nd Battalion, 7th Regiment, Toktong Pass, 1:00 P.M.: Barber's men could see the convoy in the distance, and a loud cheer went up.

From the road, ever so faintly, the men on top could hear, "From the halls of Montezuma . . ." Then they picked up the tune, ". . . to the shores of Tripoli . . ."

"At the pass we waited until the lead elements of the convoy arrived, then we went down to the road," Davis said.

He saw Taplett, moved toward him, and said:

"I'll take the tank. I've got the mission. I'll go from here."

Taplett remembered the meeting well.

"I have my orders," Davis told him. "I will take over here. My troops are already on the road and ready to go."

Taplett didn't like it, but orders are orders. He felt he should have continued as the lead element all the way to Hagaru. His point units had set a good pace; they'd blasted the Chinese off both sides of the road. Hagaru was within their grasp. To put his men into defensive positions, to slow them down, would prove costly, he felt. They were all perspiring under their several layers of clothing, and to slow them down, in some instances to stop them completely, would prove disastrous. They'd freeze.

"We moved into defensive positions to the left and right sides of the road at the hairpin turn at the pass," Taplett said.

"We suffered all kinds of frostbite casualties," he said. "When they took off their mukluks, the soles of their feet came off, too."

Barber's walking wounded went down to the road first, then the stretcher cases. Benson was with Cafferatta and heard him murmur softly, "Bense, don't let them leave me here."

"Nobody's going to leave you, Hector. You know I won't go without you.

"We were happy to be leaving," Benson said.

"Cafferatta hung over the stretcher about a foot or so," Benson remembered, "and when Komoroski saw this he yelled at a corpsman, 'You better get four men to carry this one down!' "

Finally, the few able-bodied men packed their gear and moved down to join the convoy. Five days and nights of hell had come to an end. The Chinese would soon have Fox Hill—but at what a price! Everywhere you looked there were Chinese bodies.

"Although it was only six miles to Hagaru, it took a long time to get there," Kanouse said, "and a lot of fighting.

"We really didn't know what was happening. We'd been up there and out of touch with everyone," he said. "We didn't know that Hagaru had been hit hard and was surrounded. We didn't know why the regiments were coming out of Yudam-ni, although everyone seemed to be on the road going back. But we didn't know why."

Barber was on the road now. The wounded had all been placed aboard trucks. Davis's 1st Battalion was now the point.

"I was hobbling with the aid of a stick," Barber said, "when I was told to turn my company over to a lieutenant." But he said he wasn't ready to do that just yet, and he continued walking.

"Then I thought, 'This is not only stupid, it may be criminal. I can't move well. What if we're attacked? What if we get pinned down? What if it becomes necessary to move and somebody gets zapped trying to save me?' So I said, 'To hell with this.' "

He turned what was left of his company over to Dunne.

"I followed the company for a while in case a situation came up that I could help with," he said, "but I didn't let them know I was there."

But he couldn't keep up, and soon the last man was out of sight.

He climbed into a jeep for the rest of the journey to Hagaru and was flown out.

What was left of B Company and the luckier ones in H Company, 7th Regiment, were on the road beyond the pass and close to the head of the convoy. There were some pretty fair-sized log bunkers ahead. The Chinese also had a machine gun high on a hill, and they just kept spraying this one spot on the road, daring anyone or anything to cross. B Company started up after them. It wasn't a particularly high piece of ground, but there was very heavy snow, and the going was tough.

"It was one mad, disorganized charge up through the snow," Dyrdahl said. "There was no plan. Nothing. It was 'High-diddle-diddle, right up the middle.' "

They went up, spread out in a thin line, took a few casualties, not too bad for slow going uphill, through three hundred yards of open ground. "The Chinese couldn't shoot worth a damn," Dyrdahl said.

There were about 120 of them up on top, but they were long gone by the time B Company reached the high ground. PFC Jim Beard grabbed an old machine gun, turned it around, worked on it for a few seconds, and got it to fire single rounds. Then he zeroed in on the retreating Chinese.

The company stayed on top for a while, rested, then slid down to the road and continued south.

Taplett's 3rd Battalion was just ahead of Roisie's 2nd protecting the artillery.

"About two thirds of the way to Hagaru we crossed a little stream where the Chinese had set up a roadblock," Taplett said. "But one of the prime movers had run out of gas there and blocked the road so nothing could move. The Chinese had a machine gun there and they'd already killed the driver."

It was so cold it was next to impossible to move, let alone fight.

"I couldn't understand why the column wasn't moving," Taplett said, "so I walked about a mile to where the roadblock was. The Chinese were firing, but we weren't firing back."

He looked around, spotted an officer, and in no uncertain terms let him know his feelings.

"You got a 105. You got heavy machine guns. Why aren't you firing back?"

"I can't get them to."

"Put the walking wounded to the right of the vehicles. We'll lay down a barrage on the left. Get that prime mover off the road. Then we'll go across," Taplett told him.

Just then Roisie showed up with some 3.5 rockets, and they blasted the Chinese out of there. It was all over in two hours, and the convoy was moving again.

"It's surprising how cold affects people," Taplett said.

Wounded were stacked three deep in the medical section of the convoy. They couldn't get out to urinate, so empty plasma bottles were passed to them. They were fed C rations when the vehicles were halted by fighting.

The medical train was long, about a hundred vehicles. It was in the middle of the convoy. By the time the convoy got to Hagaru, the doctors, corpsmen, and medical section were strung out from the front to the rear.

At times the Chinese were so close to the road they could toss grenades into the fires.

Corpsmen were supposed to carry carbines, wear red crosses on their helmets, and use armbands.

"You can't work on a guy and carry a carbine," Schaub pointed out, "and the red crosses on the helmets were good targets, so we didn't use them at all.

"When I worked on a guy, I gave him the .45 and told him to shoot anything that moved. And for safety's sake, I carried a .38 in a shoulder holster, too."

Two marines curled up on the back of the tank and covered themselves with their ponchos to bag a little sack time and stay warm. It didn't work out that way. They were asphyxiated by fumes from the tank's engine.

It was so bitterly cold that whenever the column stopped for a roadblock or a firefight, fires seemed to spring up as far as the eye could see in both directions.

PFC John A. Swindle was warming his hands and feet while trying to thaw a can of beans. "Next thing I knew something hit me and I was

212

laying on the ground. A corpsman ran over, looked me over, then said, 'You got hit in the lung and the back of the arm. We'll try to get a chopper and get you out of here.' "

They put him on the bottom of the jeep ambulance. There was another wounded man above him.

"We were going like hell down the road toward a 'copter pad," Swindle remembered. "Then the gooks opened up. They shot the driver. The jeep ran wild all over the road. The top stretcher broke loose, and the guy up there fell on me. Then the damn jeep hit the side of a hill and stopped."

Marines from the passing column ran over and checked the driver. He was dead. So was the marine who had been on top.

"They got another driver, put another wounded guy on top, and got us to a helicopter in about ten minutes." He was flown to Hagaru and carried aboard a transport for evacuation to Japan.

He was laying on his stretcher, wondering just what had happened, when a corpsman came by.

"Are you a Catholic or a Protestant?"

"Why?"

"You're not gonna make it."

That upset him. But it upset a lieutenant nearby even more.

"He was on a stretcher near me," Swindle said. "He'd lost both legs, but he turned to me and said, 'Don't worry, you're gonna make it.' "

Then he turned in the direction of the corpsman and shouted, "You son of a bitch! Everyone here's gonna make it!"

A Catholic priest from Milwaukee and his assistant climbed into an ambulance to check on the wounded and never got out. It was riddled by machine-gun fire.

"We were near the reservoir coming back from Yudam-ni when we saw some people walking toward us," Sgt. Lewis C. Wroblewski remembered.

"Hey, marine, can we join you?" one of them hollered.

"Sure."

They were the first of many stragglers from units of the Army's 7th Infantry Division who had stumbled into marine lines. They were the fortunate ones. Many others were bayoneted as they slept when the

Chinese surprised them on the eastern side of the reservoir. Others had been shot, and many were stranded on the ice.

"Here's a rifle," Wroblewski said to one of them. "Get up on the flanks.

"We were up in the hills on the way back to Hagaru and we went into several shacks that were abandoned," he said.

"They [soldiers] were hung like cattle in a slaughterhouse. They were hung from the roof, feet up, and frozen stiff. All their clothes were gone."

"Keep going! Keep going!" Cahill urged his men, prodding and pushing them to the limit. "If they offer us a ride, we're not taking it!

"You really had to literally kick their asses to keep them going," he said.

"We walked all the way, though. We were very proud."

Hagaru, although not yet in sight, was very close. The men could tell from the tall columns of smoke that spiraled high into the sky in late afternoon of December 3. The point units could smell the smoke. Hagaru had come through a night of hell. Most of the marines didn't know who controlled the village. They thought they would have to fight their way through hordes of enemy troops before they could continue south to the sea.

CHAPTER 9
A NIGHT OF FIRE

November 28, 1950; Hagaru, 10:30 P.M.:

The perimeter was more than four miles—close to five million square yards of ice, snow, partly destroyed buildings, tents everywhere, and very little natural cover. There was *the* road, a hospital, a landing field large enough to handle two-engine planes, and supply dumps everywhere. And a very large hill to the east that dominated the entire area.

"It reminded me of a picture of a Klondike gold camp," said Lt. Col. Thomas L. Ridge. But its appearance wasn't important. The location was. It straddled the road, the only escape route leading south to Koto-ri, and it had to be held.

It had to be defended to the last man, and with the five-to-one advantage the Chinese had, it looked more and more that it might come down to that.

Hagaru was the key. If it fell, then almost surely the division would cease to exist. Why the Chinese did not concentrate all their forces around Hagaru, quickly overwhelm it, then sit tight and wait for the two regiments to come down the road, only their generals will ever know.

Ridge brought his 3rd Battalion, 1st Regiment, into the village shortly after dark on November 26. It was one of only two top-line fighting units there, and it was understrength. Capt. Carl Sitter's G Company was still in Koto-ri, eleven miles south. So was one platoon from Weapons Company, the other battle-tested outfit in Hagaru.

Just about everyone else was in a service or support capacity. Some of these units had as few as eight to ten men. And no one knew for sure exactly what units were there. They had come up the road piecemeal from Koto-ri, found a spot to bivouac, dug in, then stayed put unless ordered to move elsewhere. It was a chaotic situation.

General Smith's headquarters was set up on November 27. The area quickly became a small tent city within a large tent city as his aides arrived and went to work. Then the large communications vans rolled in and the marines' 1st Division was operational. A very small group of staff members remained in Koto-ri simply because there were not enough trucks to move them north with the rest of his staff. But they were expected to start toward Hagaru on November 28 as part of a very large convoy of reinforcements that were desperately needed.

Hagaru was busier than an anthill. Engineers were carving out the

217

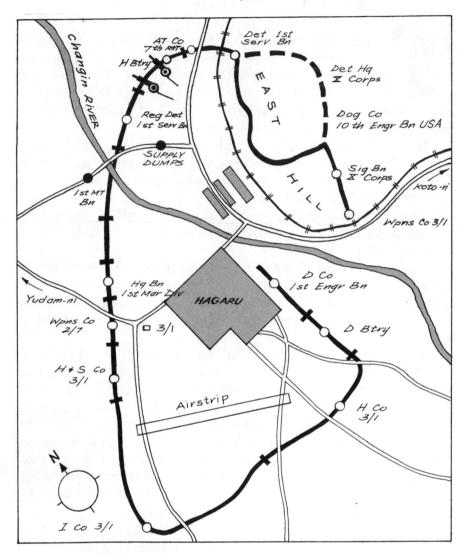

Map 9—The defensive perimeter at Hagaru and the marine and Army positions are shown.

airfield so wounded could be flown out and supplies and fresh troops brought in. They were still rebuilding the road because a lot more tanks were due in.

Ridge sent out patrols to try to find the Chinese. He had to know where they were, how many were there. He asked intelligence to try to pinpoint as best it could—with the sketchy information available—where the Chinese would most likely attack.

Would it be from the southwest? Probably.

Or East Hill? Maybe.

And in what strength?

This was important. He didn't have enough riflemen to cover the entire perimeter. He couldn't even cover East Hill and the potential attack route from the southwest. It would have to be one or the other.

Once he made this decision, he put less seasoned troops in what he felt would be the secondary route of attack.

Ridge's battalion command post was just outside Hagaru, beside the road leading north to Yudam-ni. His two rifle companies were southwest of his CP in an L-shaped area that covered close to two thousand yards. His order to his men: Dig deeper.

He wasn't optimistic.

"I knew that Litzenberg's men had taken some Chinese prisoners. He told me they were Chinese. This confirmed my feelings," Ridge related. "The Army kind of pooh-poohed the Chinese threat, but I took it very seriously."

Ridge was worried before he got to Hagaru.

"All my instincts were up," he said. "In combat a little red light goes on, and when it does, I don't double-check things, I triple-check them. It's instinct."

"The light went on before I ever got there, and it stayed on. That light never went off until I got aboard ship," he said.

Further, he was now getting bad news from his eyes and ears—the patrols and observation planes.

The patrols found Chinese everywhere, and in great numbers. The spotter planes reported the road cut in several places, north and south. His perimeter, Ridge now realized, was 360 degrees. He was surrounded.

Tanks and infantry had tried to fight their way north to Yudam-ni in the morning and again on the afternoon of the twenty-seventh, but couldn't.

Everyone knew that a decisive battle was close. It was in the air. They could sense it.

So each man dug a little deeper, added a few timbers to the front of his hole, stockpiled as much ammo and grenades as he could.

The engineers worked at a feverish pitch around the clock. Bulldozers ripped up the ground for the landing strip. Despite the danger, floodlights were used after dark. Jackhammers never stopped working on the road.

By now everyone in Hagaru knew that the 5th and 7th regiments were in a battle to the death. They talked of nothing else around the cook fires, in the warming tents, in their holes, and wondered when their turn would come.

There were fifty-eight separate marine, Army, Navy, and South Korean units in Hagaru, and more were on the way. It was crowded almost beyond belief. Hourly, more and more refugees fleeing the Chinese filtered through porous marine lines.

It was so packed with humanity, weapons, and supply dumps that had the Chinese used artillery effectively it would have been impossible not to score one direct hit after another. *it was left behind. the*

General Smith touched down at midmorning on the twenty-eighth. A half hour later General Almond flew in to discuss the Chinese attack at Yudam-ni, the gravity of the situation there, at Hagaru, and at Koto-ri.

By this time the Eighth Army on the western coast was in full retreat.

One of the greatest problems at Hagaru was exactly who was in command of what. Ridge didn't know. No one had really told him specifically what he was to do or his responsibilities.

"Before I left Koto-ri I was told verbally to go up there and take up a position," he said. But he realized quickly that one person should be charged with the defense of the area.

So he went to the division command post and talked with General Smith's chief of staff and operations, Bowser. Ridge suggested that an overall commander for the defense of Hagaru be appointed as soon as possible.

"The day I got there, Tom was waiting for me with the recommendation that I be in charge of the defense of Hagaru, that I be the defense coordinator," Bowser said.

They discussed the problem briefly. Then Bowser said:

"No, I'm not gonna do this because I'm not a tactical commander. I've got other things to worry about. I've got a battalion at the railhead at Chinhung-ni, a battalion at Koto-ri. We've got the problem at Yudam-ni. I have no business walking around here siting machine guns."

"You're gonna be the defense commander," Bowser told Ridge.

Bowser and Ridge then went to see General Smith.

"Bowser's right, Tom. You're it," General Smith told him.

"He was an ideal commander," Bowser said, "and he did a helluva job, as I knew he would. He was absolutely super."

Ridge immediately urged that Sitter's G Company and three hundred British royal marine commandos be rushed from Koto-ri to Hagaru. He wanted his missing rifle company to man the perimeter at the base of East Hill. But late on the twenty-eighth it appeared that this was out of the question for the moment.

Undismayed, he returned to his command post, anxious to find out what intelligence could tell him about Chinese intentions.

Lt. Richard E. Carey, his intelligence officer, said that he felt the attack would come at about 9:30 P.M., from the southwest.

On the basis of this, Ridge extended the H and I Company areas of responsibility from two thousand to twenty-three hundred yards, close to a mile and a third. There were great gaps in the perimeter, but they would have to be covered by crossing fields of fire.

East Hill was another worry. Since G Company was still in Koto-ri, he shifted D Company of the Army's 10th Engineer Battalion, which had been attached to the marines, over to the base of the hill along with a small force from X Corps headquarters. But he sent along an officer and a radio operator with each unit, since mortar and artillery fire would be vital. Ridge had enough problems where he was, so he put his executive officer, Maj. Reginald R. Myers, in charge of the hill situation. "Reg, this is your problem," Ridge said. "Organize it as best you can.

"I told him to get whoever he could and to keep his men alert, because he might have to repulse an attack.

"I wasn't as worried about the hill as I was about the southwest," Ridge remembered, "because if they came over the top it would be like shooting ducks.

"If the Chinese ever stayed up there, however, they'd be looking

221

down our backs, and a couple of machine guns could do a lot of damage," he added.

At about noon on the twenty-eighth, Ridge sent his junior officers through the area with instructions to anyone commanding a unit, regardless of its size, to gather at the flagpole in the village at 4:00 P.M. Ridge wanted to know what units were there, their size, and what weapons they possessed. Then he began to assign them.

"We had cooks, bakers, air controllers—everybody we could find got a hunk of the perimeter."

As usual, the forward air controllers came out best. In no time at all they had oil heaters in their bunkers. "They had the reputation of making out as good as humanly possible," Ridge said, "so I wasn't surprised."

By dark, barbed wire had been strung in double rows around most of the perimeter. Trip flares, booby traps, and mines made the approach from the southwest a deadly avenue of attack. It was well below zero, so the men drifted back to the warming tents as often as possible for hot coffee, a cigarette, perhaps warm food.

Behind I and H companies the area was bathed in light as the engineers worked on the airfield, using floodlights. The landing field had top priority, regardless of the cost. So, despite bone-chilling temperatures and snipers, the engineers continued work, their weapons across their backs or stacked at arm's reach.

Hagaru was now on a 50 percent alert, but no man slept. Snow began to fall, lightly at first, then heavily, and by 7:30 P.M. visibility, always bad, was down to nothing. By 9:00 P.M. both I and H companies were on full alert. Minutes that seemed like hours slipped by. At 10:00 P.M. it was still quiet. Was intelligence wrong?

The only noise was the bitter wind and an occasional burst from a machine gun just to make certain it hadn't frozen.

Lt. R. L. Barrett, Jr., was in a small tent just behind his 1st Platoon, H Company, 3rd Battalion, 1st Regiment. About twenty-five yards farther behind, there was a small depression. If the Chinese attacked, he'd quit the tent and move his CP back there. He'd take his platoon sergeant, two runners, a corpsman, and his phones.

He passed the word down the line: Remain fully clothed all night. Barrett then slipped his .45 into a pocket of his parka and lay down to try to grab a few minutes of rest. It never hurt to have an extra weapon.

The wind had stopped. Snow covered everything—marines, weapons, tents, tanks. And it was still falling, so heavily you couldn't see past the end of a rifle. Perfect weather for the Chinese.

At 10:30 P.M. the Chinese smashed into I and H companies, an hour later than expected, but from the southwest, just as intelligence had predicted.

Three shrill blasts from a whistle, exploding flares, and the Chinese were on the marines almost before they knew it. Small patrols of six to eight had crept to within thirty yards of the perimeter, searching for weak spots. Chinese had also crawled into a small riverbed. Then they crawled over the bank and rolled toward marine foxholes.

"It was impossible to see them until they were almost upon us," Barrett said. The rows of barbed wire, mines, booby traps slowed, but didn't stop their attack. The mines killed many. Others got hung up on the wire and were killed, and the few that got close to the foxholes in this first attack were all shot.

"When the first burst of fire came, we poured out of the tent and ran back to our tactical CP and began calling for mortar fire," Barrett said.

The company command post was mass confusion. Everyone was running from the tent to their holes, but they did manage to get in a few rounds of mortar fire. Then Chinese mortars began to lob shells on Barrett's CP.

"We thought at first they were our own, but when the white phosphorus started dropping, we knew it wasn't ours—we were not firing WP at all."

Then the Chinese were gone as quickly as they had appeared, and quiet settled over the battlefield.

But only for a few minutes. While the marines were fumbling with mittens and near-frozen fingers trying to reload M-1, carbine, and BAR clips, the Chinese attacked again.

White phosphorus rained down on them. Machine-gun fire raked their holes.

"It looked like the whole field got up and walked forward," Ridge remembered.

He had taken four tanks and positioned one at each end of his two-rifle companies so they could get the best possible fields of fire— a lateral crossfire. He didn't want them firing straight ahead, which tankers were more accustomed to doing. "The tankers looked at me very oddly," he remembered.

But it worked. Chinese were falling everywhere.

Lt. Joe Fisher, I Company commander, was behind his men, stopping at one hole to shout encouragement, changing a field of fire at another. Somehow he wasn't hit. And at six-two and 235 pounds, he was a large target. But no one ever said the Chinese could shoot.

An eight-hundred-yard chunk of ground where I and H met bore the brunt of the new attack, which never seemed to slow. When Chinese manpower ran short, fresh units moved into the assault. Their losses were staggering, but at about 11:30 P.M. they broke through the center of H Company.

Barrett was in his CP when a marine dashed through the gunfire to tell him the Chinese had broken through on the left. They had, Barrett learned for certain a few minutes later, but they had taken only two of his holes. The real trouble was in the 3rd Platoon's positions.

Barrett tried to call in the mortars, but all he could hear on the line was the company commander, Capt. Clarence E. Corley, Jr., and his radio operator.

White phosphorus was coming in again. Barrett saw a few of his men outlined against an explosion, then watched as one went down after another round burst close by.

The company CP was catching hell from enemy mortars, too.

"Suddenly I heard over the phone, 'Look out! They're coming in!' Then I heard a lot of rifle fire. Then the mortars opened up again on us—falling all around—and WP burned my neck. But luckily none landed in the CP," Barrett said.

Barrett turned to look in the direction of the company area and saw Chinese everywhere, running along the airstrip, behind the tents. Mortars were exploding all over the place. Tracers crisscrossed the CP area.

The 3rd Platoon, on Barrett's left, was almost completely overrun. Once through, the Chinese zeroed in on Corley's CP and never let up. "I thought they would go right on to the battalion CP," Barrett said. "The Chinese missed a good opportunity. They spent the rest of the night trying to wipe out the company CP. They never succeeded."

But they gave the company some anxious moments. Once they

cracked through the 3rd Platoon, they overran the mortars and forced the CP to move. Some men in the 3rd stayed in their holes and played dead. Two were stripped of their clothing. One enemy soldier sat on a marine for two hours, thinking him dead. It was a lot warmer than sitting on the frozen ground.

With the 3rd Platoon overrun and more Chinese in the company area than marines, Barrett's left flank was wide open. His 3rd Squad had been hit hard, but the 2nd and 1st Squads were in good shape.

Ridge knew about the breakthrough, the danger it presented, and sent Lt. Grady Mitchell and twenty-five men over to help out. Sgt. E. J. Hanrahan saw them coming, recognized Mitchell's voice, and ran out to meet them.

Barrett watched, saw them appear on the skyline, tried to warn them, but got there too late. A Chinese machine gun opened up, and Mitchell was killed instantly. Hanrahan fell back against Barrett, knocking him to the ground.

"I'm hit! I'm hit!"

Barrett helped him back to their hole, cut through his clothes, and gave him a shot of morphine.

Visibility had been bad all night. It was still snowing, only now the flakes were the size of half dollars. Barrett spotted what appeared to be six figures coming toward him from the airstrip. He didn't realize they were Chinese until they began to talk. One of them tossed two concussion grenades into his abandoned tent, blowing lots of holes in it.

He watched them start to set up a machine gun to fire down into his lines and wondered, "How the hell am I going to stop them and still not lose the rest of the CP?" He had no grenades.

Moments later, he had no choice. The Chinese made the decision for him. One started walking back toward his CP carrying a Thompson.

When he was about fifteen yards away, Barrett jumped up, his carbine on full automatic, and fired. So did the Chinese.

"That lousy carbine fired one round," Barrett remembered. "Fortunately I hit him, and he was able to fire only about ten rounds."

Then his Thompson jammed, and as he bent over, either to clear his weapon or because of his wound, Barrett shot him again, with his .45. The Chinese had the Thompson firing now, but the rounds were going in all directions. Then a grenade took care of him and two others who had run over. At that moment, a Chinese grenade was tossed toward Barrett, who saw it coming and hugged the side of a dirt bank. He couldn't have pressed his body any tighter against it. The grenade bounced once and landed on top of his helmet.

"I brushed my right arm across my helmet just at the right moment to knock the grenade over the small dike I was lying against."

It went off, and Barrett wasn't injured. His runner, who was lying on top of the dike, was hit by shrapnel.

PFC T. E. Nelson heard the fighting in the CP area, turned a .30 around, and sprayed, killing all the Chinese there.

But some of the rounds reached the company area, and a .50 was set up over there catching Barrett's platoon CP in a deadly crossfire that continued until first light.

"Every time we would move, one or both of the machine guns would open up," Barrett said. "We found out next morning that they all thought we were dead and that anything that moved was a Chinese."

This was at about 1:00 A.M. on November 29. For the next few hours they lay out there in the snow, freezing, unable to do anything for themselves or the wounded.

"I knew that Hanrahan was freezing—his arms and legs were beginning to get hard, and I felt sure that my runner's hands and feet would freeze also," Barrett said. "The rest of us had to crawl around occasionally to keep the circulation going."

Even that was dangerous, because any movement drew fire.

Once behind marine lines, the Chinese didn't really know what to do. Most started looting. Others ran around aimlessly. There was no leadership at this point.

Skillful night fighters that they were, they could never seem to capitalize on their gains. Had they done so, the outcome would have been different, and marine losses would have been much higher.

A few Chinese raced past a frozen marsh and headed for the bright lights and the airfield. The engineers dropped their shovels, parked the earth-moving equipment, grabbed their weapons, went after the Chinese, and drove them off. Then they went back to their primary function —building the airfield—lights and all.

Fighting was still out of control both in front of and behind I and

H companies. You couldn't tell friend from foe. Tracers flew in all directions. Each round fired had as much chance of hitting a marine as a Chinese.

It was a rough night for young lieutenants. Many were killed in the first few minutes of fighting. It was equally rough for wiremen, whose job was to string phone lines from one unit to another. H Company's CP was surrounded for a time. So was the cooking area and the company supply dumps.

"It is my personal opinion that if the enemy had decided to effect a major breakthrough at this time, he would have experienced practically no difficulty," Corley said.

Battalion and company reserves consisted mostly of walking wounded.

"I'll tell you, after things started that first night, I sure as hell began to scratch my left ear and wonder what I'd do if there was a major breakthrough," Ridge said.

"There wasn't a moment that I was sure we could hold until after the British and George Company got there," he said. "I guess that was the first bit of confidence I remember having that I could hold."

So far, only H and I companies had been hit. The Chinese didn't appear to be seriously interested in any other area of the perimeter.

At about 2:30 A.M. the breakthrough was slowly plugged, the Chinese eliminated behind the lines, and order was restored in the H and I Company areas.

At 3:00 A.M. the Chinese were back, but in different areas. First they hit the south roadblock and were beaten back. Then Ridge heard gunfire coming from East Hill. Almost immediately the Chinese came over the top and down the front side, overrunning X Corps troops who were green, untested in battle, and ROK forces who had virtually no training. None could speak English, so there was no way of telling them what to do after the Chinese struck. One marine officer, Capt. John C. Shelnutt, was killed, and his radio operator, PFC Bruno Podolak, stayed in his hole and kept radio contact with marines at the base of the hill.

Ridge rushed a few tanks, some engineers, anyone he could find, toward the bottom of the hill. Hopefully they'd stop the Chinese, or at least slow them.

Marine engineer William R. Lentz, twenty-two, B Company, 1st

227

Engineer Battalion, had been on patrol on the hill when the Chinese came over the top. Shrapnel tore into an arm, his chest, and his neck, and he was helped to the bottom. "Honestly, I didn't think we'd get out of Hagaru," he said. "I've looked back and many times counted my blessings."

By 4:00 A.M. the situation was bleak. There was very little between the Chinese and General Smith's headquarters, where the division band provided security.

But again the Chinese failed to exploit the situation. And those who got inside the perimeter were quickly killed.

The six 105s of D Battery spouted flame all night. At times their fire was point-blank. Then they lobbed shells on the far side of East Hill to break up concentrations of Chinese in rear areas. With a perimeter of 360 degrees and Chinese everywhere, it was impossible not to hit something. So most of the twelve hundred rounds fired the night of the twenty-eighth and the morning of the twenty-ninth found a target.

"Off to the right and slightly behind us on a smaller hill the Chinese had four artillery pieces," artilleryman William J. Steele, nineteen, remembers.

Sometime after 4:00 A.M. the Chinese began returning fire. One round hit a fuel dump, and for a time it looked like everything might go up—gasoline, ammunition, the whole works.

The D Battery commander, Capt. Andrew J. Strohmenger, ordered five of his 105s to stop firing. He moved the sixth a few hundred yards away, then had it fire several rounds. Its flashes drew return fire from the Chinese, revealing their location.

Then all six howitzers opened up.

"I was told later that two of their guns were put out of action," Steele said. "Anyway, they never fired at us again."

Warrant Officer Lionel S. Reynolds's Radio Repair Platoon was on the northeastern perimeter, at the bottom of East Hill.

He had thirty-eight men, all technicians.

There were one Army lieutenant and sixteen soldiers under his command, too, who were to help with the repair of communication equipment.

There also were eight soldiers from units of the 7th Infantry Division that had been overrun on the eastern side of the reservoir.

"It was so goddamn cold we couldn't dig in," Reynolds said, "and we couldn't afford the gasoline to soften the ground."

So they had to improvise. He put his men behind eighty to ninety big wire reels, each weighing about a hundred pounds. They were about three feet across and provided pretty good cover.

Reynolds's group was the last line of defense. In front of him were five tanks, and in front of the tanks a very thin line of cooks, clerks, bakers, engineers, odds and ends from other units, a potpourri of not very much of anything in the way of combat troops. Not too far in front of them was the base of East Hill, and seven ravines that led to the top.

It was snowing so hard they couldn't see the tanks until they fired their cannon. At times there was heavy sleet and, as soon as it hit the ground, it froze, turning the ravines into ice-covered chutes.

They fired their weapons every few minutes just to make certain they hadn't frozen.

Reynolds assigned the Army lieutenant and his men to his left.

"He knew all their names, I didn't, so I wanted them to be together," Reynolds said. Even then he wasn't sure he'd done the right thing.

Reynolds and his NCO's shared one tent, the rest of the men another. They were crowded in pretty tightly, so body heat kept them fairly warm.

Not so the Army lieutenant.

"I saw him putting up this little pup tent, so I walked over and said, 'Why don't you sleep with your men? It'll be a lot warmer.' "

"No, I can't do that. I'm a first lieutenant."

"So when I left him he had one of his men helping him put up this little tent and they were having a helluva time trying to drive the pegs into the frozen deck."

Reynolds passed the word up and down the line: "No smoking. You can see the light of a cigarette for two hundred yards."

The Chinese knew where they were.

"They sent a couple of rounds in here and there just before dawn," Reynolds remembered. One of his men was working on the roof of a shed they'd hastily built in which they planned to work on the radios. But he had to hit the ground really fast, and he shouted at Reynolds:

"Gunner, I don't think there's bees around this goddamn place. . . . I think they found our range!"

229

Then the gunfire picked up. A couple of mortars joined in, and a few rounds fell short of the perimeter.

Reynolds checked his men frequently that night. He told the Army officer to do the same and that if any of his men were hit to get them to the collecting station immediately. He didn't want anyone freezing to death.

Sometime after 2:00 A.M. the Chinese lofted a few flares. Then machine guns sprayed the area, and mortar and artillery rounds began to fall inside the perimeter.

One round hit a fuel dump, and the entire area burst into flames.

Reynolds had one of his gunners spray it with his .30, puncturing all the fifty-five-gallon drums of fuel. They'd burn, but they wouldn't explode, and his men wouldn't be covered with flaming gasoline.

He could hear the fighting to the southwest, but it wasn't as heavy as earlier.

After 3:00 A.M. the Chinese came down the hill, broke through the outer defenses, and reached the valley, close to where the tanks were. The tankers gunned down many of the attackers. The others reached an area just in front of Reynolds's position. Reynolds emptied a clip into one about forty feet away, and with eight rounds in his chest, he still made it another twenty feet before he dropped.

"They were crazed, shouting, 'Kill! Kill! Kill marines!' " Reynolds said.

The fuel dump lit up the sky, and Reynolds's men were backlit, making them perfect targets.

"One guy ran over to try and put it out, but that was like tryin' to piss on the Chicago fire," Reynolds said.

The shooting continued in Reynolds's area until about 4:00 A.M. Three of his men were wounded.

Those who didn't die in their mad rush, turned and ran back toward East Hill. But it was a lot easier sliding down than going back up. They scrambled, clung to brush, tried to pull themselves up, but it was solid ice, and for every foot up, they slid back three. The tanks swung toward the base of the hill and fired point-blank.

"For a few seconds there were assholes, arms, legs . . . flying in all directions," Reynolds remembered. "I couldn't believe the slaughter I was seeing."

He shook himself out of a trance, got his feet back on earth, and began to check his men. The wounded were already on the way to the collecting station, so he headed toward his left flank to see how the Army had fared.

"There was a large craterlike hole over there with a lot of bodies in it, some partially covered by a large tarp," he said. "They weren't groanin' or moanin', so I knew they were dead."

But he didn't know how many. It was too dark to count.

He looked for the lieutenant, but he was nowhere to be seen.

"He's not here," his first sergeant told Reynolds, "but all those kids down there, I know."

"Well, get them over to the collecting station. We'll take them back with us."

He spoke to a few of the other soldiers, who hadn't huddled together, who had stayed at least five yards apart, who had survived because of it.

Stray rounds were still coming in, so everyone was down. By dawn, though, it was just a wild shot now and then, a round with no one's name on it.

That's when Reynolds first spotted the Army officer. He'd been gone about six hours, and Reynolds was upset.

He was walking slowly toward him, coming from the direction of a big culvert under a road about fifty feet from where the soldiers had died.

"You know you lost some of your men last night," Reynolds said. The lieutenant didn't seem too upset about it.

"I've been looking for you for hours," Reynolds said. "Where were you?"

"None of your fucking business!"

"You were in that goddamn culvert for six hours, you no-good son of a bitch!"

Then Reynolds decked him.

"I just went 'bang!' I let him have it. I put him on the ground."

Reynolds said he wrote a report on the incident but felt that the marines never forwarded it to the Army.

"I got a letter from one of his kids about two months after we got back from the reservoir, and that bastard got a Bronze Star."

The Chinese hit H and I companies the rest of the night, and it wasn't until just before dawn that they began to pull back. A few were still running around near the airfield, and Barrett heard Lt. H. F. Johnson,

H Company executive officer, yelling, "Come on, you engineers, let's run the bastards out of here!"

About ten minutes later, the breakthrough had been closed, the line restored. He wanted to rise up, to see what had happened, to check his platoons, but he was still worried about those machine guns. It just wasn't light enough yet to take a chance.

"I slowly worked my way up to the second squad, managing to get close enough to identify myself before they spotted me," Barrett said.

They were still picking off a few Chinese out in front. Others were taking wounded into the tent.

"I walked up and down the line in a daze," Barrett remembered. Then he saw Corley and Johnson coming toward him.

"They hugged me and I don't think anyone said anything."

Then Barrett sat down and cried, became ill, cried some more.

It was a time for crying.

This was the first real combat Barrett had seen. He'd taken over the platoon about three weeks earlier, and since then all he'd heard were a lot of sea stories from the men—the landing at Inchon, the fight for Seoul.

"I thought it was routine," he remembered.

When he talked with Corley a short time later he told him, "I'm not sure I can do this every night."

Then came the unpleasant task of counting casualties, checking the names, who made it, who didn't.

His platoon suffered three dead and fifteen wounded, and half the wounded were badly frozen. In front of his holes and just inside his platoon area he counted 104 Chinese dead. There were indications in the snow that many others had been pulled away.

He put half the men back in their holes and told the other half to get some rest.

Then he went over to the company to report. There were ten dead in H Company that night, plus four from attached units. Before Corley could enter his CP he had to drag four dead Chinese from the entrance. Bodies were everywhere.

The galley was full of holes. White phosphorus landed in their food, ruining everything. The water trailed was riddled, but this really didn't matter. The water had long since frozen.

It had been close. Some marines were down to one or two clips when dawn broke. Grenades were just about gone.

by Gen. Edward A. Craig.
Marine tank slides off a narrow, winding road on the east side of the Chosin Reservoir on November 25, 1950.

Above, a long column of marines moves slowly down the road from the Chosin Reservoir. The location is a few miles south of Koto-ri. The weather is clear but well below zero. December 10, 1950.

Opposite page, marines rest by the side of the road just south of Koto-ri as they head south toward the sea and safety. December 8, 1950.

Below, marines from 5th and 7th Regiments, after fighting off Chinese attacks for three days, prepare to break out of Yudam-ni and battle their way south to Hagaru-ri. November 29, 1950.

Marines wait while the Corsairs blast the Chinese from the hills alongside the road as the column moves toward Hagaru from Yudam-ni. No date.

Above, marines march south from Koto-ri in a blizzard and sub-zero weather down an icy mountain road toward Hungnam. December 9, 1950.

Below, Chinese Communist troops, wearing quilted winter uniforms, tennis shoes, some American footgear, are captured by men of C Company, 1st Battalion, 7th Regiment, south of Koto-ri. December 9, 1950.

Above, marines of 7th Regiment wait at a power plant just south of Koto-ri for engineers to truck in a Treadway bridge to replace a bridge destroyed by the Chinese. December 9, 1950.

Below, bodies of U.S. and British marines. U.S. Army soldiers and South Korean troops are gathered for burial in a common grave at Koto-ri. December 8, 1950.

Cpl. Charles E. Price from Chattanooga, Tennessee, sounds taps over fallen marine comrades at the cemetery in Hungnam. December 13, 1950.

Gen. O. P. Smith, commander of the 1st Marine Division, mourns fallen marines at burial services at a cemetery in Hungnam. December 13, 1950.

"Their fire discipline saved them," Barrett said. "They didn't shoot unless they had a target."

Chinese prisoners later estimated that 90 percent of the attacking force had been killed or wounded.

The marines at Hagaru had withstood their first night of fire. Hagaru was still theirs. Now, with the Corsairs overhead, the village was secure, at least until dark.

East Hill still was a problem. Although the Chinese did not take advantage of their breakthrough, they were still on top and in position to stop anything that moved along the road. So just after first light about two hundred marine, Army and South Korean troops, led by Myers, started up. It was a strange mix. Hardly anyone knew anyone else. None had ever fought or worked together as a unit. They had nothing that resembled a four-man fire team.

They were lightly armed—rifles, carbines, two grenades each, but all the ammunition they could carry.

There was one definite plus on their side: the Corsairs.

"Our plane assaults were very effective, especially the napalm attacks," remembered Lt. Robert E. Jochums, who led a makeshift platoon of clerks, typists, and truck drivers.

The ground pounders knew the value of close air support. They had a special relationship with the pilots, marine and Navy. "When I landed at Wonsan," Steele recalled, "I went right over [to the marines' 1st Air Wing] and looked at the planes. Marines always feel safe when they see a Corsair. At the reservoir we knew that if we could just hold out until daylight, the planes would be there. Sure enough, they were. They never failed us."

But the really good news at Hagaru this terribly cold morning of the twenty-ninth came from Koto-ri: Sitter's George Company was on the way north. So was an Army rifle company. And the British royal marine commandos, all traveling in an incredibly long convoy that included tanks, the last of the division's headquarters personnel, and assorted other units.

There were so many vehicles and men that the front could have reached Hagaru while the tail end was still in Koto-ri.

Ridge was delighted with the news. Now he'd have Sitter's riflemen to put on the hill. The commandos, about three hundred of them, were excellent fighting men. They'd already made a number of behind-the-lines raids on the western coast of North and South Korea.

There certainly was a place for them. And the soldiers, too.

"We were very, very short of front-line fighters," Bowser recalled. "We felt we needed them to hold Hagaru, because Hagaru was a very important cog. If it wasn't there when the 5th and 7th got there, they'd have a helluva time."

Myers's makeshift company of two hundred was struggling up East Hill with the help of artillery and mortar fire. But by the time they got close to the crest, only seventy-five men were left. A few had been wounded. Most had dropped from exhaustion. Try as they might, though, they just couldn't make it all the way up. They couldn't hold their ground, for that matter, and were forced to fall back near the foot of the hill and dig in.

But they did rescue Podolak, who had been busy radioing back the location of Chinese forces up there.

In the afternoon a second attack was launched by a platoon of engineers from A Company, 1st Engineer Battalion. They fought their way up the northern side but were pinned down by machine-gun fire, then were ordered back down and told to move several hundred yards to the northeast and try again.

So Lt. Nicholas Canzona led his twenty men back up, but again they were pinned down, and around dusk Capt. George W. King, A Company commander, 1st Engineer Battalion, told Canzona to bring his platoon back down and dig in for the night. It was a standoff.

The marines at Hagaru could only be proud.

They had held a Chinese division, the 58th, at bay for about twenty hours. Chinese dead covered the ground like leaves in an autumn wind from the southwest to the hill.

But they'd be back. Ridge knew it. So did every man there.

Fisher had his men dig their holes still deeper, string more wire, plant more mines. Fields of fire were improved. Corley's men did the same. Clips were loaded. Weapons checked, then spot-fired. Warming tents were full. Hot coffee was served to all hands. Warm food was ready, too.

Then it was wait for dark. The Chinese probably would strike from East Hill, because that's where they had the greatest success.

When would the relief forces from Koto-ri arrive? Everyone knew that a tank-led force from Hagaru had tried to crash through Chinese roadblocks and link up with a relief force from Koto-ri somewhere along the road between the two points. But the tanks from Hagaru were unable to break through the roadblocks on the twenty-eighth. They barely got outside the perimeter. And the marines from Koto-ri never got out of sight of the perimeter there. They would have to try again, but in much greater strength.

CHAPTER 10

HELL FIRE VALLEY

November 28, 1950; headquarters, 1st Regiment,
Koto-ri, 3:30 P.M.:

"We'll try again in the morning with a stronger force," Col. Lewis B. (Chesty) Puller told General Smith, at the same time wondering where he was going to get the men to do it.

As Puller was talking, the 41st Commando, British royal marines, G Company, 3rd Battalion, 1st Marine Regiment, and B Company of the Army's 7th Infantry Division entered the perimeter from the south. Here was the muscle Puller needed to crack through the ring of Chinese steel that bottled up the village. There would be no turning back in the morning.

Throughout the night, Puller and his chief of plans and operations, Maj. Robert E. Lorigan, organized the relief force. First they put Lt. Col. Douglas B. Drysdale, commander of the royal marines, in charge. Puller's orders to Drysdale were brief and to the point: Fight your way through to Hagaru. There must be no delay.

Drysdale then decided that his commandos would lead the breakout and take the first high ground on the road north. Then Sitter's G Company would pass through and take the next Chinese-held hill. It would be leapfrog tactically all the way to Hagaru, with the Army's B Company in reserve.

Total strength of the convoy, now called Task Force Drysdale, would be 922 men, 141 vehicles, and twenty-nine tanks.

Stacked against them would be the equivalent of three Chinese regiments, well dug in along the hilltops, behind every roadblock, concealed in ditches along both sides of the road.

Drysdale then went over to talk to his men, to Lt. Peter Thomas; to Cpl. Dave Brady; to Cpl. Don Saunchegrow of the U.S. marines who was driving a ton-and-a-half personnel carrier with twenty-five commandos in the back. "I couldn't understand a thing they were saying at first," he said. "They were talking a fast English with a lot of Scottish thrown in. What I needed was an interpreter."

"But I could tell right away they were one hell of a rough outfit. They were looking for a fight. Like a bomb looking for a place to go off," Saunchegrow added.

Drysdale told them to dig in for the night, that there would be warm food and fires in the morning, and soon thereafter they would lead a relief column north to surrounded Hagaru.

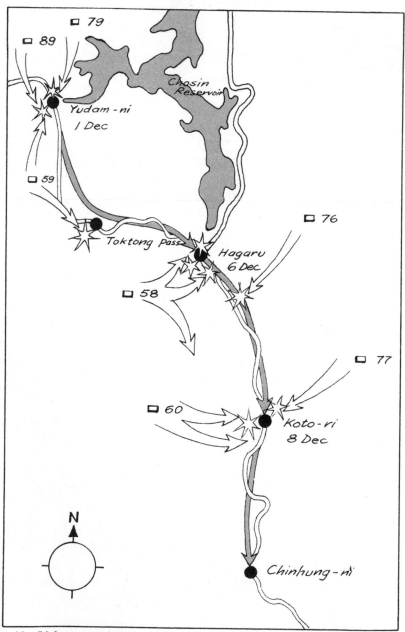

Map 10—Light arrows indicate Chinese divisions attacking Yudam-ni, Hagaru, and Koto-ri on November 28, 1950. Dark arrows show route of marines down the road toward the port of Hungnam.

"There will be heavy fighting," he told his men.

Then he left for night-long talks with Puller and his staff.

Digging in was impossible. Brady, a demolitions expert, had his men plant some charges, blow a number of holes in the ground, then toss their bags in. Saunchegrow climbed into the front of the truck, put the lower half of his body into his sleeping bag, the upper half into a poncho, and went to sleep.

Cpl. V. W. Organ chipped away at the frozen ground for an hour with his bayonet before he got a hole one square foot by four inches deep. He kept at it and in another hour had dug deep enough to find soft earth. "Wouldn't you know it, that's when the bloody picks and shovels arrived."

It was snowing very hard and growing colder by the minute, yet all the men slept soundly.

November 29, 1950: At dawn, the first thing Saunchegrow heard was someone shouting, "Where's the driver? Where's the driver?"

"It was Brady, running around the truck, looking in foxholes for me," Saunchegrow said. "He ran around that truck about twelve times shouting for me. I just lay there under about a foot of snow. It didn't bother me one damn bit 'cause I was still tired. Then he stuck a hand in the front seat so I started to get up.

"It must have scared hell out of him when I started shaking all that snow off me," Saunchegrow said. "He turned white and shouted, 'Oh, my God!' "

Then they headed for a fire to get warm and heat some food.

"I thought you were lost," Brady said.

"No, just tired."

Saunchegrow was a member of the division's Bath and Fumigation Detachment when he was told to drive over to where the royal marines were tented in Hungnam, load up, and drive them to Yudam-ni. "You should be back in a day," his commanding officer, Capt. James Dillis, said. Saunchegrow never suspected that it would lead to the ride of a lifetime.

Saunchegrow had a can of meat and beans that never really got warm, Brady a can of three meatballs—the bottom one burned black, the middle one slightly warm, the one on top still frozen.

The worst part of the morning was when the campfires began to explode as they finished eating.

"Some fool forgot to take all the grenades out of the canisters before throwing them into the fire," Saunchegrow said. "There are three grenades to a canister. Whoever it was only took two grenades out, then tossed the canisters into the flames with one grenade still in there. Several men were wounded by shrapnel."

Task Force Drysdale, 9:30 A.M.: The convoy came under fire before it left the perimeter, and once on the road, casualties began to mount. Corpsmen and ambulances tried to get the early wounded back to Koto-ri, but even this was difficult, so a platoon of riflemen went out to help.

Drysdale was in his jeep close to the head of the convoy. The commandos had thirty-one vehicles spaced about fifteen to twenty yards apart. Saunchegrow's truck, *Old Faithful,* No. 10426, was near the end of the British section.

Drysdale's leapfrog plan worked at the beginning. His men took the first hill, although Chinese opposition was stronger than expected.

Cpl. Jerry Maill, fire controller for the British 81mm mortar platoon, stood in the center of the road with Drysdale and his staff and watched the commandos take the first high ground northeast of the road. Binoculars were tight against his eyes as he watched the fighting. As he listened through earphones to the chatter between friendly units, it occurred to him that there were an awful lot of enemy troops up there, "Much more than we had expected.

"I looked around and suddenly realized that I was standing there alone. I saw the old man and his staff in a ditch waving and shouting but I couldn't understand what they were saying," he said. So he took the earphones off and right away recognized the very rapid tat-tat-tat-tat of a Chinese machine gun. "One of the bullets almost took my beret off. I got the message and needed no further invitation to join them in the ditch," Maill recalled.

The fighting on the hill was over in thirty minutes, and the commandos prepared to move on to their next objective. "Even before our troops were off the hill, the enemy reappeared as if by magic to reoccupy it," Maill said. "I knew then this would be a very long night."

"My part of the column came under attack almost from the outset," Organ said. "Running fights were the order of the day. Communications were chaotic from the beginning. The only way to relay orders was to shout them, and that didn't always work.

"We took the first hill, the Americans went up the second," he recalled. "It seemed like we were always getting in and out of the trucks, going up a hill or down a hill. All the while the Chinese were shooting at us. One marine near me took a bullet in both ankles while riding in the truck."

Then they came to the third hill, 1182, where the Chinese put up their stiffest opposition. Mortars, machine guns, and rifles forced the column to halt. Drysdale ordered the commandos and Sitter's marines to break off contact and return to the road.

The attack north had been stopped at 11:30 A.M., before it had really gotten under way.

Drysdale got Puller on the radio and told him the situation, that there were many, many more Chinese than they had anticipated.

Puller told him to sit tight, that more armor would be available to him at about 1:00 P.M. Drysdale decided to do just that—wait for more tanks before continuing the attack toward Hagaru.

Task Force Drysdale, 1:30 P.M.: Seventeen tanks were at the front as the convoy renewed its snaillike pace north. Drysdale wasn't too happy with this, though. He wanted the tanks spread throughout the column, not bunched up at the front, but the tank commander, Capt. Bruce Clark, felt otherwise.

The order of march was now the seventeen tanks up front; G Company with twenty-two vehicles; the commandos with thirty-one vehicles; B Company, en route to join the 31st Regiment, which was to the east of the Chosin Reservoir and close to the Yalu River, with twenty-two vehicles; headquarters and assorted marine units with sixty-six vehicles; and twelve tanks bunched at the rear. Four Corsairs were overhead. Artillery support came from Koto-ri. As the convoy got closer to Hagaru, the artillery support would then come from there.

No sooner had the convoy begun to move than Sitter's men were raked by machine-gun fire. The going was still slow because the tanks had to stop frequently to blast roadblocks, dodge craters in the road, and blast the Chinese off the ridges.

It was a day spent jumping in and out of trucks, only fewer were jumping back in each time.

Navy and marine pilots reported the hills ahead alive with Chinese. They said it looked as if entire hills were moving. There was no shortage of targets. Greatly concerned, Drysdale sent a tank force up the road to see how bad the situation was. Almost immediately the tanks were back, and Clark told Drysdale he felt the tanks could fight their way through but the trucks and the men could not.

Wounded were piling up at an alarming rate. Radio communication among units in the convoy had ceased to exist. Runners were now being used, but many of them were killed. Only Clark's tank radio kept the convoy in touch with Koto-ri or Hagaru. The individual units began to lose their integrity. When the column was halted by enemy fire, the trucks would disperse along the roadside. But when they got back on the road, it wasn't always in the order in which they had left it. Thus infantry units became mixed with support troops, marines with soldiers, commandos with U.S. marines. And when the trucks did roll, it wasn't necessarily with the same men who had jumped off. In the confusion that followed a firefight, the men often climbed aboard the nearest vehicle, not the one they had been on. Thus the command situation was suffering now.

To push on could mean disaster if the Chinese were massed ahead in anywhere near the strength reported. To do otherwise could be fatal to the garrison at Hagaru and the ten thousand marines at Yudam-ni.

So Drysdale had Clark radio Puller at Koto-ri, explained the situation to him, and asked if he should continue on to Hagaru.

Puller then contacted General Smith while Drysdale, worried and concerned, waited for a reply. Meanwhile, the convoy moved very slowly along the road.

Pugh lay in the hole he had scraped out of the sand after the Chinese had shot him in the knee. He couldn't feel his feet. His hands pained him terribly. He raised his head slowly, looked around, and saw nothing. The Chinese who had swarmed over the area like ants on honey were gone. He lay there for a few hours, unable to move, wondering what would happen to him. He thought he heard gunfire, but he wasn't certain. Perhaps he was imagining it. He'd lapsed in and out of consciousness a number of times since they had shot him. Then he heard it again. Rifle fire. Then machine guns. The thump-thump of mortars. He lifted his head in the direction of the road, about seventy-five yards away, and saw a long line of tanks, men, and trucks moving slowly in his direction. He managed to raise an arm, and he hollered for about half an hour. Then a marine officer saw him, went out and carried him back, and put him in the back of a jeep-trailer.

Patrick Murphy, corporal, royal marines, was riding in a truck loaded with communications equipment, much of which had been shot to pieces. Just behind were the men of the Army's B Company.

"The early part of the day was quite uneventful," he said. "We moved up the road slowly, breaking a few roadblocks here, chasing some Chinese out of the paddies. We spent most of our time with Baker Company clearing the hills to the right and the paddy fields to the left." Late in the afternoon, he said, "the firing became heavier and for the first time we ran into mortar fire. Minutes later the trucks came to a standstill and we dismounted and took cover by the side of the road. A truck about six ahead of our own was burning. Mortar bombs were falling all around it," he said. Now the Chinese were mortaring to his right. One round hit an ammunition truck and blew it sky high. Bodies flew through the air.

Murphy raised his head above the gully he was in and saw that the trucks were stopped on a straight stretch of road and that the Chinese had isolated twelve to fourteen vehicles in the middle of the long convoy. They couldn't advance because a burning truck blocked the road. Nor could they go back because of the ammunition truck that was afire. They tried, but couldn't push them off the road. They were trapped, caught between the burning trucks. The Chinese systematically began to destroy the rest of the vehicles that couldn't move. It was like a shooting gallery, the difference being that the ducks were not moving.

"Strung out along the road with the enemy holding the high ground on either side wasn't the way we liked to fight," Maill recalled. "All they had to do from their positions was point a gun downhill, fire, and they'd win a prize."

"From the time we woke up there was fighting," Saunchegrow said. "You could hear the big guns from Hagaru firing. They never stopped."

Brady had climbed into the other truck carrying the weapons platoon, and Maill was beside Saunchegrow. The two vehicles brought up the rear of the 41st Commando. "As we went up the road, the hills seemed to be getting closer," Maill recalled. "Pretty soon Chinese just sat up there and dropped Molotov cocktails on us, grenades, anything with a charge in it. As we moved up, the fighting picked up, grew in intensity. And the Chinese got bolder. They'd get closer." The 922 men in the convoy were vastly outnumbered by the Chinese.

"Imagine thousands of people standing on a corner to watch a parade. Then drop a mortar round or an artillery shell in the middle. You know you are going to wipe out a lot of them. Well, that's the way it was with the Chinese, only they were back before the smoke cleared," Maill said.

Saunchegrow's section of the convoy was getting hit pretty hard. Every time they stopped, mortar shells fell on them. A few trucks carrying Army troops had been hit and were on fire. Soon the convoy came to a halt again, then eased off to the side of the road. Minutes later several tanks roared by, heading toward the front, where the heaviest fighting seemed to be.

Saunchegrow spotted a long line of Chinese crouched in a ditch along the road off in the distance, waiting for the convoy to pass. Their arms were in position to hold a rifle, but none had a weapon. They were frozen.

"Apparently somebody had come by and taken their rifles after they froze," Saunchegrow said. "There was a long row of them. God, it must have been a mile. Covered with ice and snow. All frozen."

At 4:00 P.M. the trucks were rolling again, a few yards, stop, get out, fight again, then leap back in or get left behind. On to the next roadblock. "We were getting shot at all the time, moving or stopped," Saunchegrow said. "We stopped counting the bullets that hit the truck, but they never shot out the windshield or any of the tires. I don't know why."

At 5:00 P.M. the convoy had six miles to go to reach Hagaru, and Saunchegrow was beginning to wonder if they would make it.

The marine MP's, twenty-eight strong, were just below the middle of the convoy in four vehicles with their gear, heading for Hagaru to set up a POW stockade. Sgt. James Nash, thirty, was one of them.

"It was stop and go. We'd stop and blow up a roadblock, then we'd get back in the trucks and go on to the next one. We were like ducks in a shooting gallery. You know, going across in front of you."

The Corsairs were still overhead, bombing and strafing and napalming. But it didn't do much good. As soon as the planes were out of sight, the Chinese were back.

"I think the convoy must have stretched all the way to Hagaru," Nash said. "I was told later that some of it never got out of Koto."

A short time later the trucks came to a dead stop. Nothing on the road moved. There wasn't time to get the trucks off to the side of the road where possible.

"There were trucks in front of and behind us burning," Nash said. "We tried to turn around and head back to Koto, but we couldn't. They were burning and exploding all around us.

"As darkness fell, we were sitting there staring at each other, and there was nothing we could do. We wound up between a rock and a hard place. Stuck.

"They had us in a perfect spot for elimination," Nash recalled. "We were cut off at both ends."

At this point, the convoy was sliced in two.

The reply from General Smith left no doubt how serious the situation was: "Come ahead at all costs."

"I talked to Drysdale," Bowser said. "I told him, 'We need you guys here or we might not be here to talk about it.'

"I told him that you will have as much trouble going back to Koto-ri as you will going forward to Hagaru. . . . Whatever momentum you've got going, you've got it going in the direction of us," Bowser added.

"Aye, aye, sir, we'll be there," Drysdale replied.

"In view of this, there was nothing to do but get back into transport and, with tank support, attempt to force a way through along the road," Drysdale said.

"We had gained little ground, taken a lot of casualties," Maill said, "and the opposition up ahead in failing light promised to be as stiff as that already encountered. The old man was ordered to smash through to Hagaru at all costs, and this seemed to be to us a selfish disregard to our lovely English blood."

Nevertheless, they waited for the order to board the trucks as night fell.

The road at this point was only about five feet wider than the trucks. On the right side there was a gully about three feet lower than the road, then a few yards back a railway line that was about six feet high from the bottom of the gully. Beyond that there was a flat stretch for about 150 to 160 yards, then a series of hills that seemed to go straight up, affording the Chinese an excellent field of fire. On the left side of the road there was a flat paddy field for about two hundred to three hundred yards.

"Fine place for an ambush," Maill thought, looking down the road to a point where the hills seemed to come right down and touch the edge of the gully.

This was the beginning of Hell Fire Valley.

"The man ordered a breakthrough at all costs," Maill said, "and that is what we set out to do in the failing light of that bloody awful day in that bloody awful valley.

"It was our intention to fly like a bat out of hell up that road to Hagaru, stopping for nothing or no one," he said.

Drysdale ordered the men back into the trucks for what everyone hoped would be the last time and, with the tanks up front, began to run the gauntlet to Hagaru. With luck, some would make it. Many would not. Many would die in Hell Fire Valley. Others would spend three years in Chinese prisoner-of-war camps.

Left behind on the southern side of the burning vehicles were a few commandos, most of the Army's B Company, all those from the division headquarters, and personnel from all remaining miscellaneous units.

There were two parts to the road now. Those on the front, or northern part, were in a race to reach Hagaru. Those on the southern half were either trapped or trying to turn around and get back to Koto-ri.

The truck carrying the second section of the heavy weapons platoon was among those on the southern section of the road. However, twenty-four hours later, Cpl. Ed Cruse led the commandos, all frostbitten, through hills infested with Chinese and reached Hagaru and as much safety as could be found in a small village surrounded by hordes of enemy soldiers and undergoing attacks day and night.

Saunchegrow's PC, 10426, was now the last vehicle in the front part of the convoy and was taking fire from both sides of the road. Behind, burning trucks brightened the frozen landscape as the Chinese started to close in on the trapped men and their vehicles.

G Company, right behind the tanks, was catching hell. A withering fire raked their trucks. At every roadblock it seemed to increase in intensity.

A grenade sailed through the night and landed in the back of a truck just as the marines were jumping out to blast away another roadblock.

Only one man saw it land, then heard it clatter around. PFC William Baugh shouted a warning to the others, then took the full force of the explosion with his body. He died a short time later, but no one else was wounded.

Cpl. Robert Kopsitz, a radio operator, was near the head of the convoy with Sitter's G Company when they started to run through Hell Fire Valley. "It was hell. The firing was terrible," he said. "The flashes from the guns looked like a million fireflies.

"We'd break through a roadblock, go a few yards, then stop and do it again. The Chinese were always waiting when we stopped. And they were getting closer, growing bolder," he said. "We'd get out one side of the truck and go into the ditch, they'd be in the ditch on the other side of the road."

Then the Chinese rolled grenades across the road under the trucks and the marines rolled them back.

"It was just a question of where they went off. Our side, the other side, or under the trucks," Kopsitz said. "We lost a lot of trucks that way."

The Chinese had mortars in the hills and never stopped lobbing shells onto the road the entire night.

"We were losing a lot of trucks and taking a lot of wounded," Kopsitz recalls, "and we didn't have any place to put them.

"When the trucks were ready to make a dash to the next road-block, we'd get a warning to get all the wounded in, then we'd be off," he said.

"I didn't think we were going to make it. I don't think anyone else thought he was going to make it, either."

Then the truck Kopsitz was in roared through the last roadblock. Next stop, Hagaru. They could see the lights ahead where the engineers were building an emergency landing strip inside the perimeter. The trucks were still taking fire from both sides of the road, but not nearly as heavy as a few minutes earlier and far less deadly. "The wounded were stacked in the truck and we were really rolling," Kopsitz recalled.

Then a grenade landed in the front, killing the driver and the shot-gun. The truck veered sharply left, ran over a cliff, turned over twice, and broke through the ice of the Changjin River. Bodies were hurled through the tarp as the six-by flew through the air.

"As we started down, I remember thinking, 'Here we go down to eternity in a truck,'" Kopsitz said. Another radio operator, Wayne

Connors, landed in the river. "I pulled him out. We pulled all the wounded out," Kopsitz said. "We had to walk them, keep them moving, so they wouldn't freeze to death.

"They turned to ice that quick," he said.

There was still firing above them on the road. They could see the muzzle flashes and hear rifles and machine guns. So they decided to stay in the low ground where they were and try to walk to Hagaru.

They lost everything they had in the river—weapons, food, dry clothes. "Hagaru had better be close," Kopsitz thought as they walked between the river and the road, staying as low as possible, often moving in a crouch.

"Connors was like a robot, he was so cold," Kopsitz recalled. "He was walking stiff-legged. He couldn't move his arms."

They had gone about two hundred yards, then were unexpectedly challenged by a machine-gun outpost on the Hagaru perimeter just before 8:00 P.M. They had made it. Moments later, they passed through the lines and were put in warming tents for the rest of the night.

PC 10426, royal marines, Hell Fire Valley, 9:00 A.M.: The lead tanks had crashed through the swarming Chinese and reached Hagaru. Sitter's G Company reached the village, too, although their casualties were high.

But the commandos were still on the road, caught in the full fury of the Chinese assault in Hell Fire Valley.

Every other truck seemed to be on fire. When one vehicle was shot to pieces, the others had to stop until it was pushed off the road. This wasn't easy when it had to be done under heavy fire. "When this happened, we all bailed out to the side of the road to return fire, which came from all sides now," Maill said. "The vehicles sitting on the road were now perfect targets, and the Chinese didn't miss many."

Maill had set up a .30 at the side of the road. He'd just locked in the belt when someone shouted, "Back into the trucks! Let's go!"

"No sooner was this shouted than the truck was off, and before I had the gun dismounted," Maill said. "I was tearing along the road after the truck lugging the machine gun and surpassing Roger Bannister's four-minute mile.

"I reckon I broke it before Bannister did. I was in full kit. The enemy tactics were clear now. He was cutting the convoy into small pieces and carving up the bits at his leisure. I didn't want to be left behind as one of those bits."

He caught up with 10426, tossed the machine gun aboard, then jumped in the back, gasping for air.

This was the pattern all the way up the road, from the moment they left Koto until they arrived at Hagaru. They would pass burning or knocked-out vehicles with firefights going all around them. "No one stopped to see if they could assist," Maill said. "We all had our hands full with our own firefights, and the order had been clear: Break through at all costs.

"We were determined that somebody would, even if it was only one man," he added.

The windshield was still intact and the tires still hadn't been hit. But the rest of 10426 had been peppered. It looked like a sieve. Bullets pinged off the metal sides; others went through the tarp that covered the back, hitting men who had already been hit.

"I don't know how those guys stayed in the truck," Saunchegrow said. "The wooden floor had long since been blown away. We ran over a lot of grenades and land mines, and the only things left were some metal struts. They had their packs on top of the frame, so I guess that was the only thing that kept them from falling through."

Then, a few trucks ahead of 10426, a grenade went off under a six-by, the gasoline tank blew up, and flames and marines soared sky high. The trucks stopped, wounded were carried to the other vehicles, the burning truck was shoved to the side, and the convoy was on its way again. But not for long. A few hundred feet and the trucks came to another halt. Commando Frank Jones jumped over the side of his truck and landed in a ditch with Chinese soldiers "whose terrified reaction was to jump out and run like hell," Maill recalled. "Frank was so stunned he didn't even shoot at them. But it does indicate just how close they were to the trucks."

At this stage Maill had no idea where the rest of his platoon was. Saunchegrow's PC was still under continuous fire from automatic weapons from all directions. Commandos already wounded in the back continued to get hit again while 10426 ran the gauntlet.

"As we passed through villages the enemy stood in doorways and hurled grenades at us and fired submachine guns," Maill said. One of them burst a few feet from the left side of his head, and his ear rang for several days.

259

"I tried to find some method of operating the .30 from the back of the truck so that we could use it while on the move," Maill said, "but it presented a danger to our driver, for if we had hit a pothole or swerved violently while firing, poor old Saunche might have taken a burst up the arse."

Once again the trucks were forced to stop, either by a roadblock or a burning vehicle ahead. The commandos piled out and took to the ditch on the right. Others headed for a nearby village to try to drive the Chinese back toward the hills.

"I went around one side of a building," Saunchegrow recalled, "and ran into this Chinese or North Korean soldier who was coming around from the other side. The first thing I saw was this bayonet. Like an idiot, I grabbed it and pushed it down. Well, it knocked the rifle out of his hands and scared him and me. He took off across the field and I took off for the truck and nobody fired at anybody."

But Saunchegrow didn't have his gloves on and received a nice slice across three fingers. He didn't notice it until sometime later because "I was too scared and too cold.

"We took off in the truck again . . . got the hell out of there because they were really laying it in on us," Saunchegrow said.

He had the gasoline pedal on the floor as 10426 roared up the road, around burning trucks, the dead, the dying. He worried about the wounded in the back. He thought they must be taking a fearful battering, not only from enemy gunfire but from the shell holes as well. Saunchegrow guided the truck around most of them, but it was impossible to miss them all.

"We came up on the first part of the convoy and they were just getting hit by the worst part of the attack," Saunchegrow said. "We could see trucks on fire and guys in sitting positions being blown off the trucks. They had been sitting on the back of what must have been an ammunition truck, their legs dangling over the side, firing at the Chinese, who were everywhere now. Some were so close you could have kicked them.

"The cargo just exploded and there they were, in a sitting position, riding out into the night, oh, maybe twenty-five feet," Saunchegrow said. "But I don't recall any of them being hurt."

He stopped 10426. Some of them climbed in the back. He gathered other wounded, who had been lying by the roadside, and put them in the rear of a six-by that was now behind the PC, while other commandos took to a ditch to fight off the Chinese.

Saunchegrow then ran to the rear of the truck and unhooked a three-hundred-gallon water trailer he was towing. The tongue hit the ground and the tank collapsed—flat. "There were so many holes in it there was nothing left to hold it up," Saunchegrow said. The water had long since leaked out.

Saunchegrow then ran to the front of the truck, started to climb in, then saw Maj. Dennis Aldrich walking around as though he were in a park on a Sunday morning. "Which one of you chaps lost a glove? Come on, now, you're gonna need it before this is over!" he shouted. "Which one of you? Look around!"

"But that was Dennis," Saunchegrow said. "When we'd stop, someone always seemed to lose a piece of equipment—a glove, canteen, something that would be needed later—and Dennis would always walk up and down the road trying to find the person that lost it."

By this time the truck was a beat-up pile of metal. There were just bits of wood attached to the struts. The sleeping bags were still there. "If it weren't for them, we would have lost a lot more men," Saunchegrow said. "We hit one land mine that must have lifted the rear end three feet off the ground."

Mechanically, though, 10426 was in tip-top shape. It was also very lucky. It had to be to get that far.

"Eventually we came within sight of Hagaru," Maill said. "They were constructing an airstrip by arc light, which gave us a false sense of being home and dry."

A few hundred yards in front of them, the Chinese had attacked and set afire seven trucks. They were burning furiously. One, carrying ammunition, exploded just as 10426 rounded a curve. "The road was truly blocked now," Maill recalled, "and a fierce firefight was developing."

Running figures, Chinese and commandos, were lit up by flames from the burning vehicles. Bullets were flying. There was great confusion as the commandos tried to figure out just what to do, where they were, where to go.

"To our left front bulldozers chugged to and fro, leveling the airstrip, illuminated like a Fourth of July celebration," Maill said, "while to our right front, men were shooting hell out of each other, illuminated by burning trucks."

They couldn't move up the road any farther, not a yard, not a foot, not inches. This was as far as they could go. And they had picked up a lot of wounded from the burning vehicles ahead.

"So we decided to put all our wounded on our truck," Maill recalled, "throw a ring of commandos around it, and fight across country, which had leveled out some, toward Hagaru, and avoid that mess on the road."

When they left the road and headed for the paddy field, 10426 was moving at ten to fifteen miles an hour, which was much too fast for the wounded.

"How are you guys going?" Saunchegrow shouted.

"We can make it!" a voice shouted back.

Nevertheless, he slowed the truck to about two miles an hour, barely crawling, so they would be more comfortable.

As soon as they decided to go across country via the paddys, Maill mounted the .30 on the hood, then stretched his body near the windshield and fired across Saunchegrow's line of vision at enemy troops back on the road. Thomas, riding up front again, had a stranglehold on Maill's legs so he wouldn't slide off. Pvt. Dick Twigg, a young commando in Maill's platoon, hooked one leg around the spare tire for support and held the tripod while Maill fired.

"I was scared stiff," Saunchegrow recalled, "but you didn't even think about it because it was always the other guy who was gonna get hit."

A muzzle flash almost blinded Saunchegrow, so Maill stopped firing and put another of his men with Twigg just in case they needed some rapid fire in a hurry. Then he walked ahead of the truck over rough ground, directing Saunchegrow into the best possible path to try to give the wounded a smooth ride. "I was very much aware that there was at least one head wound in the truck," Maill said.

Saunchegrow took one last look back at the road they had just left and saw a long line of burning vehicles, perhaps twenty, and Chinese, as thick as bees in a hive, running around on the ground, hurling grenades, firing at the commandos, who were but a few yards distant. Another truck had followed Saunchegrow off the road, and both were moving very slowly through the frozen paddy, trying to attract as little attention as possible. After they had gone about two miles, Saunchegrow guided 10426 back to the road, where they picked up some walking wounded who had escaped from Hell Fire Valley and continued in the direction of Hagaru.

The truck had been on the road only a few minutes when Saunchegrow heard a voice. He didn't know if it was English or Chinese but thought, "Here we go again," and slid as much of his body below the front dash as he could just in case someone started spraying.

Then he heard it again, and he relaxed. English. Americans.

"Who goes there?"

"Peter, in his typical English voice, turned to me and said, 'It's the first time in my life I'm actually tickled pink to hear a Yank's voice.' "

Then he answered the unseen challenger, shouting, "This is 41st Commando, royal marines." Then they passed into the Hagaru perimeter.

"Glad to have you fellows here," one marine shouted at the commandos, "but who gave you the map to our minefield?"

"What minefield?" a commando hollered back.

"The minefield you've just come through!"

"No one can deny that a marine's life is eventful and at times charmed," Maill said.

They had smashed through at all costs, as ordered, and the marines were delighted to have them at Hagaru.

"But we had to wait until first light to count the cost," Maill said. "The supporting tanks had left us to our own devices and raced on ahead and most of them seemed to have survived."

"We had started off with 900 fighting men one morning, of whom 250 were royal marine commandos. By next morning, well less than four hundred had reached Hagaru," he said.

"All we had left in the world was the clothes we stood in, our weapons, and our mates, but they were thin by now, and many familiar faces were missing. My machine-gun/mortar platoon had really taken a pounding, and only Cpl. Buck Taylor and myself remained out of the noncoms along with only a handful of marines.

"Considering that we had been opposed by three regiments, it's a wonder that any of us made it."

Drysdale, wounded, bleeding, went straight to Bowser's tent.

"I remember him telling me that he had a helluva time," Bowser said. "He was very apologetic about some of the things that had happened, because he felt they could have been avoided," Bowser added.

"Well, Doug, there's no use having recriminations about it," Bowser said. "You're here, and we're damn glad to see you, and if we go down, we'll all go down together."

Specifically, Drysdale was upset over the use of the tanks. He wanted them dispersed throughout the convoy instead of clustered at the front and the rear, as they were.

"That was the hard-nosed tank commander of ours, [Lt. Col. Harry T.] Milne. He indoctrinated those kids so well that we had a helluva time with them again . . . going south. We finally overrode him and told him 'this is the way it's going to be,' " Bowser explained.

"He was a big panzer type," Bowser explained. "He wanted tanks supporting tanks all the time. He was concerned that if tanks couldn't support tanks, then he might lose them one at a time.

"Of course, if there ever was a time for him not to worry about that, this was it, because this was truly a tank-infantry thing, and not a tank-tank thing."

Task Force Drysdale, 2:00 A.M.: There were still more than four hundred commandos, marines, and soldiers caught both north and south of the point where the convoy was split in two. Some were still in Hell Fire Valley. Others were racing back to Koto-ri. But most were caught in a no-man's-land and couldn't move an inch in either direction. For the next few hours a number of trucks, tanks, and men slipped back to Koto-ri as best they could.

Those still on the southern half of the road dug in and waited for the inevitable.

"It was so quiet you could hear the snow falling," Nash remembered. "It was very late and very cold. We'd stolen some Army parkas from a field hospital at Hungnam before we started up the road, but we were still freezing.

"Every now and then a chill would run up and down my back, wondering what would happen next," he added.

"All of a sudden, out across those snowy hills, you could hear the bugles," Nash said. "First from one direction, then another. And another. All around us. It was their way of letting us know we were completely surrounded."

Then they heard the whistles. Again, from all directions.

"Then everything hit," Nash said. "Mortars, machine guns. They really lit into us."

Some of the men were using the trucks as cover, but machine-gun fire from the paddies kept coming at low level—under the trucks—and hitting them in the legs, forcing them to take cover in a ditch. It was safer, but you couldn't see the enemy as well.

"We were taking fire from every direction now," Nash recalled. The man with the most presence of mind seemed to be Lloyd V. Dirst, a warrant officer who was in charge of the twenty-eight marine MP's. "He was the only one there who had his wits about him," Nash said. "He kept us firing, told us what to do, tried to keep us organized.

"He walked out into the field to direct our fire against the Chinese. He defied their gunfire—ignored it completely," Nash said. He was about fifty yards out when shrapnel hit him in the back of the head. Nash saw him go down, jumped out of the ditch, ran out, and dragged him back through the snow. He got him into the gully, where Army medics and Navy corpsmen worked on him.

The Chinese were steadily closing in, slowly, methodically.

"They came at us in single file from a number of directions," Nash said. "We just kept knocking them down, like shooting ducks, but they just kept pouring in. The bugles, whistles, shouting, it never stopped.

"It was every man for himself now," Nash said. They were just about out of ammunition. They had more wounded on their hands than they could handle. And the Chinese were just yards away.

"Then I heard that down the road we were negotiating to surrender," Nash said.

There were only a handful of commandos in this section of the convoy, perhaps twelve at the most, and they had no officer or senior noncommissioned officer with them.

"As a consequence, we just took up firing positions in the gully looking over the railroad tracks toward the hills," Murphy said. But they were firing blind, trying to hit noises in the dark or the flash of a weapon, which wasn't too effective. The Chinese all seemed to have automatic weapons, and they just sprayed, which at times was devastating.

Lt. Joe Giddings of the Army grabbed Murphy and a few others and crept up the gully until they reached a point where they could observe the road about as well as possible on a moonless night. "From this position I was able to fire on the enemy crossing the road," Murphy said. "They were about thirty to forty yards away, dressed in white. The result was quite effective.

"We couldn't see the Chinese in the hills, but we could hear the bugles—they were not very melodious—and the screaming as they raced down toward the road and us," Murphy added.

He stayed with Giddings for about an hour, but then his carbine began to malfunction. "The action was freezing," he said. "It was bitterly cold that night, so we could not remain still ourselves for very long, as we would start to freeze."

Also, ammunition was very low. "I could hear the calls from down the gully asking for more ammunition," he said. So Murphy crawled back down the ditch, taking ammunition from the dead and wounded and distributing it to the men along the railroad bank. "I was shocked at the number of our troops who were wounded," he recalled.

Murphy made his way back to Giddings to pass out what ammunition he had left. "He didn't answer me. I think Joe was dead," Murphy said. "By now it was really noisy. The Chinese were charging down the hill. The bugles were continually sounding off. The troops that were in the gully wounded were being hit again and again, as we had nowhere to put them out of danger."

The Chinese had stopped crossing the road in front of Murphy—it was too costly. So he moved to the railway line and, although he could hear the enemy talking only a few yards away, he could not see them. So he fired at the noises, too.

Then someone down the gully suggested that they attempt to find an escape route, since it looked as if they would either be killed or taken prisoner soon.

"I don't remember who it was, although I am sure there were a couple of royal marines in the scheme," Murphy remembered. "We crossed the road and tried to make our way back down. We hadn't gone far until we ran into a group of Chinese in the dark. They were close enough to touch," he said. "But the group was too much for us to take on in a firefight, and we didn't know how many others were close by, so we had to retreat back across the road to the gully."

The lack of ammunition and grenades was now critical. Murphy made another foray down the gully but found nothing. "All the time the Chinese were hurling grenades at us," he said. "It looked like summer rain falling."

Fortunately, most of them were duds. The few that did explode, however, took a heavy toll.

But ammunition was the major problem. Murphy had none. Nor did any of the men near him.

"I walked out onto the road to search what was left of a couple of trucks when I heard an American speaking to me. I could not distinguish who he was at that time but he was very concerned with the situation, particularly the wounded men."

They stood beside the hulk of one of the trucks, lit a cigarette, then introduced themselves.

He was Maj. John N. McLaughlin, a U.S. marine and the senior officer there. Lt. Col. Arthur A. Chidester, the assistant division G-4 and the senior officer south of the roadblock, had been wounded.

"He asked me how I felt about trying to talk the Chinese into letting us evacuate our wounded," Murphy said. "I said I thought it was a good idea."

They both knew, too, that it would be light in about two hours, at about 6:00 A.M., and then marine air would be back. If they could get an airdrop of supplies, they stood a good chance of fighting their way back to Koto. But they had to stall, negotiate, talk until daylight. Could they fool the Chinese?

"We shook hands," Murphy recalls, "and started down the road."

They had gone about two hundred yards when they heard Chinese shouting. They stopped, then approached slowly, their hands upraised. They had left their weapons behind. They were suddenly confronted by dozens of Chinese. "We had apparently walked into their battle headquarters," Murphy said.

They attempted to make themselves understood but got no reply in English.

"Initially I demanded a CCF surrender," McLaughlin recalls, "but it made little impression."

"Again we tried by signs to get our message across," Murphy said. "All we wanted was to get our wounded to a safe area. However, the Chinese either did not, or did not want to, understand."

Then they heard a voice from out of the dark. An American. "We looked around and there was an American airman on a crude stretcher on the ground not far away," Murphy said. "He told us there were 'thousands of the yellow bastards' in the area, and the noises in the dark seemed to confirm this."

By now the firing had just about stopped. The marines were out of grenades. Rifles were empty. So were the carbines and machine guns. "It appeared to us that the ammunition was finished," Murphy said. "I suddenly felt exhausted." He had been fighting for fifteen hours.

The Chinese officer in charge was now making indications that he wanted them to surrender. "He held up his hands indicating ten minutes," Murphy said. "We continued to try to negotiate about the wounded, but the Chinaman would not relent."

McLaughlin was permitted to return to his men. He looked around, counted no more than forty who were able to fight, then returned to the Chinese command post.

"I could see that Major McLaughlin was distressed," Murphy said. "The Chinaman put up five fingers [five minutes]. We still tried to talk. Then the Chinese officer shouted a command and the silence was broken by God knows how many rifle bolts being thrown open and then closed. *Better Dead than Red!*

"We knew that if the Chinese opened fire they would kill everyone in that ditch. *Baloney!*

"The major was left with no option," Murphy said. "We had to surrender." *No you didn't. You Might have Fought And Escaped or even Won.*

McLaughlin surrendered to the Chinese just before dawn after getting them to agree that those seriously hurt would be evacuated.

Then word was passed to the men down the gully to lay down their weapons and come slowly down the road, which they did, but not before making the wounded as comfortable as possible.

Murphy and McLaughlin watched as the men came through and surrendered. "I could have wept when I saw men with bandoliers of ammunition around their bodies," Murphy said. "And we only needed another hour until daylight." *Read Ambush Valley*

However, it was over.

Murphy searched through a disabled truck, found a sleeping bag, some C rations, and cigarettes, and they started to move, single file, into the hills and two years, nine months of captivity that Murphy described as "an ordeal that was sheer hell." *SAVE The last Bullet FoR Yourself.*

While the surrender negotiations were taking place, Nash said, a lot of the men slipped away and made it back to Koto.

"Then word was passed that we had surrendered. We were out of everything. Ammunition. Grenades. Everything. So we surrendered," Nash said. *"Fix Bayonets"!*

They moved into the hills a short time later, and when dawn came they could see the Corsairs flying over Hell Fire Valley and what had once been a relief column of 922 men and 141 vehicles.

"MAJOR CANdy Ass!"

with was A woman! MARine leading An INFANTRY UNIT?

"NUTS"

"Low MoRAle McLaughlin was DisTRessed."

The Shores of TRipoli: 8 marines out of ammo win a hopeless battle by Fixing BAyonets And Assaulting A City Wall Defended by Riflemen And CANNoNs! They Won! Read it. Never Surrender!

"We stayed up there for a while, then came right back down on the road and walked through Hell Fire Valley for about a mile," Nash recalled.

"That was a sight I'll never forget. It had been snowing all night. Bodies were everywhere. Arms and legs were frozen in midair. It was pretty grim. Depressing," Nash said.

Then the Chinese herded them into the hills for the last time and headed north, toward Manchuria.

Five months later Nash and several others escaped and made their way back to American lines.

Pugh was delirious most of the time. He woke up once, raised the tarp, and saw that it was dark. Then he heard two men talking, then someone running.

"Who are you?" one of the men shouted.

Then he heard several shots.

"I'm shot! I'm shot!" someone cried. "Shoot him! Shoot!" one of the men cried, obviously in pain.

More gunfire and a Chinese soldier fell to the ground, dead.

Then all hell broke loose. There was gunfire in every direction.

And Pugh passed out again.

Hours later someone came by, woke him up, and told him that they had surrendered and that the Chinese were going to leave the wounded on the road with what was left of the convoy. He sank back into the trailer and lapsed into unconsciousness again.

Boom!

Boom!

Boom!

Pugh opened his eyes, his ears ringing, the trailer shaking from the force of the explosions, each one louder and closer than the last.

Boom!

Boom!

Then he realized what was happening. The Chinese were blowing up all the vehicles in the convoy. And by the nearness of the last explosion, they were very close to his trailer.

But he couldn't move. He couldn't get up, get out of the trailer.

Then he heard the grenade hit the bottom of the trailer and roll around on the other side of the ration boxes.

Boom!

"Me and the boxes of C rations went sailing through the air," Pugh recalled. "When I came to, the rations were gone, and a few of the wounded were up and walking around.

"They told me that the Chinese had taken everyone who was not wounded," he said.

"We got a jeep started and headed back to Koto," Pugh said, "but a Chinese soldier rose up from a hole alongside the road and shot them all to pieces, everyone but me, and the jeep crashed."

He crawled back under the jeep trailer and stayed there that night. The next day two Chinese soldiers saw him and pulled him out.

"They tried to get me to stand up but I fell flat," he said. "I showed them that both my legs were broken. They left, then returned a short time later with two other soldiers and a stretcher."

They put Pugh on it and carried him up the side of a hill to where they had built a lean-to. Under it were four other men, three of them shot in both legs, the other with a chest wound.

"They gave us each five boiled potatoes and left," Pugh said.

Task Force Drysdale was finished.

The exact number of casualties probably will never be known. Of the 922 men who started up that bloody road, 162 were killed or missing in action, and 159 were wounded. Many others were taken prisoner. Some died in prisoner-of-war camps. Others made their way back to Koto-ri. Of the 141 vehicles in the convoy, at least seventy-five were destroyed.

Of Drysdale and his commandos, Sitter's marines, the soldiers of Baker Company, the men in the support units, and tankers, General Smith said:

"The casualties of Task Force Drysdale were heavy, but by its partial success the task force made a significant contribution to the holding of Hagaru, which was vital to the division. To the slender infantry garrison of Hagaru were added a tank company of about a hundred men and some three hundred seasoned infantrymen. The approximately three hundred troops who returned to Koto-ri participated thereafter in the defense of that perimeter."

For those who fought their way through to Hagaru, the worst was yet to come.

CHAPTER 11
ON TO KOTO-RI

Things were looking up for Ridge. The British commandos were rested, rearmed, and reorganized. Their wounded had been taken care of.

The commandos would be used as a fire brigade. They would go where they were needed most, to the hot spots along the perimeter.

"A situation like Hagaru required that you had your best unit in reserve," Ridge said. He was aware that Drysdale was unhappy with that. However, they worked the problem out, and Drysdale accepted the assignment.

Sitter's G Company was rested as well. Some of his men were in the warming tents. They were rearmed. Much of their time was spent loading clips and getting a little warm food in their stomachs.

Fighting hadn't been too intense the previous night, so the marines were able to get their chores done—strengthen their holes, stockpile ammo and grenades, string more wire, plant more mines.

The commandos were quartered in an old garage, so broken down there was no way to keep out the bitter wind, nor the souvenir-hunting marines who were killing the British with kindness and hospitality, but would steal their magnificent green berets off their heads at the first opportunity.

Even so, Maill remembers the Americans fondly.

"I recall one dark, bitter night in the total darkness of that garage when an American voice asked, 'Any British marines in there?' "

"Yes!"

"I have a box of tea bags I received from home and I think you might appreciate them more than me."

"Well, we appreciated the gesture even more than the tea bags," Maill said. "We didn't get the chance to thank him and to this day his identity is unknown, but I, for one, have not forgotten the incident, and I hope that he returned home safely to enjoy many more cups of tea."

"That first morning in Hagaru, we were cold, freezing to death, and I was literally a walking iceberg," Saunchegrow said. Then he spotted a huge pile of flying jackets, thick, warm, fur-lined, not too far from the airstrip. So the commandos went over and tried to get some of them.

"Some Army lieutenant said his orders were to burn them and that

273

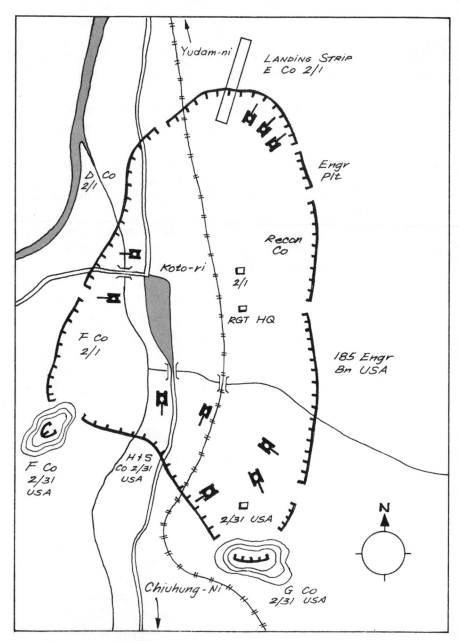

Map 11—Defensive perimeter and marine and Army units are shown on December 7, 1950, at Koto-ri.

anyone who takes one will be shot. And they burned every one of them."

The commandos went back and told Drysdale what had happened. Thomas saw that Saunchegrow was freezing, and said, "Saunche, get yourself one of our uniforms in one of the packs of the boys that didn't come with us."

"Yes, you rate that," Drysdale added. "After what we've been through, you definitely rate a royal marine uniform."

So he went out and found one that fit. "It was the warmest thing I ever had on," Saunchegrow said.

"Now, you just don't look right wearing that pot on top of your head," Drysdale said. "If you're going to wear our uniform, you just have to have a 'berry.' "

So the British colonel took his beret off and handed it to a very surprised and flattered marine.

"You really are one of us now, Saunche," Drysdale told him.

As darkness approached, Barrett's men began to drift back to their positions, wondering if the Chinese would be back. He moved what was left of his command post into the line and picked up a few men from the 3rd Platoon to help fill some gaps. Then he got word that he would be receiving a number of replacements from the engineers and an Army tank, which he planned to place near the end of the runway.

Barrett showed the tank commander where he wanted him positioned, the field of fire, briefed him on what he could expect after dark, then went back to his CP. As he was leaving, he heard the tanker say to a young marine close by, "When you start to pull out of those holes, could you give us a few minutes to warm the tank up?"

"Well, the boy in the hole, as soon as he got over the shock, told the tanker in no uncertain terms, 'Nobody is going anyplace,' " Barrett said.

H Company wasn't hit that night. In fact, it was fairly quiet all along the perimeter.

December 1, 1950: At 8:00 A.M., Ridge sent Sitter's G Company up East Hill. The Corsairs were overhead, pounding the top with bombs and napalm. When the planes departed, artillery from the village took over and continued the pounding for another hour. The Chinese lobbed mortar rounds into Hagaru.

Then, at 9:00 A.M., the first large group of survivors—about three hundred—from the Army's 31st Regiment that the Chinese had decimated began to limp through marine lines, and the enormity of the defeat on the eastern side of the reservoir began to sink in. It was not a pretty picture.— *nor a pretty fight - or lack of one* —

Sitter's men pushed and shoved their way to the top and by 4:00 P.M. had reached the crest and dug in for the night.

At 8:15 P.M. Fisher heard three bugle calls in front of I Company; then a green illumination shell exploded over his lines. The Chinese came out of the snow right in front of his company, and the battle was on. By 11:30 P.M. it was a brutal, full-scale assault on the western front. At 11:55 P.M. the Chinese began to probe the northeastern section of the defense, around East Hill. Artillery and mortar rounds exploded inside the perimeter. A few landed in Ridge's command post.

"We had fires of various sorts going in all directions that night," he recalled.

Barrett's men were deep in their holes as mortar rounds exploded in front of and behind their positions.

"I felt sure they were planning to hit us, but our mortars and artillery fire kept them from forming up," Barrett said. H Company had no casualties that night, but even so, no one dared sleep.

December 2, 1950: At 1:00 A.M. the Chinese pushed the tempo of their attack on the northwest, forcing their way to a spot just to the left of G Company on East Hill. But H Battery had already zeroed in on that area as a potential trouble spot, so most of the Chinese were blown to pieces. Others had slipped behind Sitter's men and were rolling down into the 1st Service Battalion's command post, but the Antitank Company of the 7th Regiment eliminated them.

No matter how many were killed, more took their place. By 2:15 A.M. G Company's left platoon was in trouble. Ridge sent Troop B of the commandos up there, and order was restored in a short time and the area secured.

G Company's radio was out. A bullet did it in while Sitter's company was trying to beat back the Chinese. Kopsitz slid down the hill and found an SCR-300 that worked. But the situation had worsened on top. The Chinese were between G Company and Hagaru in strength, and

Kopsitz saw artillery rounds exploding in an area he had just left, an area he thought was in marine hands.

"What the hell's going on?" he asked one artilleryman.

"The Chinese are between George and Hagaru and coming down."

The roar of the artillery was deafening. You had to shout to be heard.

"East Hill was an urgent fire mission," Steele remembered. "We didn't need fire requests from any forward observer. We'd lost most of them. At times you could see the enemy, so we just fired in their direction."

If a marine on the hill wanted artillery, he'd radio, "One white phosphorus on the hill and we'll adjust."

"On the way."

That's the way it was at Hagaru. One fire mission after another.

"I've got to get this radio up to the top!" Kopsitz shouted at an artillery officer. They stopped, and Kopsitz began to scramble up.

"You won't be able to get through!" someone shouted.

"They're cut off!" another cannoneer hollered.

All the way up he could hear Chinese. But he never saw any. Nor was there any gunfire near him. He could hear gunfire toward the top, and the din was terrific.

When he reached the top, Kopsitz went straight to the company CP and Sitter, who had been wounded. Kopsitz dropped the radio and crawled into a cave with the captain and two other men and spent the night there, warmed by body heat.

The perimeter around Hagaru was like a leaky dike that night. Plug one hole and three others appeared.

At 3:00 A.M. the southern roadblock was under heavy attack.

Both the northwestern and southwestern areas were being hit hard. The Chinese tried everything to crack the perimeter, but they could not find that soft seam, that one weak spot their strategy was based on.

By 4:00 A.M. the fighting had tapered off in most areas. The southern roadblock still was intact. It hadn't bent an inch.

I and H companies were okay, too. East Hill still was a problem, even though G Company had gained back some of the ground lost on its left flank.

The best news came at 9:00 A.M., when the Corsairs broke through heavy snow and clouds, went on station, and began to hunt down the Chinese.

Finding targets wasn't difficult. There was an abundance of them.

One flight radioed that it had spotted a large group of Chinese on a hill a half mile away.

"Forget them," his forward air controller told him. "There are targets much closer, a hundred yards away. Let's get those first."

"From the moment we arrived until we left, it was a constant battle against the cold," Barrett said.

The ground was frozen to a depth of about fourteen inches, which made digging in close to impossible. Barbed wire couldn't be strung effectively. The ground was too hard. So they strung wire through piles of bricks, then poured water on them to freeze the wire in place.

Water always was a problem. Trailers froze during the brief time it took to get from the water point to the company area. Canteens burst.

Barrett's men had hotcakes for breakfast one morning but it was so cold the syrup, although boiling when served, turned to ice before they finished eating. Mess gear could not be cleaned.

Fuel oil for stoves in the warming tents froze. To prevent this you had to keep the fuel cans within three feet of the stove.

Automatic weapons worked at half their capacity. Bolts froze. When a round was fired, the heat generated moisture in the chamber that promptly froze, preventing the next round from entering the chamber.

Grenades would not explode, or the timing would be off. Propelling charges in mortar rounds were off, resulting in many short rounds and many casualties to marines in their holes.

The cold affected the powder charges in artillery shells, making it very difficult to get really accurate fire.

The clothing worn by many marines was designed for use at temperatures down to zero, but most of the time the weather around the reservoir, at Yudam-ni, Hagaru, and Koto-ri, was many degrees below zero.

Their shoes were disastrous. Only an evil person could have devised something so deadly to the feet. They were airtight, and when you walked any distance they generated much moisture, which very quickly froze.

There never seemed to be enough daylight to do all the chores required. Feeding the men could take a day. It was such a chore that many men would skip meals. As a result, their resistance, already reduced by the cold and lack of sleep, was sapped even further.

After Hagaru's first night of fire, life for the marines became the same.

In their holes by 5:30 P.M. A 50 percent alert that quickly jumped to 100 percent.

And the sounds. You could hear the men settling down for the night.

The scraping of snow off the ammo boxes.

Rearranging grenades along the tops of their holes.

Someone slipping. Then the cursing.

The soft crunch of footsteps in the snow behind the holes. The gray, washed-out forms of squad leaders checking to be sure each man was where he should be. And awake.

The muffled sound of the platoon leaders talking over the sound power phone.

Endless chitchat. But it's important. It relieves the tension. If there is small talk going on, it means there's no trouble along the line.

The sound power is the nerve system of the rifle company. Good news, bad news travel over it.

"Replacements are coming."

"We're going to be attached."

"We don't expect anything tonight."

At times it sounds like a party line. A dirty story. A bad joke. Someone sings a song. "You like to hear that phone making some noise because you know what it's like when the phone goes out," Barrett said.

It's been dark for a few hours now. The phone talk starts to die out. It's really quiet. Too damn quiet.

"It's 2200 hours [10:00 P.M.]. Those bastards hit us the other night just about this time."

"God, but it's quiet."

"Can't see a damn thing out in front."

The right flank reports some activity to their front.

Grab the sound power.

"How! How! God damn that CP bunch, they're probably asleep. How! How!"

Quiet. Not a peep. Anywhere.

Then, suddenly, over the line, "This is How! This is How!"

Then the platoon leader may cuss them out for taking so long to answer. Or he may ask for illumination to see what's going on out front.

"One round of illumination on the way."

279

You spot the trail of sparks up over the line. Then a brilliant flare suspended from a little parachute lights up the entire area. That's the way it's supposed to be. But at Hagaru it was a bit different. Due either to the cold or faulty ammunition, most of the time it was a brief flash that plummeted earthward. A dud.

So you call for another. Then another. Still one more.

Then you hear over the sound power, "All rounds of illumination expended—no more illumination."

"You've heard it so often, you hate it," Barrett recalled. "One good round for every four or five rounds. You get bitter."

Now it's time for the platoon leaders to check their lines.

No one likes to do this. Laying in their holes, feet and legs in their bags, they're almost warm. It's not too pleasant to get out in the minus-thirty-degree weather.

They're scared, too. No one knows what's out front.

And if the Chinese attack, he's caught a long ways from his hole, his CP.

Damn a battalion that gives a platoon such a long front.

Walking up and down the line, he finds some men asleep—standing up—who are supposed to be on watch. If you haven't had sleep in a week, it's easy to sleep in any position. But a kick to the head, an ass-chewing, wakes them up. But don't threaten them with a court-martial. Just remind them of the men who have been bayoneted while asleep on watch.

The next hole. Where the hell is the next hole?

Damn this darkness.

But he finds each and every hole and talks to the men. He laughs, they laugh. It's good.

Finally, it's back to his own little world and the sound power.

But it's hard to stay awake, even with a phone stuck in your ear. Lieutenants need sleep, too.

Suddenly he leaps up.

He's been dozing. But for how long? What has happened?

He grabs the sound power.

"How! How! Were you calling me?"

A moment of panic.

Then he finds that all is well. It's still calm along the front.

One hour to daylight. This is the bad time. Will the Chinese come?

Slowly. Slowly it gets light. That last half hour seems to take forever.

Then they listen for the planes. Will the weather be good for flying?

Then you hear the growl of the Corsairs even before you can see the hills in front of you. The weather is clear.

Bless those planes, their pilots.

Another day. They can come out of the foxholes. The Chinese won't do much with the Corsairs buzzing over their heads.

The men move as if each is suffering from an advanced stage of arthritis. Bones are tired, cold. They just don't want to move, to respond to a message from the brain.

But they do. A few head for the tents to start the stoves. Others build fires along the line so those on watch can warm themselves.

Such is life at Hagaru.

As soon as the men have thawed out, eaten, they're back at their holes, digging, enlarging, loading clips.

More mines are planted. More barbed wire strung. The seriously injured are flown out.

Those wounded but still able to fight are patched up and told to stay. They will be needed again before this is over.

Barrett told his men to expect more Army troops to come through during the day. They were beginning to straggle in from all directions, and no one wanted to shoot a friendly.

Later, he heard that the 5th and the 7th had broken out of Yudam-ni and were on the way back to Hagaru.

"At the time, we didn't know they had been hit even worse than we had, and looked forward to having them to help us out," Barrett said.

"We began to get a little clearer picture of the situation and a better understanding of our position," Barrett said. "We were told that we would hold Hagaru at all costs until the 5th and 7th regiments passed through, and then we would move back to Koto-ri—which was also under attack."

Late in the afternoon, Barrett stopped sending men to sick bay with frostbite. There wasn't room there to take care of them. "We did what we could for them in the line," he said.

At about 5:45 P.M. another 260 soldiers straggled through marine lines. Most were walking wounded. Many were freezing. Very few had winter clothing. Only a few had weapons.

Overall, the night was relatively quiet. There were a few firefights, all minor. Occasionally a stray artillery round from the Chinese fell inside the perimeter. With all the men, fuel, and equipment there, it's surprising the Chinese did so little damage with their cannons. A lot of tracers flew overhead, but very few had anyone's name on it.

December 3, 1950: At 6:00 A.M., Navy planes were on station, seeking out the Chinese. Then the heavy mortars and howitzers joined in the pounding.

If a Chinese soldier showed his head, forward observers brought something down on it.

The day was the same as the others: chores to do, wounded to take care of. More wire around the perimeter. Don't forget to stockpile those grenades.

Everyone tried to spend a little time in the warming tents. If the Chinese struck after dark, you wouldn't have time to get near an oil-burning stove.

At 2:00 P.M. the mood of everyone brightened considerably.

The 5th and 7th regiments were close to Hagaru and would be in sight within four or five hours.

At 4:00 P.M. a flight of four Corsairs flew north over the road to try to pinpoint the location of the two regiments. They were about a mile and a half from the perimeter. But the Chinese were contesting every last foot of the road. Heavy fighting still was going on along the ridges. The men and trucks on the road came under plunging machine-gun fire.

A tank-infantry patrol moved north up the road at 5:00 P.M. to try to make contact with the point units but had to turn back. There were too many Chinese, too many roadblocks.

Nevertheless, the convoy moved steadily toward the perimeter, taking casualties, fighting off the Chinese as darkness fell.

Northern roadblock, Hagaru, 7:35 P.M.: "They're here! They made it!" the defenders shouted. "They're coming in!"

The point units could see the roadblock about two hundred yards away.

Davis was several hundred yards out when he spotted Dowsett running out to meet him.

"He was half running, half walking, and issuing orders," Davis remembered.

"He told me to start outposting key terrain features on in to Hagaru," Davis said.

"Where are you going so damn fast?" Dowsett asked.

"We're going to Hagaru!" Davis shouted back, and he didn't slow down for anything or anyone until he was inside the perimeter.

"When I saw the 7th coming, when I got 'em in sight, I said, 'We got it made,' " Ridge remembered.

The point units passed through the roadblock at 7:50 P.M. The column continued to arrive throughout the night and most of the following day. Pearl passed through a few minutes after Davis. "We slept in an open field that night and it wasn't too bad. It was nice just to be able to sleep," he remembered. "It didn't matter where."

Each man who crossed through the roadblock got a small bottle of liquor from the medical supplies, and that helped pass the night.

Schreiner, H Company, 3rd Battalion, 7th Regiment, one of the few to live through the night of terror on Hill 1403, was thankful to have reached Hagaru. So many hadn't. He thought it was all over, that they were safe, that they had beaten the Chinese. He was stunned to find that Hagaru was surrounded, that the marines would now have to battle their way south to Koto-ri.

"It was quite a letdown," he remembered.

Hot coffee and warm food, the first in many days, helped. But he had no mess gear, so he ate the hot beef stew out of his helmet.

"The mess personnel were apologizing for not having a better fare," he remembered, "but to us it could not have tasted better."

When Hull crossed the northern roadblock, MP's took one look at him and guided him straight to an aid station. He stayed overnight and was flown to a hospital in Japan.

Newton, the only remaining officer in H Company, 3rd Battalion, 7th Regiment, and now the company commander, gathered the survivors in a warming tent and told them the company had fought its way into Hagaru, and now How was going to fight its way out. A few hours later H Company got a much-needed shot in the arm when a dozen replacements from the artillery showed up.

Dyrdahl, B Company, 1st Battalion, 7th Regiment, couldn't have gone much farther. His toes and fingers were badly frostbitten, and he was evacuated. Nevertheless, he had no doubt the marines would get out. "We just didn't know how bad off we were," he said.

Hedrick, also from B Company, 7th Regiment, was happy to have reached Hagaru, to be able to sit down. Little things like that were so very important.

"It was so cold coming down that road we'd try to find a truck that had the motor running, then lean against it to keep from freezing. Then we'd fall asleep standing up," he said. "The only danger was that the truck might start moving suddenly and we'd be thrown under the wheels."

Fulop, the engineer, was tired, hungry, and very cold, and he needed a good, stiff drink. He knew just where to get it: Charley Med. Corpsmen always had something to drink. When he got there he saw wounded stacked three high, spread on the ground, in the backs of vehicles. More wounded arrived all the time. "It looked like a slaughterhouse," he said. He decided he could wait for that drink.

"There was plenty of snow on the ground, and under that there was solid ice all the way," said Benson, F Company, 2nd Battalion, 7th Regiment. "I think I slid halfway to Hagaru."

Cafferatta was gone. So was Barber. Both had been evacuated.

"We were taken straight to the warming tents," remembered Kanouse, F company, 2nd Battalion, 7th Regiment. A lot of warm food and hot coffee had them feeling much better.

December 4, 1950: "We were just walking down that road like we were out for an early-morning stroll," corpsman Schaub recalls.

"There were bullets flying around us and gunfire in the hills. We could see part of Hagaru afire ahead of us," he said.

"Then out of a foxhole to the side of the road steps a commando. He was neatly dressed, wearing a tie, creases in his uniform. I've never been so impressed. I knew if we had people like this on our side, we couldn't be in that much trouble. It was a terribly good feeling."

The commando snapped a typical British salute—palm out: "Good to see you, Yanks."

Once inside, Schaub warmed himself, had a hot meal, rested, then was flown out, his feet and hands badly frostbitten.

H Company, 3rd Battalion, 5th Regiment, went into Yudam-ni with close to 250 men. It was down to forty men, one jeep, a small trailer, and all the company ammo and C rations when it reached Hagaru.

"Four of us went into a little hut for a few hours' sleep," PFC Peter Hildre remembers. "One watched and three slept."

But not for long.

"Wake up!"

284

"Wake up!"

"We're moving out!"

Hildre was on his aching feet and heading toward a chunk of the perimeter.

Taplett was inside the perimeter now, his battalion in a rest status. But before he could relax, he had to find his men, and he didn't know where many of them were.

"When we came down from the hills just before going into Hagaru, it was one of the blackest nights I've ever seen. You couldn't see your hand in front of your face," said Johnson, F Company, 2nd Battalion, 5th Regiment.

As soon as they reached the road, they were peppered by plunging fire from the hill they had just left. "We couldn't do anything about it, so we just ran through it for a couple of hundred yards, and no one was hit.

"I felt damn relieved when we reached Hagaru," he said. "I thought we were safe. I didn't know we were still cut off.

"Nevertheless, it was great just to be there, to sit down and say to yourself, 'By God, I did it.' We stood in line four hours to get pancakes and bacon and powdered eggs," Johnson said, "and that was nice." He remembered passing the building that was used as a hospital. "It was solid blood from the hospital to the airstrip," he said.

Johnson's platoon was down to ten men, not all able-bodied, but five replacements were picked up. Then it was back to the war and a piece of the perimeter.

The howitzers of the 1st and 4th battalions of the 11th Artillery Regiment crossed the perimeter just before first light. Each unit was vastly understrength, having sent most of their men to the rifle companies as replacements. Their trucks were down to their last spoonful of fuel. They were full of bullet holes, but the cannons still could fire.

C Company, 1st Battalion, 5th Regiment, came down from the hills just short of the village, passed through the roadblock at dawn, and moved into a deserted building. "It was the first time I'd been in a building since I got to Korea," said Jones, the company commander.

As Murray, the 5th Regiment commander, crossed the perimeter, he spotted the warrant officer heading in his direction.

"General Smith wants to see you, sir."

Murray turned the regiment over to his executive officer, Lt. Col. Joseph L. Stewart, told him to get the men bedded down for the night, then headed toward the division headquarters.

"General Smith just wanted to talk about the situation up there. He wanted to know how things were going, the casualties," Murray said.

Murray also talked to Bowser and others on the general's staff who were busily mapping plans for the division's breakout south to Koto-ri on December 6.

They were already planning to drop a bridge at a power plant south of Koto-ri that the Chinese had blown. If it were not replaced or rebuilt, none of the vehicles would get out. There was a footpath that led behind the power plant so the men could walk out. But it would be slow going and very difficult carrying the wounded.

If details could be worked out in time, the bridge would be flown from Japan, dropped at Koto-ri, and trucked to the power plant, where the engineers would install it.

As Roisie's 2nd Battalion, 5th Regiment, began crossing the perimeter, he remained on the road, near his jeep and radio and forward air controller, just in case. His executive officer, Maj. John L. Hopkins, took the men in and put them in a battered building along with the Motor Transport Battalion. "They had heaters and it was warm and, after all, that's what really mattered—getting warm," Roisie said.

Nolan's platoon in E Company, 2nd Battalion, 5th Regiment, was the rear point, the last to leave Yudam-ni, the last unit down the road. But he didn't have it as rough as the units up front. Compared to his night at Easy Alley, the trip down the road was just a hike.

"Personally, we never came under any fire on the way back. We lost some men from frostbite, but not to enemy fire."

"The people up front cleared the way out," said his platoon sergeant, Howard Solheim. "We just had the usual snipers from the sides."

"You could always see them, though, back off the road, up in the hills," Solheim said.

He turned for one last look, saw the smoke rising from the burning supplies, the Chinese running everywhere. "I will remember Yudam-ni always," he said.

"I'll never really forget that," he said. "I don't like to think about it."

It was as cold as it had ever been and snowing heavily when Yudam-ni faded from sight. Not too many marines turned around for a last look at the village, whose name would remain forever etched in their memories.

Nolan's platoon crossed the perimeter at 12:30 P.M. on December 4. It had taken his men seventy-two hours. Front units made it in fifty-nine hours. Solheim was hobbling, his feet badly frostbitten. He limped to the nearest aid station and was tagged for evacuation.

Roisie got in his jeep with his air controller and followed the last man in; then the northern roadblock was buttoned up. Most had a day of rest, a hot meal of pancakes, coffee, powdered milk, and powdered eggs. Many junked their carbines in favor of the more reliable M-1's. They filled their pockets with clips and grenades and grabbed two or three bandoliers.

Most of the headquarters and service troops were returned to their normal duties. The tactical defense of the village was shifted to the tough, battle-hardened battalions of Murray's 5th Regiment.

G Company, 3rd Battalion, 1st Regiment, was taken off the small spot it held on East Hill and moved to a different section of the perimeter.

Murray's men now held more than half the perimeter. The Chinese would have a tough time taking the village now.

Barrett knew that the 5th and the 7th had arrived. He had a lot of friends in those regiments, and he was glad they were inside the perimeter.

"We knew that we would soon be leaving Hagaru, and that made everyone feel good," he remembered. "We were a division again and could do anything." A short time later he got the frosting on the cake: He found out that Navy had beaten Army in their traditional football game in Philadelphia.

December 5, 1950: Barrett was up early, had some hot coffee, then wandered over to the battalion command post to try to pick up some information. Would they be leaving soon? Who would be where in the convoy? Who would be the point? The rear point? He didn't learn anything, so he headed for the areas where the 5th and 7th regiments were.

"I don't know exactly what I expected to see. Certainly I didn't look for any parade-ground formations of the two regiments," Barrett said. "But I was not prepared for what I saw."

"There were long lines of bleary-eyed men, half frozen and dazed, eating off pieces of cardboard with their fingers because they had no mess gear—their first hot chow in over two weeks and, for some, the first food in three days."

Men were wandering around with blank stares, sleeping on the frozen ground. Wounded, men with frozen feet, standing around waiting for more room in the aid stations.

"It was a horrible sight," he remembered.

Then Barrett began to recognize men he had known elsewhere. Slowly, recognition came to them, and they remembered Barrett, spoke to him softly, almost hesitantly. Then he began to piece the bits together. The picture he got was horrendous.

He asked about men he had known in the two regiments.

"Killed."

"Evacuated."

"Frozen feet, flown out."

"I don't know."

"I saw his body on a truck."

But mostly they didn't have time to talk.

They were busy getting reorganized, looking for their platoons, companies, searching for warm clothing, for gloves, socks, sweaters.

There was no mistaking the hell that each had been through.

Platoons, companies had disappeared, been swallowed by the Chinese.

And now they had to rebuild, reshape, turn units that were in disarray and confusion into fighting outfits again.

"Although we had the 5th and 7th regiments and the 3rd Battalion of the 1st Regiment in Hagaru, still there were actually just enough men to make about a brigade," Barrett remembered.

The C-47s were very busy on December 4 and 5, flying out the wounded that the 5th and 7th had brought with them.

For the Chinese, what had been attainable a short time ago had now become a difficult task. They still could capture Hagaru. They had six divisions in the hills around Hagaru and Koto-ri. But it would take some time to do it, and the cost in Chinese lives would be astronomical.

At 2:00 P.M. Ridge sent a commando-marine-tank force about a half mile north toward Yudam-ni to try to bring back eight howitzers whose prime movers had run out of gas. "Try to recover them; if you can't, destroy them," he instructed his men.

The commandos moved out in a skirmish line. Half ran low to the ground, dropped, and rolled over once or twice. Then the other half did the same thing, overlapping the first group. The marines were just behind, followed by the tanks.

Maill manned a .30 on top of a small hill while the commandos descended into the valley to where the howitzers were.

"When our lads started to move down the valley, Chinese soldiers appeared on the hill opposite us," he remembered. His first bursts were on target. He could see the Chinese falling, running for cover. So he kept firing, and the Chinese couldn't move.

Then, over a rise in front of them and totally unexpectedly, Beard appeared, walking nonchalantly, as if he were out for a stroll. He stepped carefully down the road so as not to step on any of the commandos.

He'd been down at a stream for a drink of fresh water and was returning to B Company, 1st Battalion, 7th Regiment.

The commandos blew the howitzers to pieces. The tanks destroyed the six-bys, then covered the withdrawal back to Hagaru.

Forward observers had brought in mortar and howitzer fire, and the forward air controller had four Corsairs overhead in minutes, pounding the Chinese with napalm and high explosives.

"This was typical of the U.S. habit of taking a sledgehammer to crack a walnut," Maill said.

General Smith's headquarters was bustling. In addition to making last-minute plans for the breakout south to Koto-ri, he was kept busier than he liked simply answering the questions of reporters who flew in and out of Hagaru aboard the evacuation planes to see for themselves if the division was intact.

Their questions were mostly the same, and they contained two of the words General Smith disliked most: "retreat" and "trapped." So he painstakingly explained to the assembled writers, "When you're surrounded, it is impossible to retreat. We're simply attacking in a different direction."

Col. Edward W. Snedeker, General Smith's deputy chief of staff, was in Tokyo as part of a naval evaluation group. "Deputy chiefs of staff of anything don't have too much to do, so I was sent," he explained. But the situation in Korea had deteriorated so rapidly he was ordered to fly back to Hagaru immediately. He flew in with replacements and a few newsmen and went immediately to the general's command post. "There was an element of suspense there," he recalls, "because we didn't know if we were going to have Chinese visiting us or not."

General Smith told him to get on down to Chinhung-ni, at the foot of Funchilin Pass, and set up a control post "because the division is coming out."

General Barr, the commander of the Army's 7th Infantry Division, which was to the east of the marines, also flew in, to discuss the situation with General Smith.

The marine general told Barr that all his troops who had escaped from the Chinese that were wounded or suffered frostbite had been evacuated. Those who were healthy and could fight had been organized into a battalion and attached to the 7th Regiment. The marines called the provisional battalion 31/7.

While Snedeker was there, Murray and Litzenberg were awarded the Distinguished Service Cross by General Almond, who flew in to discuss the breakout south with General Smith and his staff.

"They both cried," Snedeker recalled, "not at receiving the medal, I'm sure, but at thinking how preposterous it was under this particular situation to have something pinned on you when it was better to be out with your troops."

General Almond went over plans for the breakout, then flew out. So did Snedeker.

The Chinese suffered so many casualties in their first great attack on Hagaru the night of November 29 that they couldn't really mount a second major assault on the perimeter until fresh troops and supplies arrived. They were slow in coming. Everything had to come by foot. After dark. By this time, the 5th and 7th regiments fought their way into Hagaru, had rested and reorganized, and were in the perimeter, adding a lot of muscle to the defense.

The airfield was in full operation now. Six C-47 transports could land and take off at the same time, as opposed to two a few days ago.

At 11:00 A.M. fourteen hundred wounded and frostbitten marines and soldiers were waiting to be flown out. They were everywhere—in tents, ambulances, on the ground, covered with parachutes in the backs of trucks.

By nightfall they were all gone, despite a few anxious moments. One transport lost power just after taking off and pancaked in a short distance beyond the runway. The crew wasn't hurt, but some of the wounded suffered additional injuries. Corpsman Richard P. Davis was one of the first to reach the crash. All were stretcher cases and had to be helped. "We got them all back to the aid station, then watched the artillery blow up the plane just as the Chinese tried to get to it," he said.

General Smith's thinned-down staff worked around the clock on plans for the breakout. All the wounded and the badly frostbitten had been flown out: 4,312. Several hundred replacements had been flown in. Ammunition, fuel, and C rations had been air dropped. They had so much more than they needed that hundreds of tons of supplies would have to be torched.

It was clear to all, from General Smith down to the lowest ranks, that the longer they stayed, the stronger the Chinese would get. So it was time to go.

December 6, 1950; breakout from Hagaru, 5:30 A.M.: "When we were ordered to leave, marines actually cried," Steele remembers. "The veterans of World War II didn't want to give up ground they had won without a fight, and the younger marines, like myself, felt we couldn't be beaten."

At first light Litzenberg's 7th Regiment began to pass through the southern roadblock. His 1st Battalion headed up in the hills on the right. The provisional brigade of Army survivors of the debacle east of the Chosin Reservoir, 31/7, moved up on the left. They would try to keep the high ground clear of Chinese while the convoy shot its way down the road. His 2nd Battalion was on the road, leading the way to Koto-ri, and Barber's old F Company, far understrength, was the point, the assault force. If the Chinese were on the road, if there were roadblocks that had to be blasted, F Company would have to do it, because the marines were moving south.

"We got up at 3:00 A.M., rolled up our gear, and formed up to move out," Benson said. Dunne was still the F Company commander, replacing Barber.

"He told us what to expect—sniper fire, roadblocks," Kanouse remembered. "We would march south in a column of twos. We were to open the road for the division. Our casualties would be picked up. We'd have tanks immediately behind us. We were to take care of the roadblocks. There would be people on each side up in the hills who would take care of the opposition up there."

At the same time the division broke south to Koto-ri, Murray's 2nd Battalion began the attack to capture East Hill. With the exception of a small toehold on the hill that G Company, 3rd Battalion, 1st Regiment held for a while, the Chinese had controlled the huge landmass since they captured it on November 29.

But now, with the marines passing under the hill on the road south, there was no way the Chinese could remain up there.

Marine planes arrived over the hill at 7:30 A.M. and bombed, strafed, and rocketed the top for ninety minutes. But there was very little napalm available because they had run out of tanks.

At 9:30 A.M. Smith's D Company moved up in a northeasterly direction toward Objective A, a high peak on the northern part of the hill. Surprisingly, resistance was light, and at 11:00 A.M. the Chinese unexpectedly withdrew. One marine was killed and three were wounded, and the Chinese suffered thirty dead.

Before they left Hagaru, each man loaded up on all the PX goodies he could carry. "I lived on two big bags of caramels from Hagaru to Koto-ri," Kanouse said. Just about everyone had a big supply of Tootsie Rolls.

"Hey, Lieutenant, when we gonna get this show on the road?" one of the men shouted at Lt. John Theros, a marine pilot who was pulling duty as a forward air controller, something all marine pilots did. "Don't they know there's only six more shopping days until Christmas?"

It was still too dark to see anything. Some of the marines were sighting their rifles on the hills to the left, where they knew there were Chinese.

Fox was on the road and ready to move once the go-ahead came. Right behind were four tanks.

Then came Theros and his forward air control team of ten men.

He had three flights of Corsairs upstairs, twelve to a flight, at levels of ten, twelve, and fourteen thousand feet, on call. But it was still a little too early to use them. The pilots wouldn't be able to see targets for another half hour.

One of his men carried a backpack radio, about forty pounds, line-of-sight, and not very reliable.

Ice and snow were everywhere.

"We started walking down that road as the light came up, and the Chinese started firing at us," Benson remembered. His first reaction was to dive into a ditch, but he kept moving.

He could hear bullets whizzing by, kicking up the ice, the snow, the frozen ground. But they didn't fire back. Every man kept moving.

They were almost running, but each man was lugging too much gear. But they were moving along at what probably was a record fast shuffle.

They hadn't gone a mile when the fire became so heavy the column was forced to stop, the men leaping into ditches on both sides of the road.

"It sounded like hail on a tin roof," Benson remembered.

"I don't think I ever was or ever will be as scared as I was that day."

No one knew at first where the fire was coming from.

But Theros didn't waste a moment. As soon as he heard the gunfire, he called for air.

He contacted the flight leader, told him where he thought the Chinese were, and said, "Make the first drop napalm to mark the target for all following aircraft."

The first plane came in low, about fifty feet off the ground, dropped the tank, then zoomed up and away.

It carried fifty to a hundred feet forward, hit the ground, and exploded just short of the target.

Then the other planes came in and raked the area with 20mm cannons. Their bombs were too big to drop, the planes too low. If the five-hundred-pounders exploded, the planes would catch hell.

The four tanks were ahead of Theros and to the right. He couldn't communicate with them, so he ran forward about fifty yards to where they were.

"I wanted to talk to the tank commander, to tell him to move across to the left side of the road where he could fire at the Chinese, that the planes would be firing over them and not to worry."

"I ran over there, but some guy was talking to him. I bumped him and he fell in the snow, but I was in a hurry, so I began talking to the tanker," he said.

"The guy gets up, brushed off the snow. Then I saw it was Litzenberg."

"Sorry, Colonel."

"That's okay, John. This is your show."

Benson was in a ditch on the left side of the road. Out a few hundred yards were some old shacks.

"Fire at those huts!" Komoroski shouted.

"Fire at those huts!"

One of the tanks moved across the road and parked just behind Benson. Its turret swung around until the barrel was just about over his head and pointing in the direction of the huts.

Then the gunner cranked off a round.

"Wham!"

The ground shook. Benson's head seemed to bounce off both sides of his helmet. The muzzle blast just about lifted him out of the ditch.

"I gotta get out of here. If it fires again, I'll never hear again."

So he rose slightly, turned, started to inch his way out of the ditch. But that was as far as he got.

A bullet tore through the back of his left shoulder, caromed off a bone, and came out several inches lower. He toppled back into the ditch, stunned, but not yet in pain. But he couldn't lift his arm.

Komoroski ran over, checked him with his eyes, then his hands. His fingers were warm, sticky.

"There's a lot of blood on your back. Just lay there and be quiet."

There was still a lot of shooting. Benson was scared. He wasn't sure what might happen next.

Would the Chinese get to the ditch? To the road?

Would he be forgotten in the confusion?

But when you've been hit, you're down, in shock, a lot of thoughts race through your mind, all of them bad.

The Corsairs had been overhead for some time now. Benson could hear them raising hell with the Chinese. The Corsairs were blasting the hilltops. The huts were dust.

As the firing eased, Komoroski went back to Benson and told him: "You have two choices: You can come with us, or you can go back to the airstrip and see if you can get out."

He thought about it for a minute or two. He was hurting now. So he and a few other walking wounded decided to go back to Hagaru and were flown out. The column was held up no more than thirty minutes. But it was slow going all the way to Koto-ri.

Theros was close to the point, walking or riding, always in contact with the planes, always close to the tanks, usually under fire.

Morris's C Company, 1st Battalion, 7th Regiment, was high on the right, the point in the hills. "You'd go down a little gully and you didn't know what you'd find on the other side," he remembered. His men didn't see too many Chinese up there, and when they did, the enemy usually was too far away to worry about. Kiser was up there with B Company, 1st Battalion, 7th Regiment, just behind Morris's men. "The biggest problem we had was that the Chinese now looked like us," Kiser said. "We had lost so many men by this time that the Chinese all seemed to have on our parkas. It was hard to tell them apart at a distance."

The attack south was sluggish. With each passing yard it got worse. At every turn there was a roadblock and rifle and machine-gun fire. Progress wasn't measured in feet. Just holding fast was an achievement much of the time.

The column moved another mile south, then could creep no more. Ahead was the biggest roadblock they had faced. Several drivers were killed. Eight trucks were set afire. Those behind couldn't move. There were no drivers. Everyone had taken to ditches on both sides of the road. The mortar fire set several more on fire. Then the Chinese brought up more men and machine guns.

Two marine tanks took off cross country, around the burning vehicles, looking for a spot where they could get a good line of fire. One had to turn back immediately because it ran into a ravine it could not cross. But the other tank found a well-concealed location and an excellent angle of fire from the side and fired round after round into the Chinese massed behind the timber and sandbags. Within thirty minutes the Chinese were fleeing across the countryside.

At 10:00 A.M. the convoy was moving again. A marine dropped here, there. A driver was shot. But another man quickly took his place behind the wheel to become a sitting duck.

General Smith remained at Hagaru until he was certain the breakout was a success; then he and part of his staff went by light plane and helicopter to Koto-ri. Bowser and the rest of the staff remained at Hagaru until they knew General Smith had arrived at Koto-ri; then they flew out, too.

Dead and wounded were picked up as the trucks moved slowly down the road. Then the tanks had trouble trying to negotiate a railroad embankment. Suddenly, radio contact was lost with battalion, regiment, and 31/7. But you didn't need radio contact with anyone to realize the convoy had run into a lot of trouble. You could hear it and, from the higher elevations, see it.

Trucks were burning. Drivers were being killed and wounded. A gap was developing in the front third of the convoy. A tank shot its way down the road. A good ass-chewing got several small units moving through the fire from the low hills. A battery of howitzers got through. So did some headquarters and service company troops.

But the back two thirds of the convoy was dead in its tracks. The front third had already disappeared on the way to Koto-ri.

Two tanks clanked forward, but it was too dark for them to do too much. H Battery brought a howitzer up, but it wasn't effective. No one knew where to point it. A forward observer crawled far ahead of the tank and the artillery piece and laid wire so he could direct fire. Meanwhile, the Chinese were becoming more daring. Some were within hand-grenade range of the road. But marines and soldiers in the hills took the Chinese under fire and scattered them in an hour, and the convoy was moving slowly again. But every foot was contested and would be until daylight.

December 7, 1950: The point units of the 7th Regiment were closing on the perimeter at Koto-ri. It was about 5:00 A.M., and with luck they would reach the marine roadblock in a few hours.

Morris's C Company came down from the hills on the right about a half mile out and walked in with the front third. He was so tired he doesn't remember what the place looked like. Once inside, he was put in a holding pattern, ready to back up the road if the convoy ran into a monster roadblock it couldn't crack. Even so, it was nice to be in Koto-ri, to rest, get warm, get a little warm food. Hot food was out of the question.

PFC James H. Cash had fought with the infantry at Yudam-ni, returned to his artillery unit at Hagaru, and now was back with the foot marines, high on the right, keeping the peaks clear.

"We stayed up there the rest of the day [December 6], that night, and all we spotted were three or four Chinese soldiers about a hundred yards to our right front, and they were running from us.

"I can remember this vividly because it's the first time I ever saw a whole battalion firing at three Chinese. Last time I saw them, they were still running. I don't think we came close."

He slid down to the road about a half mile out, joined the column, and walked in, dead tired, colder than he'd ever been in his life.

Kiser came down from the hills about a mile short of the village.

"We walked into Koto and had the first good coffee and hot meal in some time. It was like checking into a hotel," he said.

Of his original platoon, there were only four left.

The 2nd Battalion, 7th Regiment, was the first into Koto-ri. The 1st Battalion followed, then the 3rd. So did 31/7. All were safely in before 5:00 P.M. on December 7.

Along the way, the marines picked up twenty-two commandos who had been caught in Hell Fire Valley since the ambush on November 29–30.

The marines knew the commandos were out there. It was just a matter of locating them. A spotter plane had spotted the word H-E-L-P stamped in the snow, so food and medical supplies had been dropped.

Pearl was up in the hills with the 1st Battalion, 7th Regiment, but "all the action seemed to be ahead of us, down on the road, or up in the hills on the other side of the road."

They came down just short of the perimeter and walked in with the column. Just before they reached the northern roadblock, gunfire held them up briefly.

"I was tired, so I sat down on a stump to rest," Pearl remembered.

"Hey, Roy, do you realize what you're sitting on?" a friend asked. He looked down.

"There was a snow-covered Chinese soldier in a sitting position with his feet folded neatly under him. His head was bowed. So were his shoulders, and I was sitting on his back."

Once inside the perimeter, he searched for a big, warm engine to snuggle against. Then he tried to heat some food. Hamburgers and gravy were best because the gravy would melt and boil the meat and it took only a few minutes.

Pugh was still alive, although badly frostbitten, terribly hungry, and very thirsty. He and the four other wounded marines each had only the four or five potatoes that the Chinese had given them when they carried them up the hill and put them in the lean-to. This was five days ago.

The Chinese had built the lean-to, but it did nothing to keep out the cold and snow, and it snowed all the time. Most of the time they were unconscious.

Pugh woke up at midmorning on December 6. It was very quiet and very clear, for a change. Pugh wasn't sure how many days he had been in the lean-to, but he knew he couldn't last much longer.

Then he heard what sounded like gunfire on the hill above him and the rumble of trucks below. Then he lapsed into unconsciousness.

Minutes later he heard the roar of engines.

Trucks!

The Chinese didn't have trucks.

Marines! It had to be.

But would they see him?

Then he saw someone walking down from the hill above. No question about it. A marine. When he got closer, Pugh saw that he was wounded in an arm. They talked for a few minutes, then the wounded marine walked down to the convoy. In no time at all corpsmen and stretchers were at the lean-to and the five men were carried down to the trucks and on into Koto-ri.

December 6, 1950; headquarters, 2nd Battalion, 5th Regiment, Hagaru, 1:30 P.M.: Roisie sent Peters's F Company up East Hill to replace Smith's D Company on Objective A, then told Smith to capture Objective B, another high peak, about three hundred yards southeast of Objective A. A saddle linked the two.

It took D Company four hours to capture Objective B, but it was worth the effort. Now the marines controlled the heights above the road south. No one would be up there firing down on the convoy as it passed through the southern roadblock.

A platoon from the Army's 4th Signal Battalion and twelve marines kept the saddle clear of Chinese.

Jones's C Company and Jaskilka's E Company were side by side along the base of the hill to the north.

Although the marines had the hill for the first time since they got to Hagaru and were well dug in on top and in good position on the low ground, the Chinese weren't about to give up.

They attacked high and low throughout the night of December 6, first on the hill, then at its base.

Their losses were frightful. They came in great numbers, sometimes four abreast, marching, at times trotting, into the barrels of machine guns and Army tanks. They walked through fields of mortar fire.

When his company went into the perimeter at Hagaru, Jones was told, "Hold that ground in front of you." He did. So did Jaskilka.

"We were dug in pretty good. We were in some holes that were already there but we changed them the way we wanted them," Jones explained.

Wallingford had his 60s about fifty yards behind Jones's command post. When the Chinese struck again, at about midnight, he dropped the first few rounds out about two hundred yards, then carefully walked them in about twenty to twenty-five yards a round until they were exploding about twenty yards in front of company lines.

When it got really tight, he brought them in to about ten yards in front of the foxholes. This was a bit too close, but it worked. It stopped the Chinese.

"We felt good. We knew their tactics. We'd had waves of people coming at us, and we'd stopped them. We knew what to expect. Mass hordes. We had a couple of bad nights there. We didn't lose many people, but we sure took account of them," Jones said.

A company commander's command post might be from fifty to a hundred yards behind his men. At Hagaru, Jaskilka was ten yards back. And his CP was topside. He couldn't dig a hole; the ground was too hard. He had no sandbags, no cover.

"Whatever dent you found in the ground, that was your cover," he remembered.

He had his radio operator, his runner, and his gunnery sergeant, Barnett. Close by, within shouting distance, was his exec, Lt. Jim Roberts.

"There were so many flares, so much white phosphorus, you could clearly see columns of Chinese walking down the road from the north, trotting along, four abreast," Canzona remembered. "When they got to the front lines, they'd fan out and try to penetrate. But we were cutting them down like wheat."

"I didn't quite see it that way," Jaskilka remembered, "but I knew there was a hell of a lot of them."

When the Chinese hit, his men began firing when they were about forty to fifty yards away. Jaskilka liked it that way. Let them get in close, but not within grenade range, yet close enough so that when you fired, you hit something.

While the Chinese were being eliminated at the base of the hill, the situation was turning against the marines on top.

D Company was attacked again and again until the Chinese forced their way in.

Roisie was in his CP of sandbags a hundred yards or so behind the lines and listening on his radio to the fighting on the hill.

Canzona, an engineer, was with him when Smith radioed that Chinese had gotten into his position.

"Smith was reporting to Roisie, and as the Chinese got closer, his voice became lower and lower, finally down to a whisper," Canzona recalled.

"They're getting closer."

The sounds of gunfire and hand grenades exploding were heard.

"They're breaking through."

Roisie didn't like this.

Then, barely audible, "They're among us!" "They're rolling hand grenades at us!"

Roisie, munching on crackers, turned to his radio operator and very calmly said, "God damnit, tell them to throw the grenades back at them!"

Johnson was on the hill at Objective A in a bunker with Iverson when a shell went off ten yards away, sending a shower of white phosphorus over their heads but right at Peters, F Company commander, who was badly hit, and his radioman, who was killed.

Johnson's hole was small, hardly big enough for one, let alone two and their gear, so when the shooting stopped for a few moments both men dug furiously until they had something they could call home for however long they would remain on East Hill.

He heard the bugles just after dark; then flares burst overhead. "I looked up and saw several skirmish lines two hundred to three hundred yards away. They moved in on Dog Company on the other side of the hill," Johnson recalled.

D Company was really catching hell. So was the Army Signal Corps platoon, and the twelve marines in the saddle.

Johnson couldn't see over the hill, but he could hear someone walking on the other side, so he pulled the pin and sailed a grenade over there. Moments later he peeked over just as a concussion grenade went off in his face. Powder burns closed both eyes. Wood splinters peppered his skin.

"I panicked. I thought they'd get me when I couldn't see, so I grabbed a carbine and started to fire." But that was foolish, and he quickly realized it. So he began crawling back toward the company CP. He hadn't gone far when he fell into an empty foxhole, so he stayed there until his eyes opened.

The weather was good, and the planes were up before first light on December 7 to blast the Chinese around East Hill. They couldn't get away fast enough to escape the bombs, the rockets, and the strafing runs.

While the planes were pounding the Chinese, Fox and Dog companies on East Hill were told to pack up, come down, and prepare to leave Hagaru. The Army Signal Corps platoon and the twelve marines who held the saddle were also brought down. The two companies then came down and headed for the road leading south to Koto-ri.

As Johnson walked down the hill he passed several captured Chinese and flashed them his best smile. "I didn't want them to think we were whipped."

A few Chinese had slipped down the hill, a few others had gotten through or around Easy and Charley, but they were quickly picked off as soon as it got light.

In front of both companies there was a carpet of bodies.

"I remember walking out there with Murray and they were really piled up," Canzona said. "Bodies were very close to Easy, in many cases a few feet. A lot of them had burned to death. A lot of guys were shooting white phosphorus from their bazookas at point-blank range," Canzona added.

Marines estimated there were more than eight hundred dead in front of their holes on and around the hill.

"We did have a lot of contact with the Chinese," Roisie remembered. "I had one company that killed over five hundred Chinese trying to get in there."

Taplett's Third Battalion was on the road and moving south early on December 7. His 1st Battalion was getting ready to quit the village, and Ridge's 3rd Battalion of the 1st Regiment would follow.

Roisie's 2nd Battalion would be the rear guard. There would be a platoon of tanks followed by Canzona's small group of engineers, who would touch off the supply dumps, destroy the village, and destroy the bridge leading south.

Canzona and his men were cutting the fuses several feet long, setting the timers so they would have five to ten minutes to get out of there before everything went sky high.

While Canzona's men still were setting fuses, and pouring gasoline on the supply dumps while Roisie's men still were coming down the hill, the first dump went up, sending smoke and flames high in the sky and live ammunition exploding in every direction.

"You could see stuff sailing all over the place," Canzona said.

Rockets, tracers, and machine-gun ammunition flew everywhere. Mortar shells exploded.

Canzona didn't know what had happened, who had touched off some of the dumps prematurely. He knew for certain his men hadn't done it.

"I got pretty teed off about it," he said, "and I hoped some of it wouldn't go off underneath us."

The situation on the road south had worsened. There was still a roadblock at every turn, but now they were bigger. None was easy. Some were much tougher than others. It wasn't long before the convoy ground to a halt once again. In front of the lead vehicle was a huge pile of logs, dirt, and rocks. There were hundreds of Chinese behind it. Machine guns had the convoy under fire from both sides of the road. The first few trucks ran off the road and got around the barricade. Several were set on fire.

At this point every man in the convoy reverted to his primary MOS: rifleman. Headquarters personnel, supply clerks, motor pool, artillery, all attacked the roadblock. But it was a standoff for about two hours, until dawn, when the air cover arrived. They strafed and rocketed the Chinese. A howitzer was brought to the front and fired point-blank. It was a delicate situation in the sense that if the road were cratered by explosions, then the convoy would be delayed further.

Just after daylight the vehicles began to roll again, past dead Chinese, an estimated eight hundred who had fought to the end.

Although the trucks were moving a mile or so an hour, the situation was anything but good. The front third of the convoy, far down the road, radioed that Chinese were everywhere.

Roisie was on the road and heading south from Hagaru now. Jaskilka's company was the rear point. There were tanks with his men. Then came Canzona's engineers.

Hagaru was in flames. Ammunition still was exploding. Canzona could see the Chinese coming in from the north. "They were several hundred yards away but not looking for us," he recalled. "They were bent on looting.

"It was quite impressive," Canzona said as he watched the village go up in smoke from the center of the bridge leading south. "It kind of looked like the Fourth of July."

"As I crossed the bridge, a terrific explosion rocked the town" as the ammunition went up, Barrett remembered.

A couple of disabled planes were burning on the runway. Chinese were milling around them, not doing too much of anything. New fires were breaking out as the time fuses went off, blowing up the last of the supply dumps. The Chinese who had gotten to them moments earlier went up, too.

Jaskilka turned around for one last look and thought, "How desolate. I wonder if I'll ever come back."

Barrett wondered about it, too—the killing, the bloodshed, the night of terror.

"Forget it? I doubt it very seriously."

Thousands of Korean refugees trying to keep ahead of the Chinese followed the marines.

"One thing I'll always remember is the hostile looks of the North Korean people as we moved up to the reservoir," Steele said. "Coming down, though, they all wanted to leave with us."

One jeep was parked in the center of the bridge while the engineers discussed the length of fuses to be used.

Then, a few minutes later, it went sky high.

The commandos were with the rear guard now, and Maill remembers being told just before they left Hagaru, "It will be a fighting withdrawal, and we will withdraw like royal marines. We will shave off our beards and smarten ourselves up some."

Maill and two other commandos took up a position on the far side of the bridge leading south out of the village and, with a machine gun borrowed from some U.S. marines close by, kept the Chinese from crossing while the last vehicles left the village.

"We put so many belts of ammo through that gun that we returned a burnt-out machine gun to a slightly disgruntled marine," Maill remembered.

"My lads joked about me knocking off fifty to sixty gooks before breakfast and my reward was no breakfast, because we were on the move again without time for food.

"I have little recollection of consuming food during that period other than Hershey bars and Tootsie Rolls," he said, "which were parachuted to us along with after-shave talc, and deodorant."

The fight south was bitter and bloody all the way. It never seemed to stop.

Most of the time the sky was clear, so air support was always up there.

"Once across the bridge out of Hagaru, everyone heaved a sigh of relief since we felt sure the worst was over," Barrett remembered. "Once we get to Koto-ri we will have it knocked up, seemed to be the general consensus among the men and junior officers. We didn't know at the time that the road south from Koto—the road down the mountain—was cut and would have to be opened."

Hintsa was on the road south, his pockets jammed with Life Savers and Tootsie Rolls. He'd cut a sleeve off a GI sweater and made a stocking cap of it. He had his helmet on top of that, then the hood of his parka, and his head was still cold.

A few hours out he passed a Chinese machine-gun crew that had been napalmed. The gunner was still holding the gun handles, eyes open, scorched black. "Some wise guy lighted a cigarette and dangled it from the corpse's mouth," he remembered.

The road was littered with Chinese. "After the vehicles rolled over them they were flat as pancakes," Hintsa said. "They looked like gingerbread men."

On the road it was still stop and go. The foot troops moved. The vehicles stopped. When the trucks rolled, the marines didn't. When all went right, troops and trucks moved together. But that wasn't often.

"It was the slowest-moving goddamn thing you ever saw," said Reynolds, whose radio repair platoon moved south with the medical detachment in the back two thirds of the convoy, which was moving along at about two miles an hour and taking heavy fire every yard of the way.

A double turn in the road slowed the trucks almost to a stop. Then a flatbed trailer, whose driver was shot, brought it to a halt.

Reynolds ran forward to see what had happened. The driver was dead. The marine beside him had a hole in his chest.

"Can you drive it?"

"I don't know."

Reynolds went back to find a driver, but by the time he had returned, the truck was shot to pieces: A tank pushed it off the road, and the convoy began to move again.

The pace picked up, the sweat began to roll. Then it slowed, and the men began to freeze.

And the trucks. Were they a blessing? Or were they to be cursed?

It was easy to disable them. Easier still to shoot the drivers. They were prime targets. Moving along at two miles an hour, often less than that, the Chinese could hardly miss the drivers, the engines, or the tires.

No one who walked down that road wanted to get too close to them. They drew a lot of rifle and machine-gun fire.

So the wise hands stayed away from the vehicles as much as possible.

But were it not for the vehicles, they wouldn't have gotten the wounded out.

The gunfire never really stopped. At worst, snipers kept the marines busy. Most of the shots were wild, never drew blood, just hit the road. But occasionally the cry for a corpsman could be heard and you knew that a bullet had struck home.

Blodgett was with the 5th Regiment, driving a big tractor. But it ran out of gas a short time out of Hagaru and was run off the road.

Then he reverted back to his secondary MOS—demolitions—and wound up at the rear of the convoy, carrying forty pounds of explosives. His orders: "Don't leave any bridges standing under any circumstances."

Maill was trudging down the road, pipe lit.

He spotted what looked like a company of Chinese moving up a hill about two thousand yards out. They were too far off for small arms, so he had a tank mark the spot with smoke, then called in the planes. They napalmed and strafed the hill, and in minutes it was a charred mass. The Chinese, caught in the open with no cover, were no longer a threat.

The trucks continued to move, still no faster than a couple of miles an hour.

Several prisoners were standing by the road, their feet black and popping through their sneakers, their hands tied behind their backs. They'd be questioned; then, when they could cause the marines no further harm, released.

A marine walked over, knew they were worse off than he was, stuck a cigarette in the mouth of one of them, and touched a match to it. But another marine ran over and shouted, "Don't give the bastard anything!" and knocked him to the ground.

The rear guard entered Hell Fire Valley and saw what Task Force Drysdale had endured. For Maill and other commandos, coming back through the area was almost as bad as fighting north through the area.

"We found our dead where they had fallen in the snow, preserved in gruesome postures," he remembered. Trucks and jeeps were bumper to bumper. All were either burned or shot to pieces. Some were still smoldering.

"One of the worse sights I have ever seen, and I will never forget it," said Coutre.

"We tried to pull bodies out of the trucks but they were frozen in grotesque positions," said Kelly, E Company, 2nd Battalion, 7th Regiment, who had passed through the area earlier.

"Christmas packages with their bright wrapping paper and colorful ribbons were strewn about the area for a quarter of a mile," Maill said.

"It was a terrible sight," he added.

Sacks of mail were scattered as far as you could see.

Instead of sitting down to rest, as they had done at other stops, the marines spread out quietly and began to collect the mail. Sacks of letters and packages, the most precious gift a fighting man can receive, had been ripped apart by explosions, and the wind had blown them all over the landscape. But there was so much mail there they didn't have time to collect it all.

"The men just stood there gazing in disbelief at the wreckage, trying, it seemed, to make it go away, or tell a different story than the one that was so obvious," Barrett said.

Then the trucks began to roll slowly south in the fading light of December 7 on the last leg of the eleven-mile running battle to Koto-ri. It was still stop and go. Hurry down the road, then stop. Perspire, then freeze. At each stop, every man thought of the precious minutes of daylight they were losing. No one wanted to be on the road after dark.

"We tried to speed up because the light was beginning to go and we hoped to be within the perimeter of Koto-ri before dark," Barrett said.

Then it was one last dash for the village. The trucks sped on and left the marines on the road.

Jaskilka walked all the way. His jeep was full of wounded and frostbitten. Along the way he picked up a Korean child about three or four years old and put it in his jeep. Later, down the road some distance, he saw a Korean woman and gave it to her.

"We were under fire most of the time, but it was at long range, three hundred to four hundred yards," he said. "Nobody got hurt, but it scared the hell out of us."

The Antitank Company headquarters crossed the perimeter at about 6:30 P.M. on December 7. The 75mm gun platoon began to cross the perimeter a short time later with elements of the 3rd Battalion, 5th Regiment. Each unit had been busy from the moment they left Hagaru, pounding the hillsides, blasting buildings on either side of the road, firing at anything that could give cover to the enemy.

But the hours, the days, the nights of continual fighting were exacting a toll. The men were stumbling, falling down, sometimes walking, much of the time running, trying to get inside the perimeter before dark. They saw the trucks roll out of sight. They knew they were close.

Then word spread down the line, "Fall out to the right of the road and form companies!"

Once off the road, the men began to collapse in the snow. They simply couldn't keep their eyes open any longer.

"Get off the ground there!"

"We'll tell you when to sit down!"

"Don't let the men sit on the ground!"

"Keep them on their feet!"

"Don't let them go to sleep!"

"They'll freeze! They'll freeze!"

"Keep them on their feet!"

The officers and noncoms certainly meant well. But they weren't having much success.

"What the hell are we stopping here for?" The men groused, cursed at no one in particular.

Shouts filled the dark.

"How Company! Over here, damnit!"

Men stumbled in the paddies and ditches. They couldn't see but a few feet in any direction.

"You felt like a slave-driver moving among your men, kicking the ones who wouldn't move, snapping at them, irritated because you didn't know why you were stopping," Barrett said.

Then the company commander called the platoon leaders together.

"We learned we were just short of the roadblock that marked the entrance to the perimeter to Koto-ri," Barrett explained.

But why had they stopped?

Why the company formations?

"Why, by God, just like in the movies. We were the 3rd Battalion, 1st Marines, some of 'Chesty's boys,' and we were going to march into Koto, the regimental CP, as a battalion—and not as a bunch of stragglers," Barrett was told.

"They had to have a goddamn battalion formation," Barrett said.

"At first we were so mad we could have cried," Barrett said.

"Then, as we moved out of the paddy, a tired, dirty, cold, miserably hungry, motley assortment of men, the whole thing seemed sort of ridiculous and we forgot our anger."

As they marched past the guards at the roadblock and down the center of Koto-ri, past the regimental CP, slipping and falling on the ice, with the voices of NCO's snarling out of the dark, "Keep it closed up," previous feelings were replaced by great pride.

"I was damn proud to be a part of it," Barrett added.

Once inside the perimeter they stopped in a courtlike area made by the positioning of tents. An officer from regiment told them where to go.

"You can put ten men in there," the officer said. "There're only fifteen in there now."

The tent he pointed to normally slept six to eight.

Men were shoved, pushed, jam-packed into tents until it was no longer possible to get in the door. Only then was one considered to be full. When tent space ran out, men were given parachutes and told to wrap themselves in them and sleep on the ground.

Regardless of where they were, in a tent or on the ground, no one had any trouble going to sleep that night. For the first time in weeks they were able to take off their shoes and sleep without the worry of someone sticking a bayonet in them.

Someone else was manning the perimeter tonight.

Once Barrett's men had bedded down, he started looking for a place to sleep.

He poked his head in one tent, saw a small spot he thought he could fit into, and crawled in. It was tight. But he moved some C rations, put a machine gun outside, used another ration box as a pillow, then crawled into his bag and slept like a baby.

As soon as Reynolds crossed the perimeter he found out where the dead were and went over to check bodies, to see who hadn't made it.

He walked slowly up and down the rows. Then he spotted the bright, heavy wool shirt on a young marine.

"His mother had sent it to him on his twenty-first birthday," Reynolds said. "He asked me if he could wear it and I said, 'Hell, yes. Don't worry about your uniform now. If you don't want to wear it, I'll wear it.' "

The ground was so hard that even bulldozers could hardly dent it, so British and American dead shared a common grave at Koto-ri covered with little more than snow and ice.

Canzona's small demolitions team was the last to cross the northern roadblock. All the bridges, all the trucks, everything that might be of some use to the Chinese on the road south from Hagaru had been destroyed.

Whenever the convoy had stopped, the engineers planted antipersonnel mines, something to let the Chinese know the marines were thinking about them. It also slowed them down as they followed the marines down the road.

Refugees were a problem.

Canzona tried to keep them at a distance of two to three hundred yards but wasn't always successful. He didn't want any Chinese to infiltrate and get too close to his men.

"We were anxious to get to Koto-ri before nightfall, so we moved fast," he remembered. They didn't make it. It was well after dark— about 9:00 P.M.—when they crossed the northern roadblock and were told to settle down next to a battery of howitzers. "We didn't get any sleep at all that night," he said.

Almost immediately he learned that the division would be leaving Koto-ri in a matter of hours and head south to the sea at Hungnam. He also learned that the 5th Regiment would move up in the convoy and that Pullner's 1st Regiment would be at the rear.

"Good. Let someone else cope with the refugees, blow the bridges, let someone else have the rear guard," Barrett thought.

Then he saw Gould, the commanding officer of A Company, 1st Engineer Battalion, striding in his direction.

"He told me we had done such a damn fine job we were going to follow the 1st Marines out."

CHAPTER 12
THE SEA AND SAFETY

Geneval Smith, Bowser, Winecoff, and the general's chief of
staff, Col. Gregon A. Williams, had four bunks in the back
of a large hospital tent. The rest of the space was used as the
division's operations center.

"We were sitting there drinking coffee and staring at a map, talking
about the bridge that had to be dropped, the road, a few odds and ends.
Then I heard what I thought was singing," Bowser said.

"Excuse me a minute, General."

Bowser got up and stepped to the front of the tent.

"I walked outside, and I was right. There was a bunch of marines
in a tent a few tents away and they were singing all the old service songs
they knew."

Bowser went back inside and said:

"General, we got it made."

"What are you talking about?"

"Those clowns, in the circumstances we regard as nearly impossible,
are all sitting over there singing."

Then the brass did some hard thinking.

They talked about the 5th and 7th regiments coming in from Hagaru,
problems along the road south, the power plant, the high ground along
Funchilin Pass, particularly Hill 1081.

Lt. Col. John J. Partridge, the 1st Engineer Battalion's commanding
officer, had flown over the power plant, saw the break in the road where
a bridge had been, and knew immediately what had to be done. The
narrow footpath that led behind the plant would enable the marines to
walk out carrying their wounded if the bridge could not be replaced.
The engineers had repaired it three times, and the Chinese had damaged
it three times. Now they had destroyed it completely, leaving a drop
of a few hundred feet between the two sections of the road. If the
division had to walk out, many more dead and wounded could be
expected. Also, more than twelve hundred tanks and other vehicles
would have to be shoved over the side. The marines hadn't come this
far, through so much blood, so much shot and shell, to build the world's
biggest junkpile.

Partridge discussed the power plant with General Smith and his staff,
and the decision was made to air-drop two treadway bridges at Koto-ri,

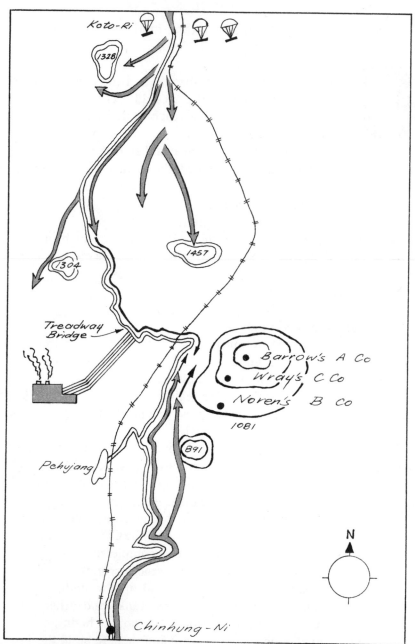

Map 12—Bridge is parachuted at Koto-ri and trucked to power plant. Arrows from north show route of marines as they take high ground on both sides of the road south. Arrows from south show route of marines as they fight up toward Hill 1081 to meet the division coming down the road.

314

then truck one to the power plant, where the engineers would put one in place. The second bridge was a backup should something go awry.

But could it be done on such short notice?

Were there parachutes large enough to do the job?

And what if it couldn't be done?

"The plan was that if that happened, well, then we would just simply ditch the rolling stock, dismount, and fight on foot carrying the wounded," Bowser said.

Woessner, Litzenberg's chief of plans and operations, said:

"I remember thinking that this was one heck of a small link to depend on to get out of there, that it was a tenuous link between these two parts of the hill that we had to depend on for the whole division to get back over."

A priority message to the Japan Logistical Command in Tokyo got things rolling.

There are four sections to a treadway bridge, each weighing two tons. That meant eight sections, one each to a C-119 "Flying Boxcar" transport plane.

The eight sections were located at an American military base in Japan and trucked to Tachikawa Air Base, just outside Tokyo. Eight Air Force C-119s flew up from Ashiya Air Base in southern Japan, the sections were loaded aboard the planes, then they flew back to Ashiya. There the Army's 2348th Quartermaster Airborne Air Supply and Packaging Company loaded the bridges, one section to a plane. Capt. Cecil W. Hospelhorn and ten paratroopers rigged and loaded the sections, then climbed aboard the aircraft for the flight to Yonpo Air Base in South Korea, not far from the seaport of Hungnam. One span was dropped there and floated to earth with a giant parachute—forty-eight feet across—attached to both ends. It worked. There were a few dents, but it was usable. It was then decided that the two bridges would be dropped the following morning.

Capturing Hill 1081 was vital. It was about a third of the way down Funchilin Pass and a short distance past the power plant, which was three and a half miles from Koto-ri. If the Chinese controlled that hill, it would be target practice as the division passed below.

Bowser wasn't too pleased with the withdrawal from Hagaru to Koto-ri. When the marines left Hagaru, they realized that the Chinese either had communications so poor they didn't know where their people were all the time, or they were physically unable to move their troops and supply them in such fashion to hurt the marines in force.

"That's the reason we launched the operation from Hagaru back to Koto-ri as . . . sort of a wagon train," Bowser said.

"It didn't work. As it turned out, it was a mistake," he said. "We never should have done it. I would never again launch a so-called division train like we did from Hagaru to Koto-ri. It was a bad mistake. We were so anxious to get moving and get out of there that I think we all accepted what looked like the easiest solution."

The breakout from Koto-ri and the fight south would be handled differently.

December 7, 1950: At 9:30 A.M., the eight C-119s arrived in a long single file over the drop zone, which had been marked with bright orange panels. All but one of the several ropes holding the bridge sections had been cut. The last rope was to prevent a premature drop. It would be cut with an ax at the same time that drag chutes pulled the bridge sections from the planes.

One very small chute was spring-loaded to throw it into the slip-stream. This chute would then deploy a larger chute that actually pulled the sections from the planes. The spring was tripped by the crew chief with a cable upon command from the pilot while another crew member cut the last rope. It took only five seconds, time that was very critical to put the sections where they were supposed to be on the ground.

The first section floated toward the panels and hit the ground. Excellent. The engineers radioed the lead plane that the drop was fine. The rest of the planes followed, unloaded the bridge sections, then headed back to Japan.

Capt. Jim Inks headed for the drop zone. His crew cut all but the safety rope. Then, on his command, the crew chief pulled the cable to release the pilot chute, and at the same moment another crewman cut the last rope.

"Unfortunately, that pilot chute mechanism failed to work, and we were past the drop zone with our load still aboard," Inks remembered.

Five of the sections so far dropped fell inside Koto-ri. The Chinese got one, and another was damaged.

Inks had the eighth.

The situation in his plane was bad and getting worse.

"We were in the floor of a canyon with a loose load in the cargo compartment and doubtful whether I had enough power to climb my overloaded aircraft over the mountains to get out of there," he said.

The canyon wasn't wide enough to make a 180-degree turn.

Inks was reasonably sure that he could have dumped the load by making a steep climb with full power, but he was miles beyond where they needed the bridge. And there was always the possibility that without drag chutes the bridge would hang up in the rear of the cargo compartment. "And that would be all she wrote," he added.

So he told the crew to stay forward of the load in case it decided to go. Then he asked his navigator to find a way out of the canyon in a hurry.

"He picked a canyon coming in from the east that he thought would continue downgrade. But as soon as we banked into it, we realized that it was upgrade and pretty steep," Inks said.

Meanwhile, his air crew had managed to get a rope across the twenty-five-hundred-pound section and secured it somewhat.

But even with the plane's full power the slope of the canyon was greater than the C-119's climbing angle.

"We were in a hell of a spot," Inks remembered.

The plane was a couple of hundred feet aboveground, just about at stalling speed, when the ridge to the left opened into another canyon.

"We skidded through it not ten feet from the rocks and started back toward the main canyon that we had just left," Inks explained.

He tried to get the plane as high as he could. His crew checked the bridge section.

Inks decided that if they could get the mechanism on the pilot chute working, they still could drop the section. His crew chief had been working on the problem and felt he had it operating.

"We made another very nervous second pass over the drop zone and our span of the bridge was delivered with the others about fifteen minutes late," Inks said.

The C-119s also dropped heavy plywood center sections that would fill the space between the two metal spans. The tanks would cross using the two spans. The rest of the vehicles would cross using one metal span and the plywood. By late afternoon the sections were loaded on four

317

trucks, and in the morning they would be driven down to the power plant.

December 8, 1950; breakout from Koto-ri, 7:00 A.M.: No one had counted on the weather turning so bad. There was nothing in General Smith's orders of the day that said visibility would be zero, that planes and artillery they had counted on couldn't be utilized.

The wind howled down from the north, blowing ice and snow into faces that soon felt like pincushions. The temperature never got above zero as the marines headed south in a regiment-abreast attack in a blizzard of snowflakes.

"The 5th and 7th regiments were abreast with specific, delineated objects they had to seize in order to uncover the road," Bowser explained. The wagon train approach had been relegated to the scrap heap.

Woessner remembered the last morning in the village.

"The whole place smelled like one big pancake," he said. "There was no limit to hot food. Pancakes, syrup, hot coffee. I think everybody had his fill."

That was pleasant. Hot food in your stomach made life on the road that morning just a bit easier.

A more somber note was the devastating losses the division had suffered. Some companies and platoons had all but disappeared. Other companies were down to twenty to thirty men, most wounded, all suffering from varying degrees of frostbite.

"We were having to fight with a vastly reduced regiment," Woessner said. "I was hoping that the Chinese would be hurt just as bad so that by comparison we would be able to do the job."

Despite the losses, the marines were beginning to feel that they would get back, that they would reach the sea and safety.

"There was no doubt in my mind that we could do it," Woessner said.

Jaskilka looked around, saw the high ground in front of the village, and knew immediately that they had to get out of there, that it was not the best position to be in. "I like to be looking down the other fellow's throat," he said.

The hills to the right and left of the road just outside the perimeter fell as planned. A few Chinese. A little gunfire.

The Army's 31/7 Provisional Battalion took its first objective on the left, then moved forward another eight hundred to a thousand yards and, with help from the 1st Battalion, 5th Regiment, pushed the Chinese off the dominating high ground on the left, Hill 1457.

Kurcaba's B Company, 1st Battalion, 7th Regiment, was the point on the road. His men would open the road south and drive the Chinese off the lower slope of Hill 1081, a long, high mass of ground that ran almost from Koto-ri alongside the road to the top of Funchilin Pass, then down beyond the power plant.

So far, so good. There were very few casualties. Fighting wasn't heavy.

Two tanks were close behind Kurcaba's men. Then came Theros and his forward air control team.

"I knew we had it made then," Theros remembered. "Leaving Koto-ri was like going to a midnight movie after all the other stuff, Hagaru . . . Yudam-ni."

By midday the situation had changed. The point was under heavy fire. The Chinese were spraying the road from both sides. Kurcaba was killed, and Lt. William W. Taylor took over as company commander.

Fighting along the road and in the foothills continued until dusk. At that time the marines had established a solid line that ran from the high ground on the left where 31/7 and the 1st Battalion, 5th Regiment, had linked up, down to B Company on the road and up into the hills on the right, where A and C companies, 1st Battalion, 7th Regiment, had joined. Rifle companies also held the high ground on both sides of the road all the way back to Koto-ri.

It was bitter cold as the men began to dig in for the night.

No one ever got smaller there. Only larger. You never took anything off. You only added another layer of clothing.

From where Morris's C Company was, he could see the Chinese out there just before it got dark. "You could look down and . . . then here came the Chinese," he said. "You could see them moving down the side of this hill, across the valley, and up our hill at us. They weren't shooting, just coming."

He tried to dig a hole but couldn't. When his shovel hit the ground, sparks flew, and it hurt all the way up to his shoulder.

Soon the Chinese were so close to Morris's line that he could hear them chattering. His men took a little fire from one side, a little from another direction. He checked his line constantly, expecting the worst at any moment.

The column now stretched two and a half miles from the south roadblock at Koto-ri. Drifts were waist high along the road, deeper in the mountains.

The road south appeared to be clear to the top of Funchilin Pass.

Northern roadblock, Koto-ri, 10:00 P.M.: The marines still inside the perimeter were faced with a mounting problem, one they hadn't expected and could do nothing about. Thousands of refugees were in the hills, on the road, held at bay by marine machine guns.

They stretched for miles along the road back to Hagaru.

They were freezing but not whimpering. Nor asking for help. Or begging. They were just waiting to follow the marines south.

Canzona and his engineers were inside the perimeter. Once the bridge was in place and the column was moving south again, when the rear guard and the last tanks had cleared the village, the whole place would go up in smoke.

They would try to keep the refugees at a safe distance, but this was a problem that was rapidly getting out of control.

The last casualties would be flown out in the morning. Later, General Smith would fly to Hungnam. Once he'd touched down safely, Bowser would follow.

Hill 1304, 11:00 P.M.: In the hills down the road the point units were trying to make it through the coldest night the men had ever experienced.

In front of Morris's C Company, 1st Battalion, 7th Regiment, on the right there was total silence. It was 11:30 P.M. and his men had not heard anything for more than two hours. He had expected the Chinese to come storming up the hill. But nothing was happening. The silence was confusing. So no one slept that night.

December 8, 1950; Chinhung-ni, 7:00 A.M.: It was snowing just as hard at the bottom of Funchilin Pass as it was at the top, but it wasn't as cold because there was a drop of three thousand feet. At the same time that the division was breaking out of Koto-ri, the marines were attacking another giant problem: Hill 1081. It was well bunkered at three levels and garrisoned by fresh Chinese troops who wanted to hold on to it as badly as the marines wanted to capture it.

While the three regiments were on their way to the top of the pass, Lt. Col. Donald M. Schmuck's 1st Battalion, 1st Regiment, attacked from the bottom. When the division passed below Hill 1081, the top had to be in marine control.

Schmuck's battalion was at the bottom of the pass to keep the flatland free of Chinese, to keep open the only link to the sea.

But the Army's 3rd Infantry Division was on the scene now and had set up a perimeter around Hungnam, the port city. Patrols had fanned out to try to find out where the Chinese were and in what strength. There were soldiers in Chinhung-ni, too, thus freeing Schmuck's battalion to head north up the road toward Hill 1081.

Several days earlier Schmuck had anticipated that someone might have to go up 1081 if the division was to get back in one piece. He thought it just might be his battalion. On December 2 he went out with a patrol north to see how far they could get up the road toward the power plant.

A lieutenant was in charge of the rifle squad. There was a forward observer along with Maj. W. L. Bates, Jr., the weapons company commander, and Schmuck. They raced up the road in three jeeps and a six-by until they got to the power plant. The drivers turned the vehicles around in case they had to get out in a hurry. Then they walked behind the plant and up the road toward the first turn. So far, nothing. But once they turned the corner, the entire area was alive with Chinese. They were talking, laughing, cooking. War appeared to be the last thing on their minds. Schmuck and the forward observer climbed a little ridge for a better view and saw still more Chinese.

"A chance of a lifetime," Schmuck thought.

In minutes artillery rounds were falling on top of their heads. They didn't know where to run, what to do.

"It was the most rewarding few minutes of my whole period of service," Schmuck later told the Army's noted military historian Gen. S.L.A. Marshall.

Then they got out of there in a hurry, driving at great speed down the road to the battalion command post.

"From that hour, I felt I was in good position to attack up the canyon, and I was confident we could carry it out," Schmuck said.

On December 7, Schmuck was told to move early the following morning. His objective: Hill 1081.

"Colonel Schmuck called us over and showed us the message that had come in over the radio from Puller: 'We have contact on four sides,'" Capt. Robert P. Wray remembered. "We all chuckled about it." Then Schmuck told his company commanders:

"Things are going to get a little sticky in the next few days."

Early on December 8, in a blinding snowstorm, Wray's C Company moved out from Chinhung-ni.

"My orders were to go about four or five turns up the road, attack up this hill, seize it, and hold it until Bob Barrow with Able Company came up behind me," Wray explained. Barrow would then take his company across a saddle to the next hill, and Wray would provide fire support from below.

The only maps they had were in Japanese and many years old.

The snow was so heavy Wray couldn't see three feet in front of his face.

"I missed the number of turns I was supposed to take and then go upward," he recalled. "I was one turn too far." As a result, his men were on the lower reaches of Hill 1081 but in an area where they shouldn't have been. But he didn't know it then.

Barrow's men were already on the march.

So were the men in Capt. Wesley C. Noren's B Company, whose job was to go up the road and clear it of Chinese. But they had to be careful. Noren didn't want any of his vehicles on the road. He didn't know just when the 5th and the 7th would come down. So to be on the safe side, he didn't want the road cluttered with any company vehicles.

Barrow knew exactly where he was, where he was supposed to be, where he was heading to begin his ascent.

"It wasn't a case of fanning out in an approach," he remembered. "Only mountain goats would attempt to climb it."

Barrow and his gunnery sergeant, King Thatenhurst, led the way up to where they expected to find the Chinese.

"We had a lot of pride and belief in ourselves," Barrow said. "We had had nominal good success [in everything we had done]. Put that all together and we were really at a kind of peak when we launched off toward Hill 1081.

"The terrain clearly presented itself as one to be held to block the rest of the marine division from coming out," Barrow remembered.

It was snowing heavily now, which muffled the sound of marching and masked the Chinese from seeing the marines.

The hill was rough from the start. With each succeeding step it became more difficult. It was like trying to scale the Alps.

"It was so steep and treacherous," Wray remembered, "that we couldn't carry more than a third of a GI can full of water." And his men didn't get close to the top.

It was hand-over-hand. Climb with one, pull with the other. You had to be part mountain goat.

It was very cold where Wray was. It was much colder on top, where Barrow was headed.

Wray told his sergeants to check the holes throughout the night. "I, myself, made three complete tours, and I fell over six men. The wind had blown snow over their sleeping bags. I'd trip over them, brush the snow off, uncover their faces, straddle them, and sit there and slap their faces to wake them up. Otherwise they'd have frozen to death. When I got 'em awake to where they'd try to take a swing at me, I knew that I'd gotten them awake enough so that they could survive."

The weather was a great problem. And a blessing. Because of it there was no air support. But the Chinese still couldn't see the marines, and surprise was a big part of the assault.

But once the weather cleared, Schmuck could call on Koto-ri for artillery fire. Back at Chinhung-ni a topflight Army outfit was anxious to join the fighting: the 92nd Armored Field Artillery Battalion, commanded by Lt. Col. Leon F. Lavoie.

He and Schmuck had met at Chinhung-ni several days earlier.

"I have tried for four days to convince General Almond that I ought to get the hell up here and shoot for you boys," he told Schmuck.

"Obviously, you need it. I've got these guns just dying to be fired."

But Almond didn't want him to go.

"I can't let you. We might endanger the tubes," he told Lavoie.

But Lavoie was finally able to convince him.

"My specific instructions are to fire all the ammo and get the hell out and back to Hamhung," Lavoie told Schmuck.

"Great. I couldn't be more pleased," the battalion commander told Lavoie. Then he showed the artillery commander around the area, particularly the neatly stacked piles of 155 rounds.

Lavoie just grinned from ear to ear.

"He didn't specify which ammo I could fire. I'm gonna stay here until I fire every damn round of this, as well as what I brought with me. Name your targets."

Schmuck had another outstanding Army outfit supporting him, an antiaircraft unit that had eighteen half-tracks of twin 40s and quad 50s.

A few of them followed his battalion up the road, and when those 40s unloaded, it was as if someone had dropped a basketful of grenades on your head.

All they wanted to do was fight. One gunner was shot out of the saddle, and two other GIs had a fistfight to see who would take over the hot seat.

"That's outstanding," Wray said.

By 10:00 P.M. a full-scale assault was under way, on the road and on 1081.

There were plenty of Chinese around. Noren could tell that by the tracks in the snow on the road; and on the hill, when the snow slackened a bit, Barrow could see them everywhere.

B Company ran into the first roadblock at 10:30 P.M. Machine-gun fire flew across the road, but it was high, probably because the Chinese couldn't see through the blinding snow and darkness. B Company machine guns and the 60s put an end to Chinese fire, and Noren's men moved on.

Schmuck was right behind Noren and, after the Chinese were routed, the battalion commander and his staff moved into their holes. Rice still was cooking.

A Company had moved higher on the hill, fighting, climbing where only eagles dared go. Barrow's men moved up in single file along a trail so narrow two men couldn't stand abreast. They grabbed anything they could get their hands on for support. They couldn't see and, because of the wind and swirling snow, they couldn't hear. They kept climbing, finally reaching a level area where they could fan out. Then Barrow gave the signal to charge. "Yell with everything you got!" he shouted at his men.

"Let's go, marines!"

"Kill 'em!"

"Over the top!"

They shouted rebel yells, anything that came to mind.

That's the way Barrow liked it. Plenty of noise. If nothing else, scare them to death.

No one could see much of anything, Chinese or marines.

But the Chinese were firing down, and marines were being hit. Then it was a long slide down the hill.

The top of the first little knob was alive with Chinese, easy targets for the marines who had closed to within a few yards. Lt. William A. McClelland's 1st Platoon worked its way up to the knob, routed the Chinese out with grenades, then dug in for the night. It was snowing. And bitter cold. The weather had turned unbelievably bad. No one slept. You might freeze. Bones were chilled to the marrow. The only thing they had to look forward to was dawn and the slim chance that it would warm up—perhaps only twenty below zero.

The climb had been almost straight up, and that more than the Chinese or the cold had taken a terrible toll.

Noren's men were dug in along the road. He set up a roadblock just in case the Chinese decided to come down the road from the north. His company had blasted away three Chinese roadblocks and kicked away all the Chinese they had run into.

Wray's men were dug in on the lower reaches of 1081.

Hopefully, the Chinese were as weary as the marines and would settle for a night of rest.

Barrow checked his men on the windswept knob. They were awake. They'd changed socks. Rubbed their cold feet. Then stomped around to get the circulation flowing again.

But it took a long time. Each hole, each man had to be checked time and again.

At midnight about forty-five Chinese hit Barrow's line, more to let the men know they were still around than anything else.

Barrow's message to Schmuck told it all: "They hit us. We killed them all. . . ."

The hardest part of life on Hill 1081 wasn't the fighting, or the cold, or the climbing. It was getting the dead and wounded down the hill. Getting one body down took from five to seven hours, depending on the route.

December 9, 1950; Hill 1304, 6:00 A.M.: Morning dawned bright, clear, and very, very cold. Morris's men in C Company, 1st Battalion, 7th Regiment, were close to freezing. It was so cold that no one could sleep. As soon as it got light, small fires were going. There was hot coffee and slightly warm food.

As far as Morris could see, there was nothing around him on the hill. He couldn't see a Chinese soldier anywhere. Why?

Because it was too cold to fight. At one point during the night the temperature had dropped more than thirty degrees in an hour and a half, to about forty degrees below zero. So the Chinese packed their gear and left the hill to try to find a place where they could get warm, build small fires without bringing artillery or the Corsairs down on their heads.

A short time later, Morris led his company back down to the road and they headed toward the top of Funchilin Pass a couple of miles away. As soon as the trucks with the bridge sections arrived, C Company would start down toward the power plant.

The twenty-two men in Barrett's platoon were huddled around some tanks at the top of the pass. The engines had been running all night, so they wouldn't freeze. Why waste the little warmth they generated? Everyone thought they'd be heading down in a short time, toward the flat land, where winter wasn't so harsh.

They quickly learned, instead, that they would remain where they were to keep the top of the pass clear of Chinese until the rear guard arrived.

Hill 1081, 7:00 A.M.: Clear, bright weather meant but one thing: They would now get the artillery and air support they had missed during the snowstorm.

Barrow could look up and see the Chinese swarming over the top, a few hundred yards above him. He saw, too, the three layers of high ground he would have to take. Every man who looked up knew then that it would be a very hard day.

"We could see the enemy on the top of the final objective as easily as they could see us," McClelland remembered.

Barrow began to direct rifle and machine-gun fire toward the lower row of hills. Then his 60s and the 81s from below dropped round after round on the Chinese. McClelland and his first sergeant, Ernest Umbaugh, kept the men moving upward. Sgt. Henry Noonkester wiped out a machine-gun nest.

They took the first row of small hills and headed toward the top, but heavy fire from a machine-gun bunker hidden on the right slowed them. Grenades quickly took care of that problem. They were about two hundred yards from the top.

There was a company of Chinese up there, and so far they had shown nothing but fight. They would have to be rooted out with bayonets. At this point the marines had done as much as they could. Now it was time for air to soften them up.

Capt. Robert B. Robinson, Schmuck's air controller, was on the hill with A Company. There was an electric power pole on the top of the hill. The planes could use it as an aiming stake. Four Corsairs were overhead, waiting for something to do. Robinson got the flight leader on a backpack radio, told him what he wanted him to do, then directed him to the top of the hill. Napalm, rockets, and high explosives turned the hill into an inferno. In the middle of the strike, Barrow's men began to claw their way to the top. One squad hit the Chinese from the right, another from the left, and a third circled around and struck from the north, something they didn't expect.

Chinese were everywhere as the marines attacked the second level, shouting like wild men. Twice they were slowed to a crawl in the last fifty yards, but they weren't stopped. Bunkers were everywhere. All were full of Chinese when the marines hit. None tried to surrender. All died.

Barrow's company rested briefly, took care of the wounded, then at 2:00 P.M. launched their final attack to gain the top of the hill. It wasn't easy. The attackers were slowed but not stopped. When they did fight their way to the top, they were shoved off for a short time before regaining the peak for good at 3:00 P.M. Again, no one tried to surrender. The marines counted 530 Chinese dead. Barrow's company had 223 men when it started up Hill 1081. It was down to 111 able-bodied men when they captured the hill. The top was burned black. Very little was left standing. The Chinese had an elaborate network of underground bunkers that they ran to when the planes were spotted.

Barrow's company took over the enemy holes, dug them deeper, added more timber, and cleaned them out. They would be up there for another day or two, until the last of the division had passed below. So they tried to make living as pleasant as possible under the worst of circumstances.

Down on the road, Noren's B Company was running into increasing numbers of Chinese. They were being shoved down his throat by the point units of the 7th Regiment. They couldn't go up the side of 1081. That would be suicide. Barrow was on top, and Wray was partway up. The other side of the road was straight down in most places. So there was nothing else to do but try to force their way through B Company. But Noren had the road well blocked, and the Chinese found only death. The 155s from Chinhung-ni took care of that. The few who tried to flee up the side of the hill became targets for the quad .50s on the half-tracks that had been repositioned along the road just behind B Company.

Funchilin Pass, 9:30 A.M.: Morris led his men down toward the power plant. There were Chinese along the way, but they pretty much kept out of his way. His men did one of two things: killed them, or drove them down the road toward Noren's company.

Partridge arrived at the power plant at about noon. The trucks carrying the bridge sections got there at about 12:30 P.M. The engineers had the bridge in place by 3:30 P.M., and the convoy began to cross. But it was slow going. One wrong move and it was a fall of a few hundred feet.

A thirteen-man patrol had earlier slipped behind the power plant and now was advancing cautiously down the road, trying to locate the front units of Schmuck's 1st Battalion, 1st Regiment. Instead they ran into a lot of Chinese who wanted to fight.

"We went around a finger in the road and ran into automatic fire," recalled Pearl, who had been the radio operator for the commander of the 1st Battalion, 7th Regiment. Due to battle injuries, Davis was now Litzenberg's executive officer. Davis was replaced by Major Sawyer as the 1st Battalion commander.

The patrol backed up but then caught fire from the rear coming from the direction of the power plant. They were now caught on the road with fire in front and back, with twenty-five Chinese prisoners who had lost their desire to fight, and a few wounded marines. Pearl radioed back to battalion on the northern side of the power plant and described their predicament. Then they sat down and waited for dark.

At 6:00 P.M., still pinned down on the road, Sgt. William H. McCormick said, "Let's try to get around them." The wounded stayed on the road to guard the prisoners and wait for the convoy, which now was crossing the bridge at the power plant.

Pearl had been on the radio with battalion. He knew that the 1st Battalion, 1st Regiment, was fighting its way up the road, that marines had wrested Hill 1081 from the Chinese.

They stumbled and slid for about a half mile down over rocks that were covered with ice and snow. Although they couldn't see a thing, the Chinese fired down at them. A bullet nicked the left calf of Cpl. Ronald J. Molloy. "I thought it blew my leg off because it was so damn cold," he said. It was painful, but he could walk.

Two hours later, they climbed back up to the road. "It was just as hard getting back up as it was going down," Pearl remembered.

McCormick, Molloy, Sgt. Eugene Suter, PFC John D. Barliss, PFC Charles B. Knudson, PFC Robert L. Lunardi, and Cpl. Edward J. Cantwell were the first to make contact with Schmuck's 1st Battalion.

"I saw a tent just off the road," Molloy said, "so I parked my Thompson just outside and went in. I was asked my name and was told to move to the rear."

When he came out, the machine gun was gone, but he still had his rifle. "I figured someone else could put it to better use now," he said.

Pearl made it about a half hour later, at about 10:00 P.M. He called Sawyer to let him know that the patrol had reached the 1st Battalion, 1st Regiment. Then he called Davis and filled him in, too. Then he fell asleep in Noren's command post.

"Later that night they woke me up to see the headlights coming down the road," Pearl said. "It was a great sight, and there was a lot of jubilation. I guess it was like seeing guys come back from the dead."

The trucks, jeeps, ambulances, and men of the 7th Regiment were crossing the bridge now and moving through Noren's company on the way to Chinhung-ni.

At times it seemed as if there were more prisoners than marines coming down the road.

A Company was still high on Hill 1081 at midnight on December 9. C Company was partway up the same hill. If the Chinese decided they wanted to fight, the two rifle companies would oblige.

Then potential disaster struck at the power plant.

The reinforced plywood paneling between the two treadway spans began to crumble under the weight of a bulldozer. The plywood fell to the ground far below, and the span on the right was pushed too far to the right. None of the vehicles, including the tanks, could use the bridge now. The bulldozer hung out there by a thread perched on the left span, but only partially on the right span. First they had to get the 'dozer back on the northern half of the road, move the right span to the left a little, then install more of the heavy plywood sections between the two spans.

There was always the problem of starting that big junk pile as soon as someone touched the heavy tracked vehicle.

Sgt. Wilford H. Prosser, a skilled 'dozer operator, climbed atop the machine, backed it carefully onto the northern side of the road, then used the front blade to maneuver the right span closer to the other span so that the vehicles could cross again. Then new center pieces were installed, and the convoy began to move south.

To show the marines that it was okay to cross, Prosser drove the bulldozer over the bridge.

December 10, 1950; Funchilin Pass, 1:00 A.M.: Commando Jerry Maill spent his twenty-third birthday walking down the pass, unaware that it was his birthday. Life by this time was down to the basics needed for survival: finding warmth, food, ammunition, sleep, surviving the next ambush, overcoming the next roadblock. He had more on his mind than a birthday.

It was dark as pitch. The road was like ice. The commandos were about a mile past the power plant. What appeared to be a small road branched off to the right. "Make sure we get the right road, or we'll wind up down the hill!" Saunchegrow shouted as he gripped the steering wheel of the personnel carrier so tight he couldn't have released it if he had wanted to.

"Come on, Saunche, come on!" shouted a commando who was out front to guide the vehicle and the royal marines.

"Sure enough, we got the wrong road and it was just too dark and too narrow to turn around. Then the truck started to skid. It went over the side about twenty feet and turned over," Saunchegrow said.

Saunchegrow, upside down, was hanging onto the steering wheel. Packs and commandos were scattered all over the landscape.

Drysdale ran down. So did Aldrich.

"Are you all right?"

"Yes."

"Okay, I'll go check the lads," Drysdale said.

"We dug out the packs, then the guys," Saunchegrow said, "but it turned out that all the oil had dripped out and there was no way to get the truck back up to the road.

"It was good-bye to *Old Faithful.* It got us up there and almost back," Saunchegrow said. "It wasn't the best, but it sure could run. I was feeling mighty sad." The commandos got back on the road south and walked down to Chinhung-ni, where they got a ride to the sea.

"Don't take your shoe off," artilleryman Wilbur Way told his friend Don Heskett as their vehicle headed toward Chinhung-ni. "I did, and the sole started to come off," Heskett said, "so I put it back on." His foot hurt all the way to the sea. They saw two Chinese soldiers walking down the road with the marines. "We picked them up and took them south with us. There was no anger. We really felt sorry for them."

Kiser led his platoon across the bridge, then down the hill into flat country, past the checkpoint that Snedeker had set up. Along the way he picked up at a food dump a large can of grapefruit and five Tootsie Rolls.

"I was so glad to be out of there I ate the Tootsie Rolls, paper and all," he said. Just past the checkpoint he and his men climbed aboard a flatcar going to the sea.

At this moment Snedeker needed about six more arms. Elements of the 7th Regiment still were crossing his checkpoint at 3:00 P.M. on December 10. It was chaotic. For seventy-two hours he got no sleep.

"It was difficult controlling the convoy when it reached the checkpoint," Snedeker remembered, "because there was no way of knowing in what order it had left."

H Company, 7th Regiment, all but eliminated the night of November 27 on Hill 1403 at Yudam-ni, came down the road with twenty-four men, most of them replacements. The first thing each man did was write home.

"We were instructed to let our loved ones know we were all right, since we had pretty much been written off," Schreiner remembered.

The convoy was moving at a pretty good pace. There was a little gunfire, but by now most of the Chinese realized they could do nothing to prevent the marines from reaching the sea.

"Everyone was feeling much happier and confident now," Roisie said. "We all felt we'd gotten out of a bad spot.

"I don't think I'll ever forget it. I'm glad it's all over with. I'm glad we got the hell out of there," he added

Then he and some of his men boarded a train at Chinhung-ni for Hungnam to board troop ships for the journey back to South Korea.

Murray passed Snedeker's control point, then spotted the Army troops a short distance beyond. "I later heard that they were a so-called rescue mission," he said. "But I, of course, didn't think we needed rescuing. I thought we'd done pretty well with ourselves."

Jaskilka walked down the pass with his gunnery sergeant, Robert Barnett.

"Those are damn good marines you've got behind you, skipper," Barnett said.

"He was right. Their average age was nineteen or twenty. They'd done everything that had been asked of them, much more, in fact," Jaskilka said. "These kids were great. They were quiet, determined. They never bitched, never complained."

When did he think the marines would get out?

"When I could smell that salt air," he said, "I knew we were in charge then."

When they reached Hungnam, he experienced a feeling of great satisfaction. "I was really glad to be on safe ground again," he said. Then he gathered his men together and told them what a great job they had done. Then they went aboard ship.

Johnson, F Company, 2nd Battalion, 5th Regiment, saw the soldiers standing alongside the road as they passed the checkpoint. "We're here to save your ass," one of them said. PFC Don Kjellman, one of the company runners, was with him.

"I saw his carbine come up to his waist pointed toward them. He was just looking blank. So I gently pushed the barrel back down and we walked past them," Johnson said.

Down the road, where the ration dumps were, Johnson picked up a one-gallon can of pickles. He was so thirsty he drank the juice and threw the pickles away.

Saunchegrow stayed one more night with the royal marines, bade farewell to friends he would have for a lifetime, then rejoined his old outfit and went aboard ship.

* * *

Jim Kanouse was aboard ship. His feet were frostbitten. A bullet had grazed a cheek. He was happy to be out of there.

But the memories. They would last a lifetime.

The Chinese soldier who was shot in front of his foxhole at Toktong Pass and crawled back about fifty feet, then took a long time to die.

The canteen of water that cost ten Chinese lives. "At the time I didn't think it was much of a price to pay for a drink. It seems incredible today."

The Chinese bodies piling higher each night.

"But most of all, I'll never forget Fox Company."

When they went aboard ship there were fifteen men in the company: two sergeants, two corporals, eleven PFC's, and no officers.

"How are you, Sarge?" an Army lieutenant asked Fulop.

"Fine."

"Can I get you anything?"

"How about a cigarette?"

"Sure thing. Here."

As Fulop paused to light up, he heard the young officer talking to a captain.

"Hey, they're marines," the lieutenant said.

"Yeah, they're marines," the captain said in a tone of respect, "and they're bringing back their dead and wounded."

"When I heard this, I didn't mind the fact that I was cold, the fact that I was hungry and tired," Fulop said. "I stood a little straighter and put my shoulders back a little."

Molloy's leg wound wasn't bothering him too much. But his hands and feet were frostbitten.

"I almost cried when I found out I was going to be put aboard a hospital ship," he said, "and had to leave my M-1 behind."

"What a good job it had done for me. It was beautiful."

Morris's C Company walked down the pass to Chinhung-ni, then caught a ride to the sea. He was glad to be out of there. But he will never forget the dead stacked like cordwood at Toktong Pass. Or the young kid who said calmly, "Don't worry, skipper, we'll throw snowballs at 'em when we're out of ammo." Or the one who shouted, "Eat shit, you

333

slant-eyed bastards," a cigarette dangling loosely from his mouth because he was so scared.

And if he had to do it again?

"I would not be very happy about it . . . there is something about being a marine, though."

Theros remembers it all very well, the walk down the pass, the Chinese.

"I'll never forget that first Chinese attack at Sudong. But I don't want to forget it. It added a lot to a guy's vertebra."

December 11, 1950: At 6:00 P.M. most of the marine units were in the Hamhung-Hungnam area. Many had already gone aboard ships for the voyage to the division's new home at Masan, in South Korea.

But the fighting had not yet ended. There were marines still on the road, engineers, tankers, and a recon platoon, with the Chinese close on their heels.

Power plant, Funchilin Pass, 8:30 P.M.: Canzona was at the bridge with a small group of engineers. So was Gould, the commanding officer of the engineers there, and CWO Willie Harrison. They had tied eight hundred pounds of explosives to the span—TNT, plastics, mines. Now it was time to wait. There were forty tanks on the far side of the bridge along with a recon company platoon of twenty-nine men under the command of Lieutenant Hargett.

There were a lot of Chinese back there, too, mingling with thousands of refugees who were following the marines down the road.

When they first arrived at the bridge, it was light. That was several hours ago. Since then, the last of the convoy—trucks, ambulances, and men—slowly passed. Now they were waiting for the tanks. General Smith wanted it that way. If one had tried to cross the bridge early but instead had caused it to collapse, then all the vehicles behind it would have to be pushed over the side.

This way if a tank damaged the bridge beyond repair, then only the tanks would be lost.

But it had been some time since the last truck had passed, and the engineers were beginning to worry.

Where were the tanks?

And recon?

They should have crossed long ago.

Then Canzona heard the rumble. It was unmistakable. Tanks.

And men in front guiding them.

They began to cross, and he kept count.

One, two, three . . .

Several recon marines crossed the bridge.

It looked as if they'd make it, even though the rest of the column had long since moved down the pass.

. . . sixteen, seventeen, eighteen . . .

The bridge was holding up well. The engineers who put it in really knew what they were doing.

. . . twenty-eight, twenty-nine, thirty.

That was it.

Where were the other ten tanks?

Across the bridge, up the road, around the first curve, nothing but silence.

So they waited.

An hour. Two.

About three quarters of a mile from the bridge, one of the tanks had lost a tread, holding up the other nine.

Instead of shoving it over the side, they tried to fix it.

Right on their heels were the refugees, and Chinese mixed in with them.

Hargett was at the very rear with several of his men.

They were alone. The tanks, their crews, the recon men.

Then Hargett heard a voice in English shout from among the refugees that they were Chinese soldiers and wanted to surrender.

He went out to talk to them, cautiously, alert. Cpl. George Amyotte was with him, a BAR pointed toward the refugees.

Five Chinese stepped forward, but they had no intention of surrendering. They had burp guns and grenades. Then more appeared from the side of the road, and the battle was on. The last tank was quickly lost. So was its crew. The tank just in front of it was buttoned up, and the crew wasn't aware of the danger. It was captured.

A Chinese grenade blew PFC Robert D. Demott over the side of the road, a drop of several hundred feet, and everyone thought he was dead.

But he landed on a ledge, unconscious, just a few yards down from the top of the road.

Now the Chinese were after Hargett, his men, and the other tanks.

At the power plant Canzona heard the gunfire. Then he saw some of the tank crews running toward the bridge.

"The Chinese have the tanks and they're coming!" one of them shouted.

Should they wait a bit longer? There were still some men and tanks out there.

"I think we ought to blow this bridge and go on down," Canzona said to Gould.

"No. Let's wait and see if we can recover any of the tanks."

So they waited.

"We didn't know who'd be driving those tanks," Canzona said.

An hour passed.

"I sure as hell wanted to get off that damn hill. Each passing hour the situation became more critical," Canzona added.

Hargett and his men were backing down the road toward the bridge, the Chinese hot on their heels.

When he got to the tanks he found seven abandoned. The one with the bad tread had been fixed and was moving toward the bridge.

Then a marine who had never driven one before climbed inside another and somehow got it rolling, past the abandoned tanks, toward the bridge.

"When we got to the bridge, I saw Nick Canzona, an old friend," Ernie Defazio, a recon sergeant, recalled.

"Glad to see you're alive," Canzona said.

"Same."

They shook hands, exchanged a few more words.

Then Canzona saw the two tanks approaching.

"Thank God, marines were inside both of them," he said.

Then the last of the recon platoon crossed.

One of the tanks failed to negotiate a sharp turn and had to back up —right into Canzona's jeep, knocking it over the side.

"I listened for it, and it took an awful long time to hit," Canzona remembered.

"We're the last ones, Nick."

"Okay, Ernie," Canzona said as he pulled from his pocket a small bottle of wine his mother had sent him.

"I've been saving this. I think this is an appropriate time to drink it."

They stood on the bridge while Canzona popped the cork and toasted each other with a mixture of wine and ice.

"I had a swig in honor of the occasion, so did Ernie, then we wished each other luck," Canzona said.

Then they got out of there in a hurry, and Harrison blew the bridge just as the Chinese rounded the last curve.

"When we finally got to the bottom of the hill, it dawned on me that I hadn't had a drink of water for a few days," Canzona recalled.

A small stream flowed from the top of the hill. Most of it was frozen, but there was a small trickle of water.

"I went over there and actually drank water. I gulped down a good pint. It tasted damn good, nice and cold. It was delicious."

When Demott came to, he was perched dangerously on the tiny ledge just below road level.

He climbed back up, saw that the marines were gone, that the bridge had been blown.

But he remembered the trail behind the power plant, so he joined the thousands of refugees heading for the sea and caught up with the marines at Chinhung-ni and received a welcome befitting one who had come back from the dead.

By 11:30 P.M. on December 11, the tanks, the engineers, and the recon platoon were inside the perimeter at Hamhung-Hungnam, and the fighting in the Chosin Reservoir campaign ended.

There would be no more looking for a place to seek cover, for a place to get warm, for something to eat.

It was over.

"You know, we would have gladly accepted death to attain our objective, but it was just so impossible," said Theros. "There were so many of them."

"I'll never forget it," said Fulop. "It was like being in a tomb, at times. Once the fighting had stopped, you could hear a snowflake falling in the deathly stillness. And the bodies. Everywhere you looked, Chinese dead, frozen in every conceivable position. One, in a crouch, had a hand grenade clenched tightly in each fist. Another was upright on his knees, a pistol in one upraised hand, exhorting his comrades to move forward. As far as you could see, there was nothing but ice statues."

337

"It was like going through a wax museum," said PFC Robert Johnson. "It was carnage."

PFC Jerry Coutre remembers well the fighting at the Chosin Reservoir:

"It was a time when attendance at Mass rose sharply."

Postscript

General Smith attended burial services in Hungnam for the last marine dead brought down from Chinhung-ni and then, at 3:00 P.M. on December 13, went aboard the U.S.S. *Bayfield,* opened his command post, and marine activity in North Korea came to an end. The *Bayfield* sailed at 10:30 A.M. on December 15, bringing to an end perhaps the most unforgettable campaign in Marine Corps history.

The ROK 1st Division departed on December 18, and by December 20 the final units of the Army's 7th Division were aboard ship. Only the army's 3rd Division remained ashore to hold the shrinking perimeter around the port city. At 8:00 A.M. on December 24, the men of the division conducted a last-minute search for stragglers, then went aboard seven vessels for the trip to South Korea.

As Christmas Eve approached, those aboard ships still in the harbor watched a spectacular explosion as the entire waterfront was blown to bits and the Chosin Reservoir campaign became a memory.

The marines were already ashore at Pusan, on the southern tip of the peninsula, and on the way by truck to Masan, about forty miles northwest, where the men would rest, rearm, let their wounds heal, and welcome replacements. Then they went back into battle, for at this point the fighting was far from over.

From October 26 through December 15, 1950, the marines suffered 4,418 battle casualties and more than seven thousand cases of frostbite and nonbattle-related casualties. During the same period, the enemy lost 37,500 dead and wounded, and many thousands more were victims of severe frostbite.

General Smith retired from the corps several years later and died in December 1977.

"Without his professional leadership, there would have been no 1st Marine Division to march out," said Gen. Craig, the assistant division commander at the time.

Craig retired in 1952 and lives in El Cajon, California. He is ninety-one.

In gathering material for this book I talked or corresponded with hundreds of present and former marines. A more gracious group I could not have hoped to meet. They invited me to their homes on weekends, holidays. I cannot recall the number of times I was asked to stay for dinner. Nor can I recall the many times there would be a pause during a discussion and I would look up from my notetaking and see a tear in an eye or on a cheek as the death of a friend or the wounding of a buddy was recalled.

My research started with two three-paragraph news stories in which I sought the names of those who had fought at the reservoir. The articles appeared in the base newspapers at Camp Pendleton, California, and Camp Lejeune, North Carolina, the homes of the marines' 1st and 2nd divisions, respectively.

Within a week I received a dozen letters, each containing several names. Then it just seemed to explode and soon I couldn't handle all the names. I talked personally with as many as I could. Many others were interviewed over the phone. Still others were handled via the postal service.

I learned quickly that many of the retired marines lived close to the two marine installations because they still had privileges at the base exchanges and because so many of their friends lived close by.

There were many problems locating homes because of faulty street signs and street numbers that were barely visible. So I learned to look for a flagpole in a front yard, a sure sign that a marine lived there. There were other signs, too. On many front porches there were artillery shells filled with sand. I saw a machine gun on one porch roof. There was a small mortar on one front porch.

I was just about through my second year of research when I stumbled onto a gold mine. I met a retired marine who had in his possession a complete updated list of all retired marines with their home addresses and their units. It was all downhill from there.

Going into their homes was like walking into a museum. Walls, rooms, and basements were filled with maps, clippings from newspapers and magazines, medals, campaign ribbons, and weapons of every description.

Certainly the most colorful individual I talked with was John Yancey, the former lieutenant who was wounded three times in the head while defending Hill 1282. I remember listening to him for the first time and wondering, "Is this guy for real?" I found out that he was, indeed, "for real." We talked over the next two years on a number of occasions, and his input was extremely important in preparing this manuscript.

Yancey was flown from the battlefield to the Navy's giant hospital at Yokosuka, Japan, for treatment of his wounds. The field jacket he was wearing then is with a daughter. He told me he counted twenty-six holes in it, yet he didn't receive a scratch on his body below his face.

PFC Marshall McCann, Yancey's radio operator and runner, was also at Yokosuka. The base locator told him that Yancey was there but didn't know where. So McCann took off in his wheelchair, headed for officer country.

"He was wearing enlisted men's clothing when I spotted him," McCann said. "I leaped out of the wheelchair and we rolled on the floor. The other officers thought we were fighting. We'd had enough of that. We were just great friends, happy to be alive and seeing each other again."

Gallagher was there, too, recovering from his wounds and damage to his back caused when a telephone pole that was blown up landed on his back during a Chinese attack as the survivors of Phillips's company fought their way down the road to Hagaru.

"Yancey was in bed when I found him. Half of his face was gone. But he still had a sense of humor and we kidded each other for a while. He was very concerned about the men and wondered what happened to them," Gallagher said.

"Yancey was the kind of person I'd read about, but never thought I'd meet in real life. He's a memory that will linger with me forever," said Gallagher, who now lives in Darby, Pennsylvania.

Yancey returned to Little Rock, Arkansas, where he had a liquor store. Several months later he received a bill from the Marine Corps quartermaster for $146.70, plus bayonet, for the carbine he lost on Hill 1282.

"They wanted me to pay for that damn weapon, so I sent them the coordinates for 1282 and told them approximately where I dropped it."

He became involved in state politics a short time later and in 1964 filed a lawsuit that brought about the reapportionment of both houses of the Arkansas legislature.

He received his second Navy Cross for the defense of Hill 1282. There are many who to this day feel it should have been the Medal of Honor.

John Yancey died May 16, 1986. He was sixty-eight.

When I last talked to McCann, he was living in Seattle.

Leonard Clements, the former lieutenant who had the 1st Platoon on Hill 1282 and who was a close friend of Yancey, was living in Chattanooga, Tennessee, when I last talked with him.

Pvt. John W. Kelly, who was in Yancey's platoon on Hill 1282, lives in Columbus, Ohio.

Sgt. Robert S. Kennemore, who purposely placed his foot on a grenade to save the lives of several others, received the Medal of Honor. Yancey told me that Kennemore, in his wheelchair, had gone into a restaurant to cash a disability check, and as he left, someone hit him on the head with a pipe and stole his money. Kennemore, paralyzed and unable to talk, was transferred to a Veterans Administration hospital in the San Francisco area.

As for Pvt. Stanley Robinson, the "brig rat" who crawled to the top of Hill 1282 when Yancey needed him most, Yancey told me that he recalled reading a brief news story that Robinson had died during a shoot-out with police in Arizona quite a few years ago. According to Yancey, an M-1 was found alongside Robinson's body.

Of Robinson, Gallagher said: "I never saw him again after that night [Nov. 27–28 on Hill 1282], but he was always there when you needed him. He was a combat bugger. I don't believe Stanley knew the meaning of the word *fear*.

"I heard that Stanley got killed about eighteen years ago in a shoot-out with the cops," Gallagher said.

Sgt. Archie Van Winkle, who was in Lt. Harrol Kiser's 3rd Platoon, B Company, 1st Battalion, 7th Regiment, and was wounded in the Battle of Sudong, was recovering slowly in the Yokosuka, Japan, Navy hospital. "It was packed, jammed. Wounded were everywhere. In the halls, doorways, outside in tents," he said.

"They put me in a room where they put wounded they think will die," he said, "but fortunately, I faked them out."

Early one morning he felt a hand on a shoulder, then heard someone whispering into an ear, "Archie! Hey, Archie! Wake up! Wake up!" He opened his eyes and saw two old buddies from his World War II days, Bob Heilman and Stonewall Jackson Price. They had gone out and brought back a large plate of fried frogs' legs and a quart of Kirin beer.

"What else could I do? I ate the whole thing."

He suffered a relapse and was taken back into that room, but he woke up five days later and they carried him out.

"You were doing so well," his doctor said. "I just don't know what happened."

"I didn't bother to tell him."

Van Winkle, a native of Alaska, retired in 1974 as a colonel and moved to Davis, California, where he built a fifty-five-foot sailboat. The last time I was with him was at Camp Pendleton, California, several years ago. At that time he said he was going to sail the ship to Alaska for the summer. He did. The next several years were spent sailing the waters around Alaska.

He was awarded the Medal of Honor for his part in the defense of Hill 698 at Sudong.

Archie Van Winkle died in May 1986. His body was found aboard his sailboat in the harbor at Ketchikan. He was sixty-one.

Kiser, when I talked to him last, lived in Escondido, California.

Capt. William E. Barber, commander of F Company at Toktong Pass, was awarded the Medal of Honor for holding the high ground at the pass until the division passed below. When we last talked he was living in Irvine, California.

Pvt. Hector Cafferatta, who was in Barber's company and who also received the Medal of Honor, lives in New Jersey. So does his close friend of many years, former PFC Kenneth Benson, who shared a foxhole with him at Toktong Pass.

When Cafferatta was informed that he would be receiving this country's highest award for bravery from President Truman at the White House, he asked if they would mind mailing it to him.

"Yes," he was told.

"So I went with him to the White House to get it," Benson said.

"He wasn't shy," Benson explained. "He just didn't feel he'd done anything special."

PFC James C. Kanouse, also a member of Barber's company, who provided much of the information about life on that hilltop, lived in Rockaway, New Jersey, until his death in February 1987.

Col. Raymond G. Davis, commander of the 1st Battalion, 7th Regiment, who led the relief force across the mountains to help Barber's company at Toktong Pass, also received the Medal of Honor. He lived in McDonough, Georgia, when we talked.

His radio operator, Sgt. Roy Pearl, was living in Park Rapids, Minnesota, when we last talked.

Col. E. W. Snedeker, General Smith's deputy chief of staff, who established the checkpoint at Chinhung-ni to keep track of the many units coming down the road, lived in Carlsbad, California, when I saw him last. His help was instrumental in putting this book together.

Col. Alpha L. Bowser, Jr., the division's chief of plans and operations, provided great insight into marine thinking during the fighting at the reservoir. Without his assistance and patience, this book would be lacking in several areas.

Col. Raymond S. Murray, commander of the 5th Regiment, was living in Oceanside, California, when I last talked to him. Col. Homer Litzenberg, commander of the 7th Regiment, died several years before I began research on this book. Col. Robert D. Taplett, commander of the 3rd Battalion, 5th Regiment, was a great help. So was Col. Harold S. Roisie, commander of the 2nd Battalion, 5th Regiment. Col. Tom Ridge, commander of the 3rd Battalion, 1st Regiment, described in great detail the defense of Hagaru. Taplett was living in Arlington, Virginia, Roisie in Branford, Connecticut, and Ridge in Potomac, Maryland, when I last talked with them.

Maj. Henry J. Woessner, chief of plans and operations of the 7th Regiment, explained to me Litzenberg's thinking as he led his regiment up to the reservoir and back.

The small-unit warfare in and around the Chosin Reservoir was perhaps the most violent in the history of fighting at or below company level. Most of my research was directed toward locating the key company commanders, platoon lieutenants, sergeants, and enlisted men.

Cpl. Marvin E. Pugh, who was captured, shot, and left to die in the snow when the Chinese cut the road just south of Hagaru, was living in Knoxville, Tennessee, when we last talked.

Lt. Felix Ferranto, who was shot in a leg and his jeep blasted by a Chinese grenade when the road was cut just north of Koto-ri, spent three years as a prisoner of war.

"They would have killed me," he recalled, "but I said in Chinese, 'My leg is broken.'

"This amazed them. I could tell by looking at their faces. They carried me on their backs to positions near Hagaru, then put me on a stretcher." Then he was taken to a Chinese field hospital far to the north. When I last talked to him, he was living in Southern California.

Capt. Samuel S. Jaskilka, commander of E Company, 2nd Battalion, 5th Regiment, provided much of the information on the marines' attack to the west the morning of November 27, and again that night when the Chinese attacked Northwest Ridge. Jaskilka went on to become assistant commandant of the corps. He was living in Annapolis, Maryland, when we last talked.

Lt. Jack Nolan, who had the 2nd Platoon in Jaskilka's company, gave me much of the information concerning the fighting at "Easy Alley." When I last talked to him, he was living in Tyler, Texas.

Capt. Milt Hull, D Company, 2nd Battalion, 7th Regiment, who described the battle for Hill 1240, was living in Plant City, Florida, when we talked. He has since died.

Lt. Harold Dawe, who led the 3rd Platoon, C Company, 1st Battalion, 5th Regiment, to the top of Hill 1240 just as Hull's company was about to go under, lived in Arvada, Colorado, when I found him.

Lt. John Theros, pilot and forward air controller who coordinated the 7th Regiment's air-ground attack south from Hagaru, was living in San Diego when we talked.

Lionel S. Reynolds, the chief warrant officer who commanded the radio repair platoon in the division signal battalion, told me about the defense of Hagaru and some of the action on East Hill. When we talked, he was living in Oceanside, California.

Lt. Ty Hill, who saw through binoculars the Chinese soldier who shot him in the leg, was living in Escondido, California, when I last saw him.

Sgt. John G. Fulop, the engineer who described the ice statues at "Easy Alley" and one of the last men out of Yudam-ni, lived in Oceanside, California, the last time we talked.

Sgt. Gene O'Hara, 2nd Platoon, H Company, 3rd Battalion, 7th Regiment, one of the few survivors of the Chinese attack on Hill 1403, was living in Milwaukee, Wisconsin, when we talked. PFC James J. Schreiner, another survivor of Hill 1403, was living in El Paso, Texas, when he was interviewed.

PFC Robert M. Johnson, F Company, 2nd Battalion, 5th Regiment, the "point" when the marines attacked west early on November 27, lives in Esko, Minnesota. Cpl. Tom Jonnell, on the same four-man fire team as Johnson, lived in Pittsburgh, Pennsylvania, when I talked with him.

Cpl. J. J. Collins, also in F Company, who was wounded when the Chinese attacked Northwest Ridge the night of November 27, provided, along with Johnson and Jonnell, much of the detail of that first attack by the new enemy.

Collins was flown by helicopter to the Army's 121st Evacuation Hospital at Hungnam. "I never saw so many casualties," he remembered. "I heard a doctor say, 'Forget him, he's not going to make it,'

345

which meant treat only the high-percentage wounded and leave the ones that are likely to die." Later he was flown to the Navy's hospital at Yokosuka, Japan. "During the six weeks I was there I saw forty-three marines who were in my platoon," Collins said. "All had frozen hands or feet, missing limbs, or multiple gunshot wounds."

Capt. Jack Jones, C Company, 1st Battalion, 5th Regiment, who led a relief force up Hill 1282 and recaptured the vital peak, was living in Fallbrook, California, when I saw him last. Lt. Max Merritt, who had the 1st Platoon in Jones's company, was living in Lincoln, Nebraska, when I talked with him.

Lt. Byron Magness, who had the 2nd Platoon in C Company, was living in Little Rock, Arkansas, when I located him.

Sgt. Roger Wallingford, who had the company mortars in Jones's company, lived in Waldorf, Maryland, when we talked.

PFC Winston Keating Scott, a machine gunner in Jones's company, was found in Eagan, Minnesota.

Nicholas A. Canzona, the engineer lieutenant who was with the rear guard all the way down to Hungnam, was living in Winston-Salem, North Carolina, when we talked. He has since died. He was coauthor of *The Chosin Reservoir Campaign,* published shortly after the Korean fighting ended by the Historical Branch, U.S. Marine Corps.

Sgt. Ernie DeFazio of the recon company, who shared the bottle of wine with Canzona on the bridge at the power plant, was living in Oceanside, California, when we last talked.

Cpl. Don Saunchegrow, who drove *Old Faithful,* PC 10426, through Hell Fire Valley with twenty-five British royal marines aboard, was a great help. He not only provided many details of the fighting but also put me in touch with many of the British marines. He lives in San Marcos, California.

Capt. Carl Sitter, commander of G Company, 3rd Battalion, 1st Regiment, who led his men through Hell Fire Valley, then played a vital role in the defense of Hagaru, was awarded the Medal of Honor. When I talked with him, he was living in Chester, Virginia.

Lt. R. L. Barrett, Jr., who had the 1st Platoon in H Company, 3rd Battalion, 1st Regiment, supplied much information on life along the perimeter at Hagaru. Most of his material came from a series of letters he sent to his mother in December and January of 1950–51. She typed them and sent them back to Barrett for editing. He then made the information available to me. When we talked last, Barrett was living in Norman, Oklahoma.

Air Force pilot Jim Inks, who flew one of the C-119s that dropped the bridge sections, was located on a cattle ranch in Llano, Texas.

Sgt. Robert Kopsitz, a radio operator with Sitter's G Company, 3rd Battalion, 1st Regiment, who lived through the fighting in Hell Fire Valley and later took part in the fighting on East Hill and the defense of Hagaru, lived in Philadelphia, Pennsylvania, when we talked.

Jim Nash, the Military Police sergeant who was captured in Hell Fire Valley and escaped several months later, was living in Riverside, California, when I talked with him.

Capt. Robert H. Barrow, A Company, 1st Battalion, 1st Regiment, whose men shoved the Chinese off Hill 1081, the last dominant high ground as the division came down the road, became commandant of the corps. He has since retired and lives on a plantation in Louisiana.

Cpl. Ronald J. Molloy, who was a member of the patrol that broke through the Chinese on the road and made contact with the marines moving up from the south, lives in Kansas City.

Concerning the much publicized battle cry of the marines at the Chosin Reservoir, "Retreat, hell! We're simply fighting in a different direction," it was never uttered by General Smith.

According to Bowser, this is what was said:

"Before launching movement south from Hagaru, I outlined the plan of attack and movement to reach Koto-ri, the location of the first marine regiment. While we were looking at my proposed plan of action, my executive officer, Lieutenant Colonel Winecoff, remarked to General Smith, 'This is a new experience for marines, retreating.'

"At that point General Smith said to both of us, 'We have to attack in order to move, so we are not retreating. We are simply attacking in a different direction.'

"I was not present at the general's conference with the press the next morning, but apparently when the general was asked by the press if it wasn't out of character for the marines to retreat, he said, 'Retreat! We're simply attacking in a different direction.' "

Col. William Sexton, the general's aide, was present at the conference with reporters and at no time did he hear General Smith use the word "hell."

"The general was a Seventh Day Adventist and four-letter words are not part of their religion," Sexton said.

So somewhere between the press conference and headlines in the United States, the rallying cry, "Retreat, hell . . . ," was born, and it is inaccurate.

In all, thirteen men received the Medal of Honor during the Chosin Reservoir fighting that involved the marines.

The Korean War faded quietly into history, seldom to be heard of for more than thirty-five years. There were no parades for the returning men, no monuments. Those who returned were happy to be able to pick up their lives. Many had fought in World War II, then had joined the reserves, only to be recalled to active duty. For them, it meant starting over a second time.

If you were in the Army, for instance, and returned to the United States through Camp Stoneman or Fort Mason, in California, you were treated to a dinner of your choice in the mess hall—steak, chicken, or pork chops, magnificent by Army standards—then sent on your way the following day, either to reassignment or civilian life. Quickly, Korea became known as the forgotten war.

The fighting continued for three years and one month. It ceased at 10:00 A.M. on July 27, 1953, when delegates of the warring nations signed a truce at Panmunjom in a small farmlike structure of wood and bamboo called "The Hall of Peace."

The peace talks were the longest in history—two years, seventeen days, 575 regular meetings between the two sides and eighteen million words spoken in a frigid and hostile atmosphere.

During the fighting, 54,246 Americans lost their lives. More than 250,000 were wounded, and 8,177 are still listed as missing. Incredibly, 389 Americans still are listed as prisoners of war.

According to the best estimates available, more than one million people died during the fighting, many of them civilians.

The invasion from the North changed warfare as we know it today. No longer would we fight to win, but rather to hold our ground, and the word "limited" became important in the language of the military. The invasion became a test of wills between the Communist world and the free world, between the United States and Russia, who used surrogates—North Korea and Red China—to do the fighting. It also brought about the firing of one of America's greatest and certainly one of its most controversial generals, Douglas MacArthur, by President Truman, who said, "MacArthur left me no choice . . . I could no longer tolerate his insubordination. . . ." The invasion raised the specter of the United States resorting to the atomic bomb once again in an effort to resolve the fighting. And for the first time, the attack by the North showed the world that the Communists would use force of arms to gain what they wanted, if they wanted it badly enough.

Of the fighting at the reservoir, noted Army historian Gen. S.L.A. Marshall had this to say:

"No other operation in the American book of war quite compares with this show by the 1st Marine Division in the perfection of tactical concepts precisely executed, in accuracy of estimate of situation by leadership at all levels, and in promptness of all supporting forces."

Should we have been there in the first place?

Gen. Omar Bradley, chairman of the Joint Chiefs of Staff when the fighting erupted, characterized it as ". . . the wrong war, at the wrong place, at the wrong time, with the wrong enemy."

Was one side victorious?

Thinking back over events that occurred so many years ago, retired Gen. Raymond S. Murray, who as a lieutenant colonel commanded the 5th Regiment, said:

"If their objective was to destroy us, they didn't go about it in a very smart way. If their objective was to drive us out of North Korea, then they succeeded."